AF269894

THE INSATIABLE MACHINE

ALSO BY TREVOR JACKSON

Impunity and Capitalism: The Afterlives of European
Financial Crises, 1690–1830

THE INSATIABLE MACHINE

How Capitalism Conquered the World

Trevor Jackson

W. W. NORTON & COMPANY

Independent Publishers Since 1923

Copyright © 2026 by Trevor Jackson

All rights reserved
Printed in the United States of America
First Edition

For information about permission to reproduce selections from this
book, write to Permissions, W. W. Norton & Company, Inc.,
500 Fifth Avenue, New York, NY 10110

For information about special discounts for bulk purchases, please
contact W. W. Norton Special Sales at specialsales@wwnorton.com or
800-233-4830

Manufacturing by Lake Book
Book design by Dana Sloan
Production manager: Louise Mattarelliano

Library of Congress Cataloging-in-Publication Data is available.

ISBN 978-1-324-10687-6

W. W. Norton & Company, Inc., 500 Fifth Avenue, New York, NY 10110
www.wwnorton.com

W. W. Norton & Company Ltd., 15 Carlisle Street, London W1D 3BS

Authorized EU representative:
EAS, Mustamäe tee 50, 10621 Tallinn, Estonia

$PrintCode

CONTENTS

INTRODUCTION

History is what hurts.

—Fredric Jameson[1]

It wasn't always this way. Today, the entire world lives under a single economic system that we call capitalism, and markets for commodities, information, services, and money span the globe. Most people alive today have never lived under any other kind of economy. Capitalism's historic rivals failed and collapsed decades ago, and there is no credible alternative system on the horizon. Capitalism's advocates claim not only that it is the most efficient, productive, and beneficial way of organizing economic life but also that it is the outcome of innate human nature, or that it encapsulates a set of moral virtues.[2] The market logic of capitalism affects every aspect of our lives, from education and healthcare to housing and childcare. Over the past half century, economic assumptions about individual rationality, maximization, equilibrium, and efficiency have been applied to more and more aspects of the study of human life.[3] The use of economic reasoning has been extended to nearly everything, from democratic deliberation to the allocation of kidneys to whether it is acceptable to poison children with lead.[4]

Market logic has been the main way of assigning value and making decisions for decades, such that many people have never experienced alternatives or realized that market values are a choice and have a history. As the literary theorist Fredric Jameson wrote in 2003, "It is easier to imagine the end of the world than to imagine the end of capitalism."[5] But even a cursory look at the world around us gives the clear impression that things can't stay this way forever. An economy predicated on infinite accumulation, mass consumption, and fossil-fueled industrialization is not reconcilable with a finite planet. The realization that the world hasn't always been this way is helpful for thinking about the realization that it also can't stay this way.

This book is a history of the economic system that we call capitalism. It explains the origins, spread, and internal dynamics of this system, with the intention of explaining to nonexperts how the world we live in got to be the way it is. The book's scope is the subset of the world economy that can reasonably be termed "capitalist," beginning in dispersed and sporadic parts of the Atlantic world in the 16th century and continuing until the global dominance of capitalism at the onset of the 20th. In other words, it begins roughly during the life of Martin Luther and ends during the life of Vladimir Lenin, and it will use each of them (Luther in 1517, Lenin in 1917, and with Isaac Newton in the middle in 1717) as an illustrative example of how the global economy changed over the course of centuries. This is a book about where capitalism came from, how it spread around the world, and how it came to be the dominant way of organizing human life.

There are good reasons to tell this history again, and in a new way. The first is the simple fact that capitalism is the economic system we live in today: It spans more of the globe and encompasses more aspects of human life than any economic system ever has before. Since at least the 2008 crisis, there has been an increasing sense that it may have gotten out of control and might now threaten democracy, society, the environment, and the habitability of the planet. But unlike countries, people, or events, capitalism is an abstraction with no agreed-upon definition and no physical location. There is no single place to find it, or single person in charge of it, and no single way to understand or study it. So how do we tell the story of capitalism?

The place to start is to think about *capital*, and capitalists, which is a form of power and group of people distinctive to capitalism. Over the past half millennium, capitalists have been among the most important agents of change in human history, and capital has been the central tool they have used to transform the world. Historians care a great deal about *agency*, by which they mean the ability of people to effect change in the world. Agency is closely related to power: In order to change something, someone must have the power to do so. A great deal of historical scholarship over the past 50 or 60 years has been dedicated to recovering and identifying the agency of marginalized people, to show that they mattered, and contributed to making the world we live in. Some scholars have argued for the agency of nonhuman things, like whales or mosquitoes or pathogens. Animals and environments certainly have power, and cause changes in human life, but it is difficult to show that they have intentions, or make decisions.

Capital is different, because capital is made by people, but it also lives longer than people do. To take only a few examples, there are many buildings still standing and factories still in operation hundreds of years after their construction; the Dutch East India Company paid dividends to its shareholders for two centuries; the Bank of England has been in operation since 1694. To be sure, capital is subject to degradation and depreciation, but in its physical embodiment and in its legal construction it lasts significantly longer than a single human life. Capitalists have been agents of change, but that does not mean that capital can be reduced to the whims and intentions of individuals.

Owners of capital can affect parts of the overall stock of capital, and in groups can make decisions that cause it growth or destruction. But even in a group, they are along for the ride. Rather than helmsmen, owners of capital are more like gut flora: necessary for the metabolism of the whole entity, capable together of causing distress, but individually unimportant, and living far shorter life spans than their collective host.

That is another reason for this deep history of capitalism. From the 16th century until today, capitalism has remade the world, both in terms of social relations and in terms of the material environment. Capital has valued, created, destroyed, and reorganized people and nature on a titanic scale. With the onset of the Industrial Revolution, capital unleashed productive power that was previously unimaginable. It has allowed for roughly a 16-fold increase in average living standards relative to preindustrial levels, even while providing for a 7-fold increase in human population.[6] But it has done so at the cost of burning fossil fuels, which has emitted carbon into the atmosphere at an unimaginable pace, as well as at the cost of all manner of other kinds of environmental and social destruction. Capitalism has remade the world for itself, but in doing so, it has made itself coterminous with the world. Writing from the vantage point of a quarter of the way through the 21st century, it is clear that anthropogenic climate change will not be stopped, and probably not even substantially mitigated, and that capitalist markets are utterly inadequate tools for addressing the problem.[7] The world I live in will be destroyed within my lifetime. The question of what kind of world will follow it is entirely a question of whether we all manage to kill capitalism or it kills us first. It is therefore instructive to find out how it was born, what it has killed along the way, and what has happened to past attempts to kill it, or at least to tame it.

■ ■ ■

What is capitalism? Capitalism is an economic system constituted by markets in the factors of production, which are land, labor, and capital.[8] It is not a matter of commodity markets: There is evidence of people buying and selling produce or handicrafts in contexts as varied as ancient Greece and communist China. I am also skeptical that capitalism depends on cultural or intellectual attributes like rational calculation, profit motives, or making decisions with an orientation toward the future. It is very possible to find people showing those attributes in not especially capitalist contexts, and vibrantly easy to locate examples of capitalist people acting irrationally or with a weak grasp of future outcomes. What makes capitalism distinctive as an economic system is that individuals can buy and sell the things that produce all other things.

Markets in the factors of production require a large set of legal, political, and institutional arrangements. There need to be contracts, and courts to enforce them, which tends to imply a government. Rather than thinking of a separation between the state and the market, or the public sphere from the private, governments have been at the heart of making capitalism since the beginning. Governments make markets, charter companies, issue money, produce financial instruments like permanent debt, and are often made up of capital owners. At the same time, especially in the early modern period, chartered companies acted like governments, especially in colonized spaces. Plantation oligarchies created their own slave societies, early industrialists policed the domestic morality of their workers, and mining corporations ruled company towns. Still today most capitalists run their companies like little despotic governments, and most projects for more unfettered capitalism are projects for private power and private governance. The relationship between governments and capitalism has mostly not been antagonistic. They have been partners, and governments have mostly provided stability, enforcement, and military backup to the activity of capitalists, while also increasingly trying to impose some order on the chaos of capitalist markets.

Most importantly for capitalism, there needs to be a legal concept of private property rights, which need to be unitary and alienable so that specific people can be the sole owners of specific things and have the ability to buy and sell them. Private property as we know it represents an owner's ability to call on violence, usually legitimate state violence, in order to exclude all other humans from some subset of the world. Private property does not exist without exclusion, without the credible threat of violence, and without recognition of the legitimacy of the violence claim. When people buy and sell property, what they are exchanging is that right of exclusion. When private property is bought and sold in markets, value is allocated through *prices*, rather than through custom or tradition, so capitalism has an unusual relationship to value, relative to other economic systems. For these reasons, historically it makes more sense to think of capitalism as a spectrum rather than a binary. The Dutch Republic almost certainly had private property and markets in the factors of production before anywhere else, as well as relatively neutral contract enforcement.[9] In most of Europe and the wider Atlantic, markets for capital—indeed, *international* markets for capital—preceded wage labor and enclosed, alienable land rights.

One of the most distinctive and strange features of capitalism is that its workings are the unexpected, unintended, and unknown collective outcome of innumerable individual decisions. Private costs and benefits can diverge from social costs and benefits; private control of resources and infrastructures and services can prove contrary or objectionable to democratic or community values. Astute observers have long recognized this point. When Adam Smith referred to "an invisible hand" (a phrase that appears only once in the thousand pages of *The Wealth of Nations*), he used it to refer to the strange way that the pursuit of individual self-interest also produced unintended social benefits. More pessimistically, John Maynard Keynes analyzed the Great Depression of the 1930s as partly resulting from what he called the "paradox of thrift," which happened when people were worried about the future and saved money instead of spending it, with the perverse result that nobody spending money accentuated the depression, thus bringing about exactly the bad future that people feared in the first place.

Capitalism itself was not planned by anyone, or intended by anyone, but rather has been the surprising and often accidental collective outcome of individual decisions. Many of those decisions have been taken out of self-interest, to be sure, but self-interest oriented toward survival.[10] It is common among critics of capitalism to claim that capitalism (or at least its modern form) depends on accumulation for the sake of accumulation, and profit for the sake of profit. But firms and people try to accumulate and earn profit in order to survive. A firm that is not profitable will be driven into extinction by its competitors. Accumulation is the surest way to survive periods of scarcity. And this, too, is a historical phenomenon. In the world before capitalism, people could survive through mechanisms and institutions of local custom, kinship, or common access to subsistence, but usually could not accumulate enough extra to produce anything different in the future. The basic feature of capitalism is that it has undermined or dismantled most of those traditional sources of survival, and today nearly everyone is dependent on markets in order to live. Workers are dependent on labor markets, sellers on commodity markets, and even rich capitalists mostly on capital markets—but also markets for their goods, the costs of their inputs, and so on. And thus a paradox: Although capitalism has produced a dizzying range of consumer choices, it has also silently produced a range of compulsions. We are free to choose within capitalist markets, but not free to live outside of them altogether.[11]

A struggle to survive almost certainly has shaped all human

societies, but capitalism is unusual in that survival is obtained through market exchanges, and its specific form of resulting social hierarchy is that of the ownership of capital versus its absence. The need and desire to accumulate capital is specific to capitalism, a different form of the desire to accumulate power, tribute, or prestige in other societies. The control of capital thus places some people at the top of the social hierarchy, with a stronger ability to determine the chances of survival for themselves and other people. The dependence on markets for survival means that capitalism introduced a new and specific form of social warfare that has shaped human history for the past 500 years, which is the struggle for control both of capital and over the share of output divided between capital and labor. Thus, another strange paradox: Even the richest and most powerful capitalists are themselves subject to the same struggle for survival in the markets as everyone else, and the same variety of unexpected consequences by which the individual struggle for survival produces collective disasters, ranging from speculative bubbles to interminable depressions to climate catastrophe.

The systems of money, finance, labor, and industry explained in this book are still with us today, but nobody who created them intended that, or could have predicted it. That is not to imply that everyone participated equally and willingly as rational price-taking individuals in the market. Inequality is a feature of all human societies, but inequality expressed through the unequal ownership of capital is unique to the capitalist economy. Throughout the entire time span covered in this book, the richest 10 percent of people controlled a continually increasing 60 to 80 percent of all wealth, and the median person died with nothing.[12] Ownership of capital also means disproportionate social, cultural, and above all, political power. It means disproportionate influence in the kinds of short-term decisions that then have longer consequences, as well as disproportionate effect in continuing to reinforce the systems those decisions created. But ownership of capital does not grant knowledge, foresight, competence, or coordination. Spanish conquistadores in the 16th century did not intend to produce a global monetary system and 150 years of price inflation, but they did anyway. Dutch merchants in the 17th century did not intend to reshape consumer behavior and labor markets by selling their delicious tropical products, but they did anyway. British industrialists in the late 18th century did not intend to usher in an age of fossil-fuel consumption and anthropogenic climate change, but they did anyway. And on the other side, nobody intended to produce a 16-fold increase since the year 1800 in average living standards around the world. In each case, it paid *individually* to make these decisions, without intending or even understanding the collective outcome, just as today it pays individuals and firms to render the earth climatically uninhabitable, even though catastrophe is no one's particular intention.

This book takes class conflict as its central engine, but in a different way than previous generations of scholars and critics. Class conflict does not have to take the form of immense groups of people, conscious of themselves and their efforts, undertaking concerted intentional mass actions. It can be the expression of thousands or millions of individual, short-term decisions based on imperfect information.[13] When a landlord raises the rent or a factory owner moves to a place with lower wages, that is class conflict. So too when workers strike for higher wages, or when governments bail out banks or central banks support asset prices through quantitative easing. Economists are used to thinking that the sum of numerous individual decisions can add up to unintentional or even paradoxical consequences. The creation, expansion, and persistence of capitalism through class struggle is one of them. The immense historical changes described in this book together added up to the world-spanning system of capitalism, but they were mostly all driven by the short-term imperfect choices of millions of workers, merchants, and above all, owners of capital, all of them struggling for survival against one another.

. . .

This book is not several things. It is not a history of economic growth: There are many such histories, covering well back into the 16th century.[14] It is not a history of global trade: There are already excellent histories of trade during the past half millennium.[15] It is not a history of the Industrial Revolution and afterward, although industrialization will play a vital role in this book's story.[16] It is also not a history of "the economy," whether the economy of Europe or the Atlantic or the globe, nor a history of the concept of "the economy."

For many economists, who ostensibly know the rules and workings of capitalism better than anyone, the term "capitalism" is not useful. They prefer to think in terms of a set of conceptual tools and analytical models that could be applied anywhere, to any context; and in the case of behavioral economists, even to contexts without markets or economic activity as most people would recognize it, like within families, or at school. Some even go further, and might argue that capitalism has no history, because it is an expression of human nature, of what Adam Smith called the "natural propensity to truck, barter, and exchange."[17] According to that view, the history of capitalism is the history of successfully opposing and removing governmental obstacles to natural free market activity. Further, a social system like capitalism cannot be statistically represented, and modern economics works through isolating individual variables that are then deployed in models and subjected to statistical testing. Things that are not amenable to conceptual disaggregation or statistical testing are also not amenable to economic modeling, with the weird result that economics cannot "see" capitalism.

Almost no historian would agree with the human-nature view. Free markets have proved difficult enough to find in the wild, let alone a single thing called human nature that is permanent across time and space. Since the financial crisis of 2008, many historians have turned to economic subjects, and some have formed a subfield known as the "history of capitalism," or sometimes the "*new* history of capitalism."[18] That field has been famously unwilling to define what it means by "capitalism," not as an oversight, but as a methodological choice, on the grounds that to do so would be limiting, and could exclude important subjects from analysis.[19]

In the absence of an agreed-upon definition, studies of the varieties and characteristics of capitalism have proliferated. A nonexhaustive list of adjectival capitalisms that have been the subject of book-length studies in the past 10 years includes adventure, asset-manager, cannibal, corporate, disaster, green, imperial, narco, neoliberal, pandemic, platform, racial, rentier, settler, shareholder, spiderweb, surveillance, sustainable, vaccine, war, and welfare capitalism. To that list could be added the more traditional historical variants: merchant, commercial, industrial, and financial capitalism; as well as liberal, late, and global capitalism. Each of these studies is valuable for understanding the world we live in. But many are not about capitalism at all: They are about surveillance, pandemics, and wars as they exist today, and since capitalism is the current global economic system, by necessity those subjects are analyzed in the permutations that exist under capitalism. Other studies are about one aspect of capitalism: components like shareholders, rentiers, and welfare systems. Seeking to fill the void, some scholars have recently produced histories of the word "capitalism," intending to show that the emergence and development of the concept sheds some light on the real-world processes that it denotes.[20] These too are valuable, but they are also not about capitalism itself, but rather are about how scholars and theorists have thought and argued about capitalism.

This profusion of adjectival capitalisms has meant that we can find capitalism anywhere, from ancient Rome to the Soviet Union, and in anything, ranging from emotions to natural disasters. There have been two unfortunate results. One is that it is difficult to build cumulative knowledge without an agreed-upon subject. The second is that, by expanding the historical, geographical, and conceptual scope of capitalism to potentially encompass all things at all times, it has become difficult or even impossible to find noncapitalist or precapitalist histories. And the absence of noncapitalist pasts makes it difficult or impossible to imagine a noncapitalist or postcapitalist future.

This book intends to deflate and diminish capitalism. It conceives of capitalism as an economic system: one that interacts with politics, the state, culture, gender, race, the environment, and technology, and indeed often uses, reconfigures, or instrumentalizes those things, but is still separate from them. This book seeks to understand capitalism *historically*, which is to say, not *theoretically*, in the manner of economists, sociologists, or other social scientists. Scholars trained in institutionalist economic history will find plenty of evidence here that conforms to their models. Marxists will find no shortage of exploitation, expropriation, and class struggle. The only group that will be disappointed is those who are looking for naturally occurring free markets functioning efficiently and rationally.

This book covers a lot of ground very fast. We will touch on many subjects that are probably unfamiliar—like wages of mine workers in Bolivia in the 1550s, mulberry trees in southern China in the 1620s, Dutch cheese in the 1640s, consolidated English annuities in the 1680s, whale blubber in the 1780s, and teredo worms in the 1850s—but which nevertheless are integral to telling the material history of the capitalist system. I have tried (and failed) to keep endnotes to a minimum, including only canonical works or references for very specific facts, and I have tried to draw on the past 20 years of research as much as possible. Especially in the earlier periods covered by the book, there are still many questions that are hotly debated, many questions with answers that are only sketchy estimates based on limited surviving evidence, and many questions that still have not been answered at all.

All books have a scope, and covering a global economic system over the course of a half millennium necessarily means I have left out a lot of interesting and important stories. Most crucially, some readers may find it Eurocentric, especially chapters 2 and 4. But it is worth remembering the origin of the word "Eurocentric," which was coined by the radical French Egyptian economist Samir Amin in 1988.[21] He meant it to refer to scholars who take Europe to be the necessary global norm and all other societies to be "backward." Instead, he argued, Europe was abnormal, and I agree. Instead of, say, observing that Britain had the Industrial Revolution and asking why other places did not, it makes more sense to recognize that the Industrial Revolution was a weird thing to have. Furthermore, Europe was not abnormal because it was in some way superior. Its rise to global dominance during the capitalist period owed much to accidents, unexpected consequences, and violence.

In addition to a geographical scope, the focus on capitalism requires decisions about inclusion and exclusion of economic activity in different times and places. It is essential to remember that throughout the entire time span of this book, most people lived in rural settings, working in mostly subsistence or near-subsistence agriculture. Those settings were definitely economies, and can be studied as such, but they were mostly not capitalism. Likewise, well before the beginning of this book, many parts of the world, especially the Indian Ocean, were places where merchants conducted trade in order to earn profits. Those merchants might well be accurately called capitalists, and they also might well have owned capital in various forms, but that did not constitute capitalism, because those merchants always constituted a very small percentage of overall economic activity, did not provoke lasting structural change to economies or societies, and did not have sufficient political power to make laws and institutions to protect their interests. There were capitalists before capitalism, and noncapitalist economies after capitalism, but this book does not focus on either of those things.

In this book, capitalism is conceived as a kind of machine: It obeys the dumb, inhuman logic of its own unthinking operation. It cannot stop growing or expanding, even when that need threatens the existence of the machine itself and the planet the machine inhabits. Like all machines, it was made by people, and like many machines, it has made people different in response. Its history begins with the monetization of the European and Atlantic economies in the 16th and early 17th centuries. The sudden flow of silver into the Spanish Empire and then into the wider world produced a Price Revolution that not only scrambled relative prices but also led to more kinds of economic activity happening in markets, for money, rather than through custom, tradition, or community reciprocity. As more rents were denominated in cash, more farmers and peasants produced agriculture for sale in a market instead of for subsistence, and more landlords enclosed land and common grounds. The 17th century, then, saw the emergence of capitalist agriculture, a limited land market, and a growing landless labor force. The Dutch Republic was almost certainly the first capitalist polity in the world, and the large-scale wars of the late 17th century led to the need for states to borrow large sums of money. Those needs led to the Financial Revolution of the early 18th century, which created private capital markets, especially in Amsterdam and London. Overseas trade and marketization together pushed people to work longer hours for market wages—as did the enclosure of land and the loss of access to their own means of subsistence. By the middle of the 18th century, the private land market, wage labor market, and capital market together, as well as a new mass of wage-earning consumers, created the conditions for the British Industrial Revolution.

The Industrial Revolution was an astonishing transformation both of economic life and of the relationship between humans and the planet. It was a "metabolic rift," drawing down a finite stock of incredibly dense energy in the form of fossil fuels, and marshaling it to mechanized production that could produce vastly more output than anything ever had before.[22] That output raised human living standards, but at the cost of carbon emissions, deforestation, biodiversity loss, and the construction of an energy regime that has proved both destructive and difficult to transcend. The burning of fossil fuels was an addition to prior forms of energy usage, and even intensified the consumption of wood and animal power. From then on, economic life has entailed the continual addition of energy sources, not a series of transitions from wood to coal to oil, with a renewable one now on the horizon.[23]

Industrialization remade everything, but most of all, it lowered the costs of exporting empires and markets, so Europeans spent the 19th century doing just that. Imperialism forced more of the world into a single capitalist market system, centered around Britain. "Forced" in many ways: some financially through debts and indemnities, some peacefully through trade, and some violently, most notoriously in the case of the Belgian Congo. By 1914, capitalism was the dominant economic system in the world. It experienced a profound cataclysm between 1914 and about 1933: Its leaders crashed into the First World War, a slaughter of human beings on a previously unimaginable scale. The war in turn became an explicitly anticapitalist worker's revolution, starting in Russia in 1917. By 1921, it threatened all of central and eastern Europe, and potentially farther, as old hereditary empires collapsed in disarray. The 1920s were years of instability and crisis, culminating in 1929 with the outbreak of the Great Depression. By 1933, it looked to many observers, even observers sympathetic to capitalism, that the age of capital was over. While the capitalist West had years of grinding depression, the Soviet Union managed to complete its first Five-Year Plan in only four years. The Nazis came to power in Germany in 1933, appearing to usher in a more "modern," intentional, and aggressive successor to capitalism. If ever capitalism was going to collapse, 1917–33 was the moment.

But the insatiable machine survived. Those years were the last years in which history could have turned but didn't. The basic fact of the survival of capitalism has been the single most significant factor shaping world history ever since and will continue to be so for the imaginable future. The horizon of conceivable social transformation has not moved far beyond the terms of the communist imagination of 1917–33. In some ways, those years were one end of history. And therefore, that is where this book ends. There has never again been a serious, credible threat that global capitalism would be overthrown and replaced by another economic system. It may consume the world, it may substantially change in character, but there is no real alternative. Imagining a radical alternative requires first the recognition that the world around us is not permanent, natural, and inevitable. It hasn't always been this way. It was made by people, which means it can be unmade by them.

Martin Luther in 1517: The World Before Capitalism

History is the process of change over time, and the history of something as big and complex as capitalism can easily lose sight of the tangible experience of the people living through it. For that reason, at the beginning, middle, and end of this book we will pause briefly to orient ourselves by looking at the economic world of a convenient, well-known, profoundly weird, and temperamentally apocalyptic historical figure. The people themselves are not important, which is exactly the point. These are snapshots of the economic world each one inhabited—economic processes that were outside the control, and usually the understanding, of these famous figures and everyone else around them.

In October of 1517, a 34-year-old monk named Martin Luther (probably) nailed his famous Ninety-Five Theses to the door of All Saint's Church in Wittenberg, in what is now eastern Germany. Chief among his many complaints was the Catholic Church's sale of indulgences, which had become not only widespread but even mandatory for many priests, in order to generate funds to pay for the construction of Saint Peter's Basilica in Rome. Luther's protest began the long and complicated process of the many Reformations that shook the foundations of morality and authority in Christian Europe.[1] The Lutheran Protestant Reformation, and later the Swiss Calvinist Reformation as well as the many varieties of German Reformations like the Anabaptists and Unitarians, were not only a threat to the power and prestige of the Catholic Church but also a political threat to the rulers of Europe who derived their authority from a claim to divine approval. Most immediately, Luther's Reformation unleashed civil conflict and rebellion throughout the lands of Charles V, who was the heir to the Hapsburg dynasty. Thanks to his many grandiose inheritances, Charles ruled over territory that today comprises Austria, much of northern Italy, the Low Countries, and Spain. He was also elected Holy Roman emperor, which meant he nominally was the sovereign authority over most of what today is Germany. As king of Spain, he also ruled the rapidly expanding Spanish Empire in the New World, which at the end of his reign began to produce a planet-enveloping wave of silver.

The story of the Reformations is rich, complex, and vitally important to the history of modern Europe and America. But it is not our story. It is true that many theorists and historians have seen a connection between the practices and ideas of the Protestant Reformation and the emergence of capitalism, or at least a "spirit of capitalism," in England and the Dutch Republic.[2] That too is a fascinating body of thought and scholarship that is very closely related to our story, but it is not the story of this book. Instead, Luther marks a convenient reference point, a widely recognized historical moment that can focus our attention on the condition of the world right before the dawn of capitalism.

Luther was born in 1483 in the small town of Eisleben, in central Germany. When he was born, probably at least 90 percent of people in Europe and around the world lived in rural settings, mostly working in subsistence agriculture. Their households were both production and consumption units, meaning they made or grew most things that they consumed.[3] Most people worked about 150 days a year, with very busy times during planting and harvest seasons and lots of idle time otherwise.[4] Diets consisted of 1,200 to 1,800 calories a day of the cheapest available cereal grain: varieties of wheat or rye in Europe, millet in Africa, corn in Central America, quinoa and potatoes in South America, rice in much of the rest of the world.[5] That monotonous diet would be supplemented with eggs, milk, cheese, fish, or vegetables when available, and meat on special occasions. (Luther himself struggled with the diet: He was very bad at shitting, which afforded him plenty of time to cultivate his grievances.) In Europe at least, most people lived in single-room dwellings without windows and families all slept in the same bed. Most people owned one or two sets of clothing, mostly made of unbleached and uncolored wool. Most people were short and slight due to childhood malnutrition, and diseases scythed regularly through their weak immune systems. By any conceivable standard, their lives were miserable, boring, uncertain, short, and full of tragedy. By modern standards, nearly everyone on earth lived lives of grinding, unthinkable poverty. But it isn't quite right to think that a subsistence economy was permanently balanced at the edge of starvation. It produced enough food to continue indefinitely, but without much surplus, which meant that disasters—whether wars, droughts, floods, or otherwise—could cause widespread misery, and the paltry surplus meant that only a relatively small urban non-food-producing population could be sustained, and thus a limited division of labor.

As with all preindustrial societies, European society was fundamentally a rural, peasant society. Scattered across the continent were hundreds of towns populated by a few hundred people, and each of these towns had an economic hinterland of perhaps 50 to 100 square miles, with the bulk of all agricultural and household production produced and remaining in that area.[6] A small amount of output moved among these areas, consisting largely of luxury goods or marketable surpluses. The relatively few wage laborers mostly lived in these towns, and the relatively few merchants traveled or arranged trade among them. For peasants, "the market" was a literal, physical place, somewhere they would travel to visit on market days, to buy luxuries or sell their surpluses. It might have been one of the few occasions when they would meet people from elsewhere and learn news and stories from outside their local area. It was also the main place where money was needed: Households did not need money for their own production and consumption, and trade among locals, who knew one another and went to church together, was mostly unmonetized, done through exchanges in kind or through keeping running debts with each other.[7]

There were many circuits of long-distance trade, mostly organized around large bodies of water, mostly conducted by small ships that could not sail in open ocean. The Indian Ocean was a vibrant, multilateral trading zone, as was the South China Sea.[8] The Mediterranean remained a trading world, but less than it had been before the Muslim conquests. Europe turned inward, with trade currents mostly running along navigable rivers. Some threads of trade connected the different zones, like the Silk Road across central Asia, or the trans-Saharan caravans. But in general, long-distance trade was in small amounts of luxury goods, and mostly conducted by ethnic or religious communities who were bound by trust and kinship. Most people never experienced those goods or the procedures of that commerce, or did so only rarely.

When Europeans did encounter protoindustry, trade, and commerce, it was almost always tightly regulated by government officials, guilds, customs, or local powers. Writing of 17th-century England (more than a hundred years after Luther), the radical historian Christopher Hill reminds us that the typical Englishman lived "in a house built with monopoly bricks . . . heated by monopoly coal. His clothes are held up by monopoly belts, monopoly buttons, monopoly pins. . . . He ate monopoly butter, monopoly currants, monopoly red herrings, monopoly salmon, monopoly lobsters."[9] Many places had sumptuary laws, which regulated consumption. In the year of Luther's birth, for example, England enacted a second Act of Apparel, restricting sable, ermine, velvet, and satin brocade to knights and lords, while damask and satin were allowed for people who had a yearly income of at least £40.[10] These laws were probably rarely enforced, but they indicate how little economic activity was subject to markets and individual preferences, not just in land, labor, and capital or the methods of production, but also in consumption.

In 1517, wage labor was an unusual exception all over the world. European peasants were often serfs, not owners, meaning they lived on rented land and had to pay a variety of lords, priests, and judges, either by delivering a share of their produce or, often, by working a set number of days each month. They were legally bound to their plot of land, meaning they could not leave if they wanted, and they certainly could not sell their land, but they also could not be fired or evicted. Serfdom came with a set of customary privileges and obligations, and serfs were often keen to assert their rights. But they were not free. There were other forms of unfree labor as well: Guilds controlled entry and exit to trades, servants had no legal personage separate from their masters, indenture bound laborers to employers for set periods of time, and although slavery was not yet widespread in Europe it certainly existed.

Other places had other forms of unfree or bonded labor. Russian serfs were even more tightly controlled and had fewer rights than those in western Europe. There were widespread systems of Islamic slavery in the Middle East, Indian Ocean, and East African economies, as well as systems of captured slaves in West Africa.[11] The Aztecs had enslaved laborers who could be bought and sold as well as peasants who could be temporarily conscripted by temples and local nobles into larger projects.[12] In South America,

Incan peasants were subject to a labor draft called the *mita*, which was later taken over by the Spanish conquistadores. But although unfree labor was the norm, with a few exceptions there was not yet the form of permanent, heritable, racialized chattel slavery that would emerge in the Atlantic economies, especially in the 17th and 18th centuries.[13]

Both global and European population ebbed and flowed from generation to generation, but fundamentally remained static across centuries, held back by truly ferocious rates of infant, childhood, and maternal mortality. Low average life expectancy was a reflection of the fact that about half of all babies died before the age of five. People who survived childhood could expect to live into their 60s. European population growth was also unusual in that it was subject to what is known as the "European marriage pattern."[14] Unlike most everywhere else in the world, Europeans married relatively late (in their early 20s instead of in their teens), and an abnormally high percentage of them never married, perhaps as high as 5 percent, mostly because they entered religious orders, which meant married women had one or two fewer children each, and a relatively large number of women never had children at all. Thus, the European population seems to have grown more slowly than that of South or East Asia. The great interruption was the Black Death of 1347–51, which killed between a third and half of the population of Eurasia, and from which the European population had only begun to recover in Luther's time.[15]

The relatively stagnant population and the preponderance of people living and working in subsistence agriculture meant that the desperately poor preindustrial world was also one of relative economic equality *between* societies. Of course there were profound and solid social, political, and gendered inequalities *within* societies, and of course kings and popes lived amid grandeur while most people lived in single-room dwellings with dirt floors.[16] But that pattern of inequality was roughly consistent across space, unlike the sharp modern gaps between countries, and even kings and popes died of illnesses and suffered from toothaches like everyone else. Even as late as the 1820s, the richest countries on earth (Britain and the Netherlands) were only three to five times richer than the poorest countries, whereas today the gap is more than a hundred to one.[17]

I do not mean to suggest that economic life before 1500 was stagnant or unchanging. There were many phases of expansion and contraction, population growth and decline, commercial flourishing and imperial fiscal crises. There is good evidence of extensive economic growth when new lands, goods, and people were added to production, and certainly some productivity improvements in agricultural techniques. There was probably an efflorescence of economic growth in China under the Song dynasty, circa 960–1276, partly driven by a new strain of rice.[18] However, all over the world and over the course of perhaps 20 generations, most people lived in rural settings, mostly working in subsistence agriculture, and trade was always and everywhere of small scale, as were monetization and market relations. Nowhere were free wage labor markets a norm, nor free land markets, nor capital markets, and there were no banks, stock markets, or joint-stock companies. There was one notable exception, which is that a land market had existed in China since the mid-Tang dynasty, circa 800 CE.[19] Land could be freely bought or sold or rented, although there were a variety of legal and customary restrictions that meant the land market was not a smooth mechanism of resource allocation. In northern China, tenancy was the norm, mostly held by at-will tenants with little bargaining power, paying as much as half their output in rent, while in richer and more commercialized southern China, owner-worker systems were the norm. But even this private market existed mostly with benign neglect from the state, not through the rigorous enforcement of property rights and contracts, as under capitalism. Most agriculture was done by small-scale tenants or owners, not by large landlords employing wage workers, and the rural economy remained nonmonetized until well into the 16th century.[20] The wage labor sector in China, as elsewhere, remained a tiny fraction of economic activity.

By 1517, the world had seen no sustained economic growth, nor sustained population growth. In fact, the world I have described here remained the norm for most people in most parts of the world throughout the entire time span of this book, and some elements persisted well into the 20th century. Indeed, the United Nations has estimated that 2007 was the first year when the majority of human beings lived in cities instead of rural areas.[21] The life of rural agricultural workers in Siberia, inland China, sub-Saharan Africa, and India in 1917 would have been touched more often and more deeply by capitalism than the rural life of 1517, but capitalism still did not shape and determine *every* aspect of their lives, even their economic lives.

What kind of change was imaginable in this world? Luther was an apocalyptic thinker, and his ideas were spread through a vital new technology: the printing press, which had been invented by the German goldsmith Johannes Gutenberg around the year 1450. Print would go on to play a vital role in the development of capitalism, transmitting price lists, important news, advertisements, and policy disputes all around the world. The rise of literacy and secular education were also important drivers of economic development. Luther's vision of the possibility for radical change was very different from our own. Luther had no concept of a new economic system, or an environmental catastrophe. But Luther was not the only apocalyptic thinker of his time. His ideas precipitated a tectonic crisis of political legitimacy and unleashed a series of continent-wide wars, sometimes featuring millenarian protocommunist sects like the Anabaptists, who sought to overthrow the social order. The radical theologian Thomas Müntzer predicted an apocalyptic social leveling, ultimately producing a kind of egalitarian utopia. Müntzer's teachings helped provoke the widespread uprising of the German peasants in 1525, and have served as a kind of progenitor inspiration for later communist thinkers, from Friedrich Engels to Ernst Bloch.[22] The Anabaptists were a radical nonconformist sect that took the egalitarian, pacifist, and renunciatory injunctions of the Bible seriously and tried to organize communal living, before being ruthlessly persecuted by the authorities and other Protestant sects. But although these years saw a crisis of the old order and a profusion of utopian or apocalyptic egalitarian thinking, it was still organized around theological rather than economic ideas. There was not yet a capitalism to revolt against. The horizons of Luther's and Müntzer's thought were anchored to their time, and a reminder that even people who have a powerful effect on the course of history are unable to imagine what consequences will follow from their actions, or how the world is going to change.

CHAPTER 1

Money, 1415–1650s

When most people think of capitalism, they think of money. Capitalism is associated with making money or with a greedy love for money, and capitalists are people who have a lot of money. And that intuition is right: The origins of capitalism cannot be told without telling the history of money. To be sure, capitalism involves a great many other aspects and processes, but there is no capitalism without money, and the slow beginning of the monetization of the global economy between 1415 and the 1650s unsettled the old customary world of exchange and production, clearing the way and creating the incentives for capitalist economic activity. At first this monetization was relatively shallow, as a common coinage became recognized and used at trading ports around the world, and it took a long time for money to predominate in daily transactions. But once begun, the process did not stop. Further, the actual activities of mining, transport, minting, and bullion selling were in private hands from the beginning, conducted for private profit, so the "money industry" was one of the first capitalist sectors of the global economy.

Between about 1415 and about 1570, Portuguese and Spanish merchants, sailors, and soldiers circled the planet in search of spices and gold. They found them, and many more things besides. Their explorations initiated titanic, wrenching processes of historical change: the conquest of the Americas and the deaths of probably 90 percent of their Indigenous inhabitants; the enslavement and forced transportation of millions of Africans; the reconfiguration of enormous territories and environments into production of cash crops for international sale or to generate provisions for gigantic newly created mining cities. In 1545 two enormous mountains of silver were discovered in the new Spanish Empire, one in Zacatecas in northern Mexico and one in the high mountains of Potosí in what is now Bolivia. The wave of silver those mountains unleashed spread slowly around the world over the next century in a process known as the Price Revolution. Beginning in Spain and spreading then to the commercial centers of Italy, France, and the Netherlands, then to their trading partners in England, the Baltic, and the Ottoman Empire, and finally reaching India and China, the unbelievable inflows of silver led to more than a century of continual price increases. By modern standards of inflation, the rate was very low, but by the standards of the 1540s, it was unprecedented and incomprehensible. As with modern inflation, the overall rate obscures a lot of difference: Some prices rose rapidly, others more slowly, others not at all. The uneven and unpredictable rate of price increases in different areas, markets, and types of economic activity enriched some groups of people and ruined others. By about 1650, the world was encircled by a single monetary system, based on the silver Spanish "piece of eight" coin, and the commercial world was monetized and presided over by a newly enriched commercial class, at the expense of some landowners and most wage laborers. New World silver and the Price Revolution did not create capitalism alone, but capitalism could not have emerged without the conditions they produced.

The voyages of discovery and conquest themselves could not have happened without several institutional and technological preconditions mostly developed in the late Middle Ages. Italian merchants developed double-entry bookkeeping in the fourteenth century, which made business accounting easier and clearer, and they adopted Arabic numerals instead of the cumbersome Roman system. Genoese and Venetian sailors developed better maps and compasses, which made open-sea navigation possible. Portuguese and Spanish sailors developed caravels, a new type of ship with triangular sails that could sail into the wind and in open ocean.[1] Florentine and Genoese bankers developed systems for currency exchange and commercial loans. Each of these was a component of the later world of early capitalism, but they did not together amount to capitalism any more than a pile of eggs, sugar, flour, and baking powder amounts to a cake. Instead, it took the promise of profits to make it pay to apply these technologies and techniques.

Likewise, capitalists existed all over the world, in the form of merchants conducting trade on a price-conscious rational basis for the purposes of making profit. Such merchants could be found from the Azores in the Atlantic to the Sahara to northern China. In some places in West Africa, private textile manufacture was already produced by wage labor.[2] But nowhere were these merchants politically dominant, nor was society run for their benefit and according to their preferences. To use a strange contemporary parallel, today there are communists and anarchists in the United States, but that does not mean there is either communism or anarchism. The monetization of the early modern world is a story made by capitalists, driven by the accumulation and destruction of capital, but it was not yet a world of capitalism; rather, it was a necessary step in its making, both through the destruction of the old social world and by the empowerment of the new.

■ ■ ■

The story of the global monetary system begins in the unprepossessing city of Ceuta, on the northern coast of Morocco, opposite the Rock of Gibraltar. Today it is still legally a part of Spain, an autonomous low-tax city that serves as a giant duty-free shop and a place where people in Morocco can buy alcohol. In 1415, it was a major commercial port that connected the trans-Saharan caravan trade to the Mediterranean. At that time, the Italian Renaissance was just beginning, and city-states like Florence, Milan, and Venice were among the richest and most powerful places in the broader Mediterranean world. But commerce in the western sea was dominated by the Genoese Republic, whose merchants had seized and ransomed Ceuta in the year 1235. By 1415, they had established a trading agency in Ceuta, as well as some of the first modern banks in Genoa itself, and their sailors were among the most technically skilled and knowledgeable in the world. Indeed, the case has been made that the first "cycle" of capitalism could best be described as the Genoese cycle.[3]

In addition to the beginnings of the Italian Renaissance, another sweeping historical transformation was underway in the Iberian Peninsula: the Reconquista, or the defeat and expulsion of Islam from continental Europe. The war of the Christians against the Islamic caliphates had been ongoing for centuries, but by about 1250, the great strongholds of Seville and Córdoba had fallen, leaving only the very southern kingdom of Granada under Muslim rule. There was nothing modern or capitalist about this war: It was a religious conflict, conducted by divine medieval kings for the control of territory then governed through old royal land-grant systems. By 1415, Portugal and the kingdom of Castile (which would later become what we now know as Spain) were rival forces in the Reconquista, each trying to outdo the other in the capture of remaining Muslim territory. The Portuguese capture of Ceuta in August of 1415 was an extension of that process.

There were several reasons for King John I of Portugal to cross the Strait of Gibraltar and invade North Africa. The first was religious: For the Portuguese, there was no reason for the Reconquista to end when all Muslims had been forced out of Europe, instead of defeated everywhere on earth. There was also a political reason: In 1385, Castile tried to take over Portugal and failed, but many Portuguese nobles joined the Castilian side and were subsequently wiped out in their defeat at the Battle of Aljubarrota. With them gone, the commercial merchant class became the most powerful faction in Lisbon and wanted to take over markets from the Genoese. The military elite wanted more conquest, because that meant more glory and more land to be distributed to them as rewards. And there was another economic reason: The population of Portugal had slowly been recovering from the catastrophe of the Black Death in 1348–50. By 1415, it had recovered enough that food was becoming scarce, and Portugal had no access to gold or silver to import food from elsewhere. Ceuta offered a solution to everything: more conquest, markets taken from Genoa, and access to the ancient breadbasket of North Africa.

The invasion succeeded, but like most successful military exploits, it created more problems than it solved. The city was immediately surrounded by Muslim forces and put under siege, so it required a continual drain of resources and did not actually provide access to farms and food. But upon taking the city, the Portuguese discovered something else: It was the end point of gold caravans crossing the Sahara. They realized that they could probably get to the source of the gold if they could sail around the Sahara, and so their expeditions into the Atlantic began.

From 1418 through the 1440s, Portuguese sailors explored, charted, and sometimes conquered a small Atlantic island empire. The Atlantic was a kind of rival imperial project to continued invasions of North Africa: There was no single, coherent unified plan for expansion, and it was far from certain that the Atlantic plan would work, because it meant continued competition with Genoa. In 1418–24, Portugal settled the islands of Madeira, about 320 miles west from the coast of Morocco. Then in 1424–27, they settled part of the Canary Islands, 250 miles farther south. Then in

1427–31, it was the Azores, some 900 miles out into the Atlantic. Most of these places had been known to sailors, but for the first time they were permanently settled, with land titles distributed to settlers by royal authority and official recognition from the pope. The Canary Islands had been under conquest by Castile for years, involving a wholesale genocide of the Indigenous Guanches, but the others were uninhabited. Madeira especially became integrated into the European economy as a sugar producer, and by its height around 1510, it had 200 plantations and was probably the largest sugar producer in the world.

Everything changed in the 1440s. In 1442, a ship returned from the Sahara with a cargo of African slaves, and according to one historian, their sale in Lisbon "caused something of a sensation."[4] More ships set sail right away, and in 1445, Portuguese traders made contact with African merchants from the city of Wadan, now known as Oudane, 200 miles into the Sahara in what is now Mauritania. The African merchants had come to the coast looking for salt and were willing to pay in gold. Finally the Portuguese had found what they failed to find in Ceuta: a way around the Saharan caravans, and direct access to African gold. Long before Africa began to feature in the history of capitalism as a source of enslaved labor, its currencies, metals, and export commodities connected European markets to internal African markets and eventually Asian markets.[5]

Portuguese exploration continued along the coast of Africa, with settlements and conquest in the Cape Verde Islands in the 1450s–60s and São Tomé and Príncipe in the late 1470s–90s. In the first decades, this expansion continued to be medieval and patrimonial in form: A member of the royal family would own a monopoly on commerce to West Africa, and he (always a he) would license individual voyages at his discretion, for a payment. That meant merchants would bear the cost of the initial payment plus the costs and risks of the voyages, so only a few rich merchants could participate and would mostly undertake only voyages that were known to be profitable. Then in 1469, a merchant named Fernão Gomes bought the monopoly to trade in the Gulf of Guinea on the condition that he explore an additional 300 miles down the coast every year. That he did, and directly organized fleets, because he knew that having paid for the monopoly, he would enjoy all of the profits he could find. In 1471, he found a thriving town at a place called Elmina in what is now Ghana, complete with an alluvial gold source, which, as one historian put it, "opened up opportunities for commercial wealth far in excess of the small-scale profits obtained up to that time from single-ship trading."[6] He returned in 1482 with 10 ships and built a permanent fortress at Elmina. Within a few years, an average of 12 ships per year were making the round-trip voyage from Lisbon to Elmina, carrying gold. These ships delivered about 8,000 ounces of gold in 1487–89, rising to as much as 22,500 ounces in 1494–96.[7] That was a trivial amount by

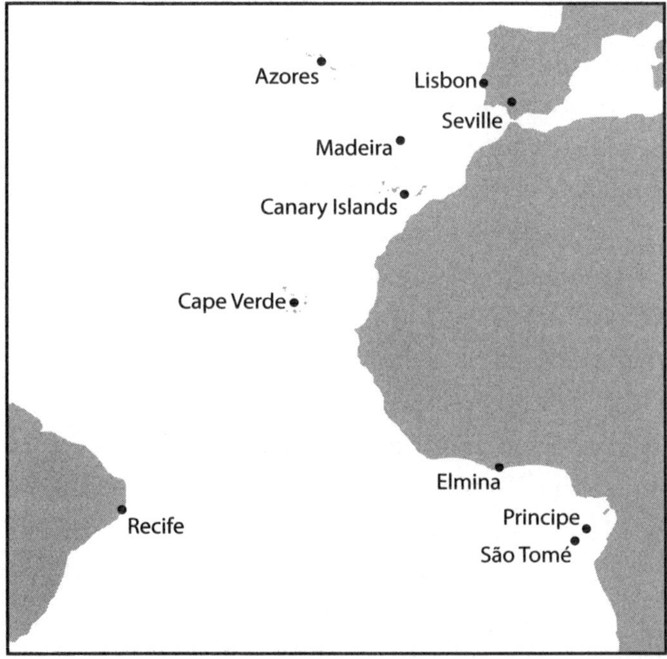

The Portuguese Atlantic empire, circa 1550

the standards of a continental economy, but an enormous amount for a small cash-poor kingdom, and an unimaginable amount for the individual merchants.

But in order to obtain gold, the Portuguese needed something to sell. At first they sold cloth, but it took a lot of cloth to get gold, and Portuguese wool was not especially popular in sub-Saharan Africa. Instead, the answer they found was slaves.

It is essential here to note two things. First, the history of money and gold was connected to and indeed depended on slavery from the beginning. And second, Europeans initially got involved in the African slave trade because they were looking for gold, not because they were looking for slaves. In order to buy slaves, they needed something to sell, so initially they got involved in a kind of complicated arbitrage trade among goods, slaves, and gold, rather than being involved in a specialized slave trade as would be the case in later centuries. Portugal had a near monopoly on the Atlantic slave trade for a century, and although there are no reliable records of how many Africans they sold to other Africans for gold, they forcibly delivered about 800 people per year to Portugal, and by the end of the century, Lisbon had a substantial African population.[8] Over the next 350 years, the Portuguese enslaved some 5.85 million people—more than the British Empire did, but unlike the British, they mostly transported people from a relatively concentrated area around Angola to Brazil, so Portuguese slaving did not reconfigure the Atlantic economy writ large.[9]

The wild success of the Elmina gold trade incentivized even more exploration. Bartholomeu Dias rounded the Cape of Good Hope into the Indian Ocean in 1488; Vasco da Gama reached India in 1498; in 1500, Pedro Álvares Cabral took advantage of the winds to swing far out into the Atlantic and stumbled upon Brazil; and in 1519, Ferdinand Magellan led (but was killed halfway through) a voyage that circumnavigated the globe.

When the Portuguese reached the Indian Ocean, they discovered a vibrant trading world. Lacking the manpower, firepower, or financial power to dominate it outright, they focused on excluding all European rivals. They declared possession of an ocean empire, the Estado da India, or State of India, in which they claimed the whole Indian Ocean as theirs, just as kings and emperors claimed ownership over landed territory. Their territory would be encircled by forts where they would collect and process the fruits of their trading and plunder, to be sent back to Portugal in fleets, and these forts would also serve as bases for raiding, safe harbors for their licensed merchants, and positions to enforce their monopoly on access to the Indian Ocean. By the 1550s, there were about 50 forts spanning from what is now Goa, on the west coast of India, to Macao in southern China. Every year five or six large ships left Lisbon full of silver, guns, and sailors and a different five or six would return full of pepper, spices, jewels, and silks.

The Estado da India was a final medieval attempt to keep a huge overseas empire under direct royal monopoly, because the rights to trade in spices, ivory, and horses were all royal possessions, and the whole territory was ostensibly governed by a viceroy directly appointed by the Crown. This system mostly failed. Many of the colonies and trading posts governed themselves autonomously and pursued their own interests, and many of the sailors and soldiers stayed in Asia and intermarried with locals, producing a mixed diaspora population instead of a body of state employees. The Portuguese entry into the Indian Ocean broke the older Arabic monopoly on the East African trades without successfully establishing a new Portuguese monopoly in its place.[10] It was so easy to evade royal enforcement that many forts and merchants traded for themselves instead, or contracted with cheaper rivals. The Portuguese Empire was less of a coherent political unit with border enforcement and governance and more of a diverse set of separate trading communities, some relatively integrated into existing social structures, others creating new settlements from scratch.

There was a lot of latitude for local private initiative and not much control, coordination, or intentional policy direction from the center. But it set the machine in motion.

■ ■ ■

As everyone knows, in 1492, Christopher Columbus was discovered by Native Americans. He was born in the Republic of Genoa, and as a young man took part in the Genoese trading voyages to England, Ireland, Lisbon, and Madeira. He was on a voyage to Elmina in 1482–85, and in 1492, he was hired by Ferdinand and Isabella of Castile, who had just succeeded in driving the last Muslims out of Granada. In this way, he combined in himself all of the elements of this early trading world, from the trade of Genoa to the Portuguese gold in Africa to the Reconquista in Spain.

Since Castile was still the rival of Portugal, and Portugal had been enjoying such success finding gold in Africa, Ferdinand and Isabella decided to fund Columbus in an attempt to reach the Indian Ocean by sailing across the Atlantic. He was looking for spices and lands to conquer, but he was also looking for gold. In fact, he was *obsessed* with finding gold. Between October 12, 1492, when he first made landfall in the New World, and January 17, 1493, when he set sail back for Spain, his diary mentions gold at least 65 times.[11]

And find gold he did. The Indigenous peoples of the Caribbean islands gathered it from rivers and used it for decorative purposes, especially the Taíno of the island of Hispaniola, which today comprises Haiti and the Dominican Republic. Starting with Columbus's second voyage in 1494 through about 1525, the Spanish conquistadores seized and exploited essentially the entirety of the gold in the Caribbean, probably taking more in the first two to three years than had been produced over the previous millennium.[12] Columbus tortured and murdered Indigenous people to learn the source of their gold, and eventually enslaved thousands, forcing them to gather the alluvial gold dust. Much of the forced labor was women and children, since the men were either killed or shipped back to Spain as slaves, and the combined effect destroyed the basis of the subsistence agricultural economy, leading to a wholesale collapse of the Indigenous population. Together, Portuguese gold from Elmina and Spanish gold from the Caribbean amounted to something like 700 kilograms per year at its peak arriving at Lisbon and 1,000 kilograms at Seville. In 1500, Columbus and his brothers were arrested by a new Spanish governor and sent back to Spain as prisoners, charged with mismanagement and abuse of his powers. The Crown refused to honor its contract with him, and he and his heirs spent decades in litigation, suing for a share of the profits from the conquest of the New World. By the 1520s, this first "gold cycle" was exhausted.

The story of blood, money, and capitalism may well have ended there, with an Atlantic extension of the medieval Reconquista to a new continent and a wave of plundered gold arriving in Spain. But the promise of more gold, more territory and titles, more converted Christians and prestige, was enough to provoke further conquests, with perhaps world history's most appalling loss of human life. Between 1519 and 1521, the conquistador Hernán Cortés joined with some Indigenous allies to conquer Tenochtitlán, the capital of the Aztec Empire, killing perhaps a quarter-million people in the process. Tenochtitlán became Mexico City, the capital of New Spain, and the Aztec Empire shattered in defeat and despair. Smallpox and social dislocation stampeded through the Indigenous population, killing perhaps eight million people and creating millions of internal migrants. Further epidemics throughout the 16th and 17th centuries killed probably at least 80 percent of the preconquest population. In the 1530s, the conquistador Francisco Pizarro arrived in the Incan Empire, in what is now Peru. The Incan Emperor Huayna Capac died from European smallpox, which kicked off a war of dynastic succession that allowed Pizarro to gather some resentful Indigenous allies and conquer the Incan Empire. As with the Aztecs in Mexico, disease, state disintegration, and continued warfare produced death and social disaster on an incredible scale.[13] In the course of three decades, the social and political world of the Americas had been destroyed. And then in the 1540s, something new took its place.

According to tradition, in 1545 a Native Andean man named either Gualpa or Guanca was chasing either a llama or a deer up a steep peak called Potoc'chi and discovered an outcrop of silver. Or he was knocked down by a gust of wind, possibly sent by God or *a* god, and found his hands were covered in silver dust. Whatever the case, control over the new silver strike that he found was immediately wrapped up in a civil conflict among the Spanish conquistadores scrambling to mine it. Already by 1549, some 5,000 Andeans held in encomienda servitude were at work in what became known as the Cerro Rico, or "Rich Hill."[14] The encomienda system was a semi-feudal form of forced labor, in which colonial authorities had the ability to demand at will the labor of Indigenous people within a given territory. Meanwhile, in Mexico, a conquistador named Juan de Tolosa had spent the early 1540s in a series of small wars against Indigenous people, and sometimes was given stones laced with silver as tribute or gifts. He traced the silver to its origin and, after many failed lines of investigation, organized a permanent settlement at the silver mines in Zacatecas.[15]

The simultaneous discoveries of Potosí and Zacatecas in 1545–46, followed by the application of a new mercury-amalgam process in the Mexican mines in 1559–62 and Peru in 1570–72 unleashed a wave of silver unlike anything the world had ever seen before, and an economic and colonial bonanza as people rushed to get a piece of the plunder. By the 1570s, Potosí had a population of over 50,000, making it the largest city in the Western Hemisphere and larger than all but 10 European cities.[16] By the early 17th century, its population was over 120,000.[17] It is 13,200 feet above sea level in the

Andes, and about 1,416 miles from the coastal port at Lima. That enormous population had to be fed, provisioned, sheltered, and paid by supplies brought on pack mules or llama trains, an arduous two-to-three-month journey of thousands of animals struggling under the weight of their cargo up the sides of the Andes.[18] Zacatecas, meanwhile, was on the frontier, in the desert of north-central Mexico, nowhere near the established population centers of the Aztec Empire. Stanley and Barbara Stein, the historians of early modern Spain, describe the consequences:

> Zacatecas's rapid evolution from frontier to settled community during the forty years between 1550 and 1590 transformed surrounding semiarid grasslands into cattle ranches producing beef, hides for ropes and sacking, large quantities of tallow for candles. More distant forests became lumber sources for mine timbers and smelters. Producers in the fertile Bajío in the south and in the Aguascalientes valley soon satisfied demand for wheat and corn. On the highway (*camino real de tierra adentro*) north from Mexico City hundreds of miles away moved the basic mining inputs of mercury, iron and steel bars, and hardware imported from Europe along with other valuable European imports of Rouen woolens, Breton and Dutch linens, Asian silks, and even Persian carpets. Mine workers bought woolens and other goods and, in fact, were frequently paid in overpriced textiles rather than silver pesos. Cattle ranches along the highway provided oxen and mules for heavy two-wheeled carts and mule teams freighting goods from Mexico City to Zacatecas and beyond and back to Mexico City over a combined distance of more than 1,500 miles.[19]

In the frantic boomtown of Potosí, mine owners, mostly Europeans but also including some Andean Natives and some free Africans, scrambled for claims. These were private entrepreneurs, and as two economic historians record, "Anyone who discovered minerals could stake a claim of 160 by 80 *varas* (approximately 440 by 220 feet) along or across the vein and could additionally pursue a continuous vein outside the claim. Miners had to continuously work their claims and submit production to the treasury for minting and to pay taxes. Taxes consisted of a royalty of at most 20 percent (known as the quinto), plus additional (but much smaller) assaying, brassage, and seigniorage taxes related to the minting of coins."[20] Soon open-air pits gave way to shafts and scaffolds, creating a boom in blacksmiths and engineers, including enslaved Africans, and a proliferation of Andean women running market stalls to feed and clothe the workers.[21] Women and children worked in crushing mills, and miners worked round-the-clock shifts carrying shoulder sacks of 50 or 75 pounds of ore out of the dark shafts. Any nearby trees were cut down to build the mine supports. The city, divided into Spanish and Indigenous sectors, filled up with merchants and moneylenders who advanced funds to miners and prospectors, with notaries and officials who recorded claims and sales, and with llamas that could carry weight in the high altitudes. Exposed hillsides were soon riddled with wind furnaces to melt the silver, venting lead fumes from the smelting process.[22]

In the early stages, the mines were worked by a mix of paid Andean workers, enslaved Africans, rented day laborers called *mingados*, forced encomienda laborers, and Spanish overseers. But mines were very difficult and time-consuming to dig in an era before controlled demolition, and the silver got harder and harder to find, while demand only continued to grow. In 1572, the reforming Viceroy Toledo decided to reintroduce an Incan system of forced labor called the *mita*, or "shift." The area around Potosí was divided into 17 districts, each of which was to provide the mines and mills with 16 percent of its able-bodied men each year. That should have produced 13,500 workers, who would work underground in three shifts of 4,500 men at a time.[23] This created a kind of underclass, raising the wages and prestige of the rented day-labor *mingados*; the *mita* draftees were paid 10 pesos a month, if they were actually paid at all, and they suffered truly horrifying levels of disease, injury, and death.[24] They were not slaves: They were paid, and the work was not permanent or heritable. But the *mita* was a brutal and cruel form of coerced labor specific to the mines, and it was abolished only in the early 19th century. It predated the Spanish conquest but was now turned to new purposes, for profit instead of prestige.

Continued silver production required an amalgamation process developed by German miners and Spanish merchants that used salt and mercury to separate silver from rock. Fortunately enough, the Spanish Crown possessed two enormous mercury deposits, one in Almadén in central Spain, and the other at Huancavelica, near Lima in Peru. The Crown kept these mines for itself, unlike the privately run silver mines. It instituted a *mita* in Huancavelica, probably more deadly than the one in Potosí, given how dangerous a substance mercury is. The liquid metal was poured into sheepskins and carried by mules down to the Pacific coast, to be shipped south, then carried up the Andes by llamas.[25]

By law, all of the silver of the New World empire that was shipped back to Spain had to be taken directly to the House of Trade (Casa de Contratación) in Seville, 54 miles up the Guadalquivir River. The colonial officials there recorded the number, weight, and fineness of all precious metals, as well as the people and merchandise, on every returning vessel. They also received reports from the colonies of silver shipments, and were watchful of discrepancies.[26] This soon became a vast colonial bureaucracy. From the House of Trade, specialized merchants would buy the silver and sell it to traders and financiers who needed it for their own operations. In 1608, the government ruled that only firms of two or more partners could operate as silver merchants, leading to the legal concept of a limited joint partnership, which was part of the origin of the modern corporation. But despite the efforts of the Spanish Crown to concentrate and control the flows of silver, Seville soon had a remarkably cosmopolitan mercantile community, full of shipowners and captains as well as merchants and bankers, ranging from Castilians and Andalusians to Basques, Aragonese, Genoese, Portuguese, Flemish, and Germans.[27] In return, these merchants and captains outfitted their ships for the return voyages, supplying everything the booming mining colonies needed, including handling reexports from elsewhere, so Flemish cloth or English hardware would be shipped first to Seville, then sent along by Sevillian merchants to Lima or Veracruz. Many of these merchants traded on credit, meaning they needed constant access to bankers and financiers.

At least, the silver was *supposed* to arrive at Seville. In the New World, only a few ports were licensed to receive goods from the Old World and formed the shipment points for outbound silver. They were Veracruz in Mexico, Cartagena in Colombia, Amatique and Trujillo in Honduras, and Nombre de Dios and Portobelo in Panama, as well as Lima in Peru. At each of these places, silver would wait and be gathered until it filled a fleet of ships, which would travel together in a convoy with armed escorts to fight off pirates and rival navies. In 1628, the Dutch managed to capture an entire silver fleet, in what might be the largest heist in world history, and in 1656, the English managed to chase a fleet off from Spain, but otherwise the convoys worked. The problem was costs. Every merchant who had silver in the convoy had to contribute to its costs, so every merchant had an incentive to smuggle silver through other means, or not declare its true value to the convoy authorities, or transport it secretly through other ports. As some merchants chose to smuggle their silver, the cost of the convoys fell more heavily on the remaining merchants, increasing their incentive to also smuggle. By the 1630s, Spanish government representatives were writing memoranda complaining that since the Crown couldn't smuggle or exempt itself, it was paying more than its fair share of the convoy costs.

On the other side of the world, every year starting in 1565 two giant ships called galleons sailed from Acapulco on the west coast of Mexico to bring silver to China, where it would be exchanged for porcelain, ivory, and silk. In 1571, the city of Manila in the Philippines was founded as the Spanish trade entrepôt, so that became the destination for these ships, giving them the general name of the "Manila galleons." Chinese traders managed to wrest permission to conduct foreign trade from the otherwise hostile Ming government, and began shipping silk and porcelain to Manila in exchange for silver, complementing the Portuguese-dominated trade from Canton and Macao that had been established in the 1550s.[28] From that moment on, a substantial and continuous trade route crossed the Pacific for the first time in human history, so 1571 is a plausible date for the specific year that the global economy was born.[29]

World spanning they might have been, but the silver flows were leaky. A huge amount of the silver stayed in the New World, paid in wages to workers, who in turn paid it to farmers, landlords, and local merchants, as well as to international merchants bringing goods from the authorized ports. Indeed, surprisingly enough, recent research has indicated that wage workers in the New World were among the highest-paid workers in the world.[30] To be sure, they also lived in some of the most expensive places in the world, as the continual flow of metal money produced a localized inflation. But they were paid, and paid relatively well, although the work was grueling and they were not free subjects as we would understand them today.

This fact is of vital importance to the history of capitalism. It is true that in the early years of the Spanish conquest, the conquistadores used forced-labor systems. They used the *mita*, which had previously been an Incan system, and they used the encomienda, which was adapted from the Old World. They enslaved people and sent them across the Atlantic, and forced others to work to death pulling gold out of rivers. But those forced-labor systems predated the conquest: None of them were new, and none of them were inherently capitalist. Instead, the truly new labor institution that came with the Spanish conquest was widespread wage labor. And wage labor is the capitalist mode of labor *par excellence*. For all the debate over the connection between capitalism and Atlantic slavery, the more fundamental point is that the conquest of the New World meant the invention and introduction of wage labor.

■ ■ ■

A lot of the silver stayed in the New World and monetized its economy through systems of wage labor and long-distance trade. A lot of it leaked, through smuggling or illegal diversions, remaining in private possession, and entering into Dutch, English, or French mercantile trades. But a lot of it, never less than half the total produced, made the trip to Seville, where about 20 percent went into the vaults of the Spanish Crown. The rest went into private hands. And from Spain, it mostly flowed out again, through three channels.

First, the Spanish Crown paid for its wars. Throughout this period, Spain was governed by the Hapsburg royal family, who also held title to lands in Austria, northern Italy, the Netherlands, and the office of the Holy Roman emperor in what is now Germany. Charles V combined all these crowns into one person, and spent his long reign dealing with the Protestant Reformation that began in 1517 and that by 1525 had erupted into generalized warfare and rebellion across Germany. He viewed himself as the great defender of Christendom against its enemies, which meant enormous, sustained warfare all over the world, against Protestants and Muslims as well as his French rivals. His son, Philip II, united the crowns of Portugal and Spain and inherited many of his father's offices (though not the Holy Roman Empire or Austria-Hungary, which went to Philip's uncle Ferdinand), and that meant he probably had personal rule over more of the earth than any other single person in history—in fact, the Philippines are named for him. He too saw himself as the defender of Christendom, which meant wars against Dutch Protestant rebels, sending the Spanish Armada against newly Protestant England, involvement in the French religious wars, and more wars against the Ottoman Empire.

This was all very expensive, and it meant paying (or trying to pay) troops, especially those fighting a long, long campaign against the Dutch, who in 1568 began a rebellion against the Spanish Hapsburg rule.

Silver would be shipped from Seville to Genoa and then be carried by pack-mule trains through northern Italy and along the Rhine to the Netherlands.[31] More silver made it to the Low Countries by sea, especially to Antwerp. Between 1566 and 1654, the military treasury in the Netherlands received at least 218 million ducats from the Crown, but it was never enough: Wages were constantly late, sometimes as much as six years in arrears.[32] The army in the Spanish Netherlands mutinied 45 times between 1572 and 1609 over their unpaid wages.[33] The wars were so expensive that the Crown soon began borrowing from bankers, promising to repay with the next year's silver fleet. It borrowed from Genoese bankers first, then from the Fuggers and the Welsers, who were banking families in Augsburg, in southern Germany. It borrowed from the Schetz bankers in Antwerp, and from any corporate body with a pool of capital, like monasteries and convents, or cathedrals and hospitals.[34] Soon it had mortgaged the next seven years of silver revenues.[35]

The struggle to pay for the wars and the upkeep of empire led the Crown to issue debt instruments called *juros*. These were something like lifetime pensions, at first given as rewards for heroic service. Over time, their repayment extended from one life to two lifetimes to perpetuity, and they were granted in exchange for a lump-sum payment and intended to be repaid out of future silver revenues, usually at the rate of about 5 percent of the principal amount each year.[36] These sort of perpetual annuities were common across late medieval and early modern Europe, but they had all sorts of problems. They were difficult to sell to someone else, and they were repaid only as long as the government had revenue to pay them—not paying a pension for a while was different from defaulting on a debt. The government was stuck paying them forever, but could also cash them out or renegotiate them at will. When the Crown borrowed from Augsburg or Genoa, it got money in exchange for *juros*, and the Genoese went on to sell the *juros* to other merchants and bankers all over Europe.[37] (In 1531, the Bourse in Antwerp in the southern Netherlands was founded specifically as a place to centralize the trade in *juros*, a process that had vast consequences, as we shall see.)[38] The Crown kept issuing more and more *juros* as the century and the wars dragged on. As the monetary historian Dennis Flynn puts it: "In 1522 *juros* consumed 36.6 percent of the Crown's ordinary revenues; the proportion never fell below 52.9 percent after 1527. After the bankruptcies of 1557 and 1560, *juros* actually exceeded ordinary revenues by 3.9 percent; the proportion never fell below 86.2 percent for the rest of the century. In 1598 they consumed 96.5 percent of ordinary revenues."[39] As the Crown's debt grew heavier and interest payments mounted, it found it was unable to repay its creditors, and the Spanish Crown defaulted in 1557, 1560, 1575, 1596, and 1606.

So this was one conduit for the flow of silver out of Spain: slow, late wages to soldiers, and interest payments to bankers. The second conduit was through trade. Spain mostly did not develop competitive exports, partly because the continual flow of silver was such an attractive source of profits, so people focused on obtaining a slice of the silver rather than taking a gamble on textile manufacturing or handicraft exports. Instead, silver arrived in Seville and enriched the silver merchants and ship captains and other members of the merchant community there. Those merchants in turn, flush with cash, bought goods (and bid up the price for them, with important consequences) either for their own consumption or to send back to the New World. Those goods arrived from all over Europe and, indeed, from around the world.

The spices, jewels, and silks from the Portuguese Estado da India would often be shipped to Antwerp, which became a giant clearinghouse for European commodity trades. Spanish merchants would buy them there, either for reexportation to the Americas, or to send back to Spain for their own enjoyment. As with overseas goods, so too with silks from northern Italy, grain from Brittany, and linens from Anjou, while more money went to pay the wages of the thousands of seasonal laborers who crossed back and forth between France and Spain, following the rhythm of the planting and harvest, producing crops to sell for higher prices.[40] Antwerp, and later Amsterdam, was the end point of a trade corridor that ran from northern Italy along the Rhine River to the coast, and connected to another trade circuit from the Baltic. The Baltic was especially important for cheap subsistence goods. As one historian puts it:

From the Baltic came the necessities of life of western Europe: grain (wheat and rye), lumber, hemp, hempseed, flax, flaxseed, bar iron, tallow, wax, leather, skins, furs, potash, ash, and naval stores. Because these were basic commodities not available elsewhere, this trade was fundamental to western Europe and commonly ran a deficit that, in the case of Russia, was about twice the value of imports from western Europe. It is assumed that the deficit was made up by importing bullion, largely silver coins. In the late sixteenth century and certainly by 1600, the Dutch were dominant in this trade, but they were displaced by the English about 1700, and this meant that large amounts of specie flowed to the east to settle the Baltic accounts. Settlements were effected through Holland in both centuries.[41]

Indeed, by 1650, something like 1,000 Dutch ships carried goods from the Baltic, exceeding their English rivals by a factor of 13 to 1.[42] Connecting the Baltic hinterland to the rest of Europe via the Netherlands was a huge undertaking: "Polish grain frequently took 9 months to a year for transport to the major distribution centers of Western Europe: the grain had to be hauled by cart to the river banks (feeder rivers to the Vistula), carried by barges (sledges in the winter) to the Vistula, and in the spring floated in larger barges or river boats to Danzig," where it was shipped to Amsterdam and then transported onward around Europe.[43] This meant that Spanish silver flowed into the Low Countries, partly inadvertently and partly illegally, where the trade conduits met in a giant commercial center, and from there it dispersed up the Rhine and into the Baltic.

Some of the silver went east to Venice, where it bought spices and other luxuries from the Ottoman Empire, and from there entered into Ottoman circulation. But an enormous amount went around Africa to the Indian Ocean, and ultimately to China. Indeed, the simplest statement of the global monetary system in this period was that Europe was the central transshipment point between the world's main supply of silver in the Americas and its main destination, which was China.

The government of the Ming dynasty, which ruled from 1368 to 1644, tried to monopolize foreign trade and exclude private merchants, but its efforts broke down by the middle of the 16th century.[44] From that point on, foreign trade posed a political problem, between some factions of the government who wanted to preserve a state monopoly and those who wanted to allow private trade but to tax and regulate it. The presence of Portuguese and Dutch traders allowed for an outflow of luxury goods and an inflow of silver. China was such a large economy with so many people, and its government was so extensive and in need of so much tax revenue, that China's appetite for silver was nearly limitless. Some silver came across the Pacific on the Manila galleons, probably about 7.5 percent of Peru's output in 1572–1600.[45] Other silver came from Japan, which used the mercury "cupellation" method that had been learned from Koreans as early as the 1540s. Japanese silver began the "silver age" in Asia, and by 1550–1600 accounted for 60 percent of China's silver imports.[46] Japanese silver output peaked in the 1620s at about 130 to 160 tons per year, most of it shipped to China first by the Portuguese and then by the Dutch, who wrestled for control of a monopoly trading station near what is now Nagasaki.[47] The rest of the silver came from Europe.

Silver continually flowed to China because Europeans had a powerful demand for Chinese luxury goods like porcelain, silk, and tea, while Chinese consumers wanted essentially nothing that Europe could produce. Instead of swapping roughly equal values of goods, Europeans had to buy Chinese exports with silver. But that also meant more and more Chinese people produced these exports in order to obtain silver, which they then used for their own consumption or to pay taxes. As one economic historian puts it, "Silver accounted for 93 per cent of the European cargo values to China and 79 per cent of the India-bound cargo. With American silver, the European companies in Asia bought cotton and silk textiles not just for European consumers but also to trade for slaves and gold in Africa."[48] Figure 1 below gives exports of silver carried from Europe to Asia by the Dutch East India Company between 1600 and 1795: some 574 million guilders in all.[49] Together, Chinese silver imports exceeded domestic production by a factor of 8 in the 1550–1600 period, and probably by a factor of 20 in 1600–1650.[50]

Until the 1620s, the inflows of silver to China produced an overall mild price increase—not so much new commerce as price increases in already commercialized activity, especially the luxury goods market.[51] Then the 1620s–40s saw a sudden, sharp inflation: Prices nearly doubled, and mostly remained at the new high level through the 1660s. The reasons were not primarily due to imported

Figure 1. **Dutch East India Company silver exports, 1602–1795**

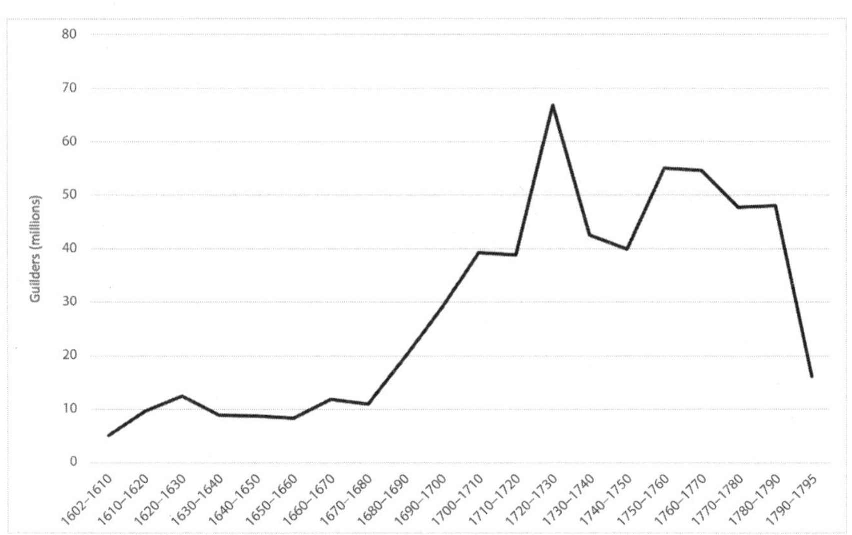

silver. The late Ming were continually fighting peasant rebellions and Manchu invasions in the north and, faced with the need for more revenue, debased the currency in the 1620s and 1630s.[52] In desperate straits, the last Ming emperor allowed paper money in 1643. People refused to accept it, and there was no system of distribution to disseminate it throughout the enormous territory, so the paper money rapidly crashed into hyperinflation.[53] Food prices especially spiked, though the historian Timothy Brook argues that this was due to crop failures from the climatic distortions of the Little Ice Age.[54] Either way, the Ming dynasty fell in 1644, replaced by the Qing dynasty, which was mainly comprised of the successful Manchu invaders from the north.

But it too struggled to govern the monetary system, and reinstated the prohibition on private foreign trade. Despite ending the paper money experiment and returning to a silver standard, inflation continued into the 1660s, after which China experienced two decades of depression and sharp deflation.[55] Agricultural prices and incomes collapsed, so farmers were unable to repay loans or pay taxes, and the crisis was widely understood by the Qing state as a monetary problem possibly stemming from the ban on foreign trade (though, again, it could have been partly the result of climatic changes producing gluts instead of dearth). They were probably half right: the historian Richard von Glahn argues that the deflation was the result not of too little supply of silver but of too much demand, possibly driven by recovery from years of famine and war.[56] People lost confidence in land ownership and investment as profitable activities, preferring to hold silver instead. Deflation seemed to confirm their fears, leading to a spiral as more people held more silver instead of spending it, thereby taking it out of circulation and depressing prices yet further. This view is consistent with Brook's view on climatic gluts producing "dearth amidst plenty": Too many good harvests collapsed food prices and thus returns to agriculture. In this way, price oscillations, climate change, and government policy together produced inflation in the 1620s–40s, the collapse of the Ming dynasty, then depression in 1660–90.

The arrival of Spanish silver reconfigured economic activity all around the world. I mean "reconfigured" in a very specific sense: People either changed what they were doing to suit market demand or did more of it to have extra to sell. A serf growing grain in northern Poland might otherwise have grown only enough for his family to get through the winter, but if he could sell his excess to Dutch traders, he might try to do so (which would likely involve some struggle with the feudal owner of his estate), and that might mean hiring more workers or investing in drainage or pack animals or trying out new techniques of crop rotation. He and his family might increase both the extent and intensity of their production, in order to have more for the market. Another serf might have grown a mix of grains and vegetables and livestock for his family and his local community, but might shift to specializing entirely in growing hemp to sell in the market, and use the proceeds to buy food and equipment. Some serfs or peasants (or their wives and children) might produce handicrafts to sell, in a process known as "protoindustry." Workers might sell their labor on rest days to make extra cash. More and more farmers, workers, artisans, and landlords would likely reorient their production away from tradition, custom, and subsistence and toward maximizing output in order to produce a marketable surplus to sell for money. We should imagine both push and pull factors. People who had the power and autonomy to decide for themselves might choose to produce more or work more for the market, but people without decision-making power would find they had no other choice.

In this way, the arrival of money and markets remade landscapes, and the lives of the people in them. Grasslands in Mexico were converted to cattle ranches to feed and supply Zacatecas, while the forests of Madeira were burned to make space for sugar production. Vast aqueducts were built in the Andes to supply Potosí, and swaths of upriver Hunan were converted to rice production in order to feed the growing numbers of people in Jiangnan who had converted their land to mulberry trees, because silkworms live in mulberry trees, and the silk would be exported to Japan via Dutch traders in exchange for silver.

In other words, the silver money industry was itself a capitalist venture, and it spread capitalism everywhere it went by monetizing exchange and incentivizing people to orient their activity toward producing marketable surpluses. But the history of money has one other essential component to the creation of capitalism, and that is a phenomenon known as the Price Revolution.

■ ■ ■

The historical phenomenon known as "the Price Revolution" refers to the fact that between about 1515 and about 1650, first in Spain, then in northwest Europe, then in the rest of Europe, and then all over the world, moving east at a pace of about 1,000 miles every 10 years, prices rose continually and inexorably. Figure 2 below shows the price levels for England, Brabant (meaning Antwerp), and Spain.[57] All three places showed sustained and dramatic increases, especially after 1540. But notably, the price increases were not the most extreme in Spain, confirming the story that most of the silver eventually flowed elsewhere and that other economies were more marketized and monetized. Figure 3 shows the production of New World silver.[58]

The Price Revolution began before the discovery of Potosí and Zacatecas. Part of it was provoked by the early "gold cycle" from Elmina and the Caribbean.[59] But a large part of it was an earlier output of silver from mines in Austria and Hungary, including from a place called Joachimsthal in what is now the Czech Republic—*thal* means "valley" in German, and the *thaler* produced there is the origin of the word "dollar." In 1490–1520, the mines of central Europe were producing 25,000 to 32,000 kilograms of silver per year, far less than the New World would do later, but a considerable boom in its own right.[60] As with other examples, this boom was based on technologies known previously, especially about how to separate silver from copper and how to pump water out of mines, but it was only in the 1450s that the price of silver had gotten so high that it paid to do these things. Much of this silver was exported via Venice to the Ottoman Empire or via Antwerp to the Estado da India, but it still started the monetization dynamics I have described, and some localized price increases.

But of course the true wave of silver came from the New World after the 1540s. There is a temptation to think about the Price Revolution purely in terms of the quantity of money: The amount of physical money in Europe increased by perhaps a factor of 10, so of course prices rose. But the reality was more complicated, and there is not a direct, neat relationship between the places and times where money increased the most and the places and times where prices increased the most. This point is made even more compli-

Figure 2. **Price indices for England, Brabant, and Spain, 1401–1650**

Figure 3. **Average annual production of New World silver and European arrivals, in tons, 1501–1800**

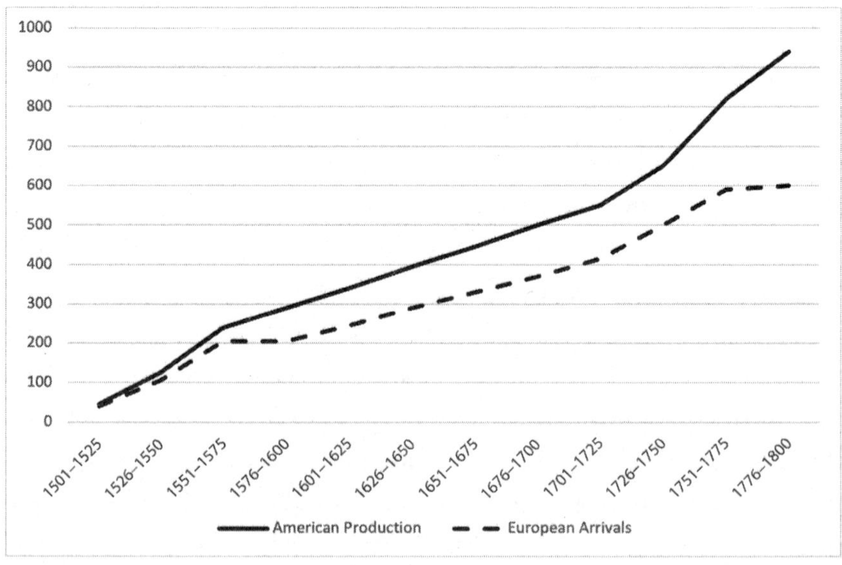

cated by the fact that governments often debased their currency, meaning they altered the silver content of coins without changing the face value. Different places did that to different degrees and at different times, leading to all sorts of variation in prices.

Further, it is essential to remember that many prices were controlled by customary rules or government regulations. Many grain prices, for instance, were capped by governments in order to avoid riots during periods of scarcity. Many land rents were paid in kind or, in the most traditionally feudal parts of Europe, were paid by providing days of labor to the landlord. Some leases were for 99 years or more, so they could not easily be adjusted. Some but not all wages could change rapidly, and many prices of many commodities could change. What this meant is that newly enriched merchants with access to silver could compete against one another and bid up the price of some things, but not all. Merchants selling goods with rising prices would in turn get richer, and they too would buy more things and contribute to rising prices. Workers whose wages could not or did not increase would find that their standards of living declined, as their stagnant wages could not keep up with rising prices. Landlords who could not renegotiate their rents would find that they too had to pay higher prices, and sometimes higher wages for servants or artisans.

Direct silver imports drove price increases in Spain, then increased Spanish demand drove price increases elsewhere, and when Spain's trading partners developed a greater demand for money, many European and Ottoman sovereigns responded by issuing more currency, especially a variety of low-quality coins that circulated below face value.[61] In this way, higher prices were transmitted even when actual physical silver was not.

The net result of the Price Revolution, then, was not only the monetization of the economy, and not just general inflation, but also class redistribution. On balance, urban wage workers lost out. Landlords tried to keep up by converting their leases into money rents wherever possible, or by implementing new agricultural techniques to raise output. Those who succeeded got richer, those who failed got eaten by their more successful competitors. Some manufacturers did well, if the prices of their goods rose faster than the prices of their raw materials, but others did badly because the price increases went the other way. And a class of merchants did very well indeed as they took advantage of rising prices. So a new commercial capitalist class was enriched and empowered, along with some manufacturers and some landlords, especially those who could fully take advantage of the new institutions of the monetized economy, and all of it at the expense of wage workers.

· · ·

The standard economics explanation for what money is has three components: Money is a store of value, a medium of exchange, and a unit of account. That explanation tells us both too much and too little.

Too much, because actual historical money sometimes did only one or two of those things. And too little, because in the real world, money is also a power relation. For that reason, money (or some money) is an expression of government sovereignty and a set of political goals.[62]

At the beginning of the history of capitalism, many people seldom used money at all. There was not enough: Late medieval Europe went through a "bullion famine" with far too little of the physical precious metal for the number of people and transactions. This problem was compounded by "the big problem of small change": The smallest coins in circulation were an amount of silver that would constitute perhaps a week's wages for an adult male worker, which meant they were useless in everyday transactions. (Imagine trying to buy a cup of coffee with a $500 bill, and the barista can try to make change only with other $500 bills.) Instead, most people used two solutions. First, they kept running tabs with one another and would only periodically (if ever) settle up and exchange whatever amount of money was the remainder. That system could work, but it was limited in range, because someone would probably trust only another member of their local community, and in scope, because while you might let someone run up a tab for groceries, you probably wouldn't let them do that for an entire ship's cargo. As a result, most small communities were tied up in webs of mutual indebtedness, and many transactions took place in kind instead of in money, as custom and tradition demanded. The other solution was to use what are called "fiduciary moneys," meaning nonmoney tokens that serve accounting purposes. A shopkeeper might give out wooden tokens or stamped pieces of tin to represent the value of transactions, and these might circulate in a local area. Individuals and governments alike used notched pieces of wood called "tallies" to indicate debt obligations. In each case, these local quasi-money solutions served as media of exchange, but they represented units of account that were determined by the government (so a stamped piece of tin meant one shilling, say, and a shilling was a unit determined by the English government) and, most importantly, they would not be accepted for international trade or for payment of taxes. International merchants wanted money they could reliably spend in other places, which meant gold and silver. And governments wanted payment of taxes in the coin of the realm, which represented their sovereign power.

A bewildering variety of types of money circulated all over the world. Most rural, traditional economies were not monetized at all. Most towns had monetized exchange, but of the fiduciary and mutually indebted variety. Most border areas would have several different moneys equally in circulation, usually exchanged by weight of the metal. In the eastern Mediterranean, for instance, "coins were weighed and assayed and sewn up in bags or purses with the amount stated on the bag by the money-changers and attested by the government, with strong penalties for misspecification."[63]

The other solution to long-distance trade was a paper credit instrument known as the "bill of exchange," which, like double-entry bookkeeping, emerged in late medieval Italy.[64] These were promissory notes much like modern checks: When I pay my rent, I write a check from my account at Citibank, and it goes to my landlord's account at Bank of America. Citibank and Bank of America can accumulate large amounts of payments they owe each other, and settle up the difference only periodically. Many of the payments will cancel out, and a small amount will change hands, and the system of payment between me and my landlord depends on the two banks having a relationship with each other. (There was an important distinction, which is that a bill of exchange was a "you pay me," not an "I owe you," so it would be initiated by the receiver, not the payer.)

In the early modern world, merchants would keep these bills of exchange, and settle up (or more likely, roll over their balances) at quarterly or annual fairs held in major commercial cities like Lyon or Brugge or Barcelona. These bills of exchange could be signed over to someone else, which meant they circulated as a kind of money, or at least as a medium of exchange, although only in commercial circles, and usually only within small networks of people who knew and trusted one another. Their purpose was to make payments across distances without having to move physical money around, which was risky and expensive. That meant more velocity of circulation than would otherwise have been the case, and they also were a way for merchants to extend short-term credit to one another rather than pay for everything in cash.

Different parts of the world had different monetary solutions, all trying to balance the demand for ways to make private payments with the demand for states to collect taxes. Aside from the failure with paper money in the late Ming, China was on a de facto silver standard for taxes and commerce, but had to obtain its silver from Japan or the New World, and still used copper for small-scale daily transactions. The Mughal Emperor Akbar introduced a unified silver standard to most of India between the late 1550s and his death in 1605. From 1477 to 1690, the Ottoman Empire ran on silver, but different types of coins of different weights: Anatolia was on the *akçe*, Egypt on the *pare*, the Iraq-Persia border zone on the *sahi*, and the Balkans on the *penz*.[65] Many parts of sub-Saharan Africa used the cowrie, a mollusk shell indigenous to the Maldive Islands in the Indian Ocean. The cowrie was not a sign of primitive backwardness but rather a brilliant currency solution: Since the source of the cowries was far away, their supply was limited and they were essentially impossible to counterfeit. The presence of these currencies allowed powerful Africans to convert wealth drawn from captives and from commodity exports into stores of value.[66] Wampum, used on the east coast of North America, was another form of shell money. Portions of West Africa used cloth currencies until well into the 19th century: The French colonial government of Senegal officially recognized them as legal tender.[67] As we will see, after the late 17th century, African slaving polities introduced units of account often based on iron or copper bars or ounces of gold: These were ways to value bundles of goods and human cargoes without continuing the inflation initially caused by European slave buyers.[68] Colonial Mexico sometimes used cacao beans, meaning money literally grew on trees.[69] And until the English currency reforms of 1717, essentially all of Europe was on a silver standard for most commercial activity but when possible used gold for long-distance trade, because it carried much greater value for much less weight.

Throughout Europe, most actual coins in circulation had no numbers on them, and no direct relationship to the official unit of account. In France, the unit of account was the livre, but there was no such coin as a "livre" in circulation. Instead, the most common coin was an ecu, which usually was three livres. "Usually," because the government could (and did) decide to change the relationship between the écu and the livre whenever it wanted. King Louis XIV did that 40 times during his long reign. The most important and most widely circulating coin in the early capitalist world was the Spanish peso of eight reales, with the "peso" being the name of the coin and the "real" the unit of account. This was the "piece of eight" made famous by pirates and their parrots. Changes in the relationship between the unit of account and the actual coin in circulation were known as augmentations.

Physical money was also constantly subject to governmental manipulation, either restampings, when people would be required to return their silver to the government mints, which would give it back to them stamped with a lesser value; or debasements, when mints would mix in lesser metals so a coin of a certain face value would contain less than its official weight in actual silver. Governments did these things all the time for the same reason Spain mortgaged its silver payments and issued *juros*: because there was never enough money for all their wars.

In addition to the class-distribution implications of New World silver, there were the imperial consequences of the Price Revolution. When cheap Spanish silver arrived in new parts of the world, it had the tendency to undercut and replace the existing currencies. When Spanish silver reached the Ottoman Empire, local mints found it was cheaper to buy foreign coins and melt them down to remint as Ottoman coins instead of mining new silver.[70] That meant the silver mines lost their customers and went out of business, which in turn meant the Ottoman Empire became dependent on European silver supplies and lost its monetary autonomy. It could either produce less currency, or debase the silver content in it, which it chose to do in 1585–86. The elite janissary troops were paid in coin, so when their wages were reduced in value by the debasement, they revolted in an episode known as the Beylerbeyi Incident, and successfully demanded the execution of the monetary official in charge.[71] Much later than our current period, when the flow of silver from Latin America was disrupted by the Napoleonic Wars and the independence movements led by Simón Bolívar, China lost its source of currency, producing severe economic and political dislocation. Industrial textile exports from Britain to West Africa in the 18th century produced inflation in the cloth currencies, so people switched to European coin, thereby undercutting their monetary independence. And so on. Whether intentional or not, international and intercontinental monetary flows frequently deranged imperial power relations.

Even Europe was full of monetary dislocation and its political consequences. When one small principality debased its currency, merchants would take their money to a neighboring polity and exchange it for an equal amount, then return and remint for a larger amount of the initial currency. This arbitrage process would spread debased currency into the neighboring areas, and provoke competitive rounds of debasement and inflation.[72] In 1619–21, starting in northern Italy and spreading through Germany, a spiral of debasements and inflation produced a period of monetary turmoil known as the Kipper- und Wipperzeit, or "seesaw times," as various small principalities debased their currencies to try to quickly produce new funds to fight the Thirty Years' War of 1618–48.

There are two important points to all of this monetary confusion. First, the history of "sound" unified money is partly the history of the increasing centralization and effectiveness of state power. But paradoxically, although states have grown more capable of forcing out other kinds of money, they also have fewer options for tampering with the money supply. Despite the popular worries that modern fiat currency isn't backed by anything, early modern sovereigns had a far wider variety of tools at their disposal for monetary manipulations than modern governments with independent central banks. Second, the monetary chaos meant that there was a reward for establishing stability. The Bank of Amsterdam, established in 1609, was one such solution. It was an exchange bank, where merchants from around the world would arrive and deposit their various currencies in the bank and be credited with a common, unified bank money that they could then use in their various dealings with one another. That stability and intelligibility gave Amsterdam an enormous advantage as a location for international trade after the fall of Antwerp to Spanish forces in 1585.[73]

. . .

The Portuguese and Spanish Empires circled the globe, unified the world trading system on a single silver currency, reorganized and reconfigured vast territories and populations, enslaved millions of people, and precipitated incredible loss of life. They did these things not for profit, but out of religious conviction, imperial competition, a drive for landed conquest to satisfy their military nobilities, and out of necessity to pay for their wars. They were not capitalist empires, and their goals were not capitalist goals. But their imperial projects created, enriched, and relied on a growing class of capitalists, from the silver miners of Potosí to the merchants of Seville to the bankers of Genoa, the landlords of England, and the traders in Antwerp.

The fantastic wealth of the New World did not enrich Spain, and the Estado da India did not vault Portugal to European hegemony. Portugal was never actually able to control the Indian Ocean trade, the gold from Elmina never rivaled the inflow of silver from the New World, and the trade in Asian luxuries mostly went through Antwerp until 1585, and then Amsterdam. Spain mostly squandered the silver on wars. Spanish kings soon learned that direct access to funding from incoming silver meant they did not need the consent of any representative or intermediary body to start wars or raise taxes: Instead, they could use American silver to begin wars and dare the local governments to withdraw tax money later. Their debts grew ever heavier, and the political power of the silver merchants grew ever stronger. As Stanley and Barbara Stein put it, "Seville's mercantile interests came to dominate the Casa de Contratación, the customs house, elements of the colonial bureaucracy, and the Consejo de Indias (Spain's colonial office), absorbing and in fact exercising public functions behind a façade of state regulation. In modern parlance, the private sector manipulated the public sector of a patrimonial state."[74] Ever short of funds, the Spanish state sold off government offices and created new noble titles to sell, which expanded the set of people exempt from taxes, and turned the government machinery into a series of extractive private offices.[75]

Conquest and plunder did not make Spain rich and powerful, and the increasing political power of the capitalist class gutted the state rather than rendering it more efficient or durable. The true beneficiaries of Spanish silver were the merchants who benefited from the Price Revolution, and especially the Dutch, who helped smuggle silver out of the New World, who dominated the commodity trades that were paid for with New World silver, and who soon supplanted the Portuguese as the predominant traders in the Indian Ocean, shipping silver from Europe to buy Asian goods and to monetize the Indian Ocean commercial zone.

Just as Spain was paradoxically hollowed out by the silver flows, so too were other empires undermined by the wave of money. The German lands, cut apart by religious wars that began with the Lutheran Reformation, also went through years of monetary instability. The Ottoman Empire became dependent on European money supplies by the end of the 16th century. And all the while, silver poured into China, carried by Dutch and Portuguese ships from Europe, by the Manila galleons from Mexico, and by Dutch merchants shipping it from Japan. As two economic historians put it, "The declines of Imperial Spain, the Ottoman Empire, and the Ming dynasty by the 1640s were all linked to the global silver market."[76]

The Price Revolution was one of the first unintended global economic transitions that created capitalism. The Portuguese and

Spanish conquistadores were looking for gold and silver, but had no idea that they would produce inflation and imperial decline. The miners, shippers, smugglers, and merchants were looking to get rich from the spigot of precious metal, not contribute to the monetization of the world and the shift from customary exchange to numerical price relations. None of this was intentional, nor even very well understood.

By the 1650s, Spain and Portugal were in decline, and their empires were huge, rich corpses feasted upon by their more agile rivals. The new techniques of money, banking, and finance that were tested out by desperate Spanish governments were soon vastly improved by the Dutch and then the English, giving them a permanent advantage in funding wars, and also creating a new set of capitalist institutions. That process, from roughly the 1650s through about 1720, is known as the Financial Revolution.

CHAPTER 2

Finance, 1650–1720

After money, when most people think of capitalism the next things they probably think of are banks, corporations, and the stock market. And they are right to do so. Financial institutions are essential to the functioning of capitalism, and have been since the beginning. They are themselves capitalist institutions, and they allow for the accumulation and investment of capital in an economy writ large. As the previous chapter described, the spread of money throughout the early modern world created some of the vital preconditions for capitalism, opened up many (often bloody) opportunities for the creation and accumulation of capital, and in the direct, physical processes of mining and minting themselves, followed capitalist market relations. In some places, monetization and prices led to a reorientation toward market production. But money and commerce alone would not have made capitalism, and the story of the last chapter left us with some capitalists and some capital, but capitalism only as a thin web spanning a few parts of the world, perhaps something like a strange subculture of enthusiasts. The creation of finance in the 17th and early 18th centuries solidified and expanded capitalism, placing it at the center of social, polit-

65

ical, and economic life, as well as making it an integral part of great-power conflict. Finance did so in a few distinct ways.

What is finance? First, finance is a way of pooling savings or resources to accomplish economic pursuits that are too expensive or too slow for any individual to pursue alone. The classic example is long-distance trade, because a ship full of cargo was probably the single most expensive thing any merchant or commercial group would ever buy, and ships are "lumpy" goods, meaning you need to buy the entire thing (half a ship is not very useful), and sea voyages take a long time, so investors would not be repaid until their ship returned, having successfully sold its goods elsewhere. In the medieval period, trade was mostly conducted over short distances and in small ships, and would be organized by partnerships that lasted only for the duration of a single voyage, or that comprised ownership of a single ship.[1] A few merchants could come together to pool their resources on one voyage, and then would cash out from the proceeds several months later. But those systems were wholly inadequate to the huge, expensive ships that made the journey to East Asia, nor were merchants willing to part with their capital for the 18 to 36 months that a voyage might take. Long-distance trade needed more capital; once that problem had been solved, it also created new methods for capital accumulation. And accumulated capital in turn wants further investment for continued returns, leading to more participation in other forms of finance, like stocks, bonds, or insurance.

Along with trade, finance was essential for governments, and the main thing early modern governments did was fight wars. As we saw with the unhappy experience of Charles V and Philip II, even a continual flow of silver was not enough to pay for all the wars of a global empire. Early modern states lacked a professional administrative bureaucracy, so they could collect little in taxes, and anyway, they could tax either their desperately poor peasants (which they did) or their richer aristocracies, which they preferred not to do for political reasons. A limited, poor tax base and no professional tax bureaucracy meant very little and very unpredictable tax income. Sovereigns made money in other ways, through selling government offices, through direct ownership of land, through sales of monopolies, through various fees, and through manipulating the value of their coinage.[2] Still, it was never enough. They also needed to borrow constantly. But lending to kings and princes was a risky proposition. They would often default, leaving their creditors with no recourse, because there was no way to sue a divinely appointed king who was the source of all law.[3] Their small and unpredictable incomes would make it difficult for them to make payments on time, even if they wanted to. They also might lose their wars, leaving them without the plunder they expected to use as repayment. Many sovereigns resorted to forced loans—a kind of tax on merchants and capital owners, which could provoke capital flight—and they mostly could obtain credit only at very high rates of interest (because most sovereigns were not subject to usury laws, which capped or banned interest payments for regular people) and even then, only on a short-term basis.

Over the course of the 17th and early 18th centuries, and especially in England between the 1680s and 1720s, a wave of institutional change known as the Financial Revolution transformed all of that. Building on earlier Dutch examples, England professionalized its tax bureaucracy, nationalized the sovereign debt so it was no longer the personal debt of the legally immune sovereign, and tied specific revenues to repaying the debt, which in turn was consolidated into long-term permanent tradable bonds. It also created a proto–central bank in the form of the Bank of England to manage the debt, *and* created a secondary market in shares of joint-stock companies, including those of the Bank itself. Thanks to these changes, England was able to borrow more and more money over the 18th century to pay for fighting and winning a series of increasingly expensive wars against its much more populous and powerful French rival.[4] Finance was indispensable to military success just as

it was to long-distance trade, and indeed, early modern governments thought that trade and war were just different versions of
great-power competition.[5]

Finance enabled capital accumulation beyond individual savings, allowed for and profited from long-distance trade, and paid
for the global wars that created English hegemony. The success of
trade and war finance created a class of capitalists who were very
much at the heart of the English state, helping to ensure that the
political hegemony of England was also a capitalist hegemony.

This chapter tells the story of the rise of finance, from the
early fumbling attempts of the Hapsburgs to pay for their wars,
to the Dutch revolt and the emergence of the Netherlands as the
first capitalist society, to the English Financial Revolution and the
triumph of finance at the heart of a global empire. The story of
money was a global one, from Mexico and Peru through Spain
and the Low Countries to China and Manila. The story of finance
is very European and, indeed, essentially a Dutch and English
story. The specific form of banking institution known as the "public bank," which was intended to facilitate commerce, government debt, and currency stability, was indigenous to Europe and
emerged only in the 16th and 17th centuries.[6] Joint-stock companies and their attendant form of alienable, permanent capital also
emerged in Europe in the 17th and 18th centuries. None of this is
to suggest that Europe was the norm and the rest of the world was
behind—rather, a specific corner of Europe was unusual, and created new forms of capitalism in order to solve immediate military
and political problems, and those forms went on to have immense,
unexpected consequences, in part because they allowed for ways to
marshal more resources to commit more violence.

■ ■ ■

The Hapsburgs' insatiable appetite for money was one of the driving forces that structured the world of finance before the Financial

Revolution. Their main procedure for borrowing was the sale of *juros*, the origin of modern debt instruments, and there was a lot of room for improvement.

The counterpoint to the pull of the Hapsburgs' financial gravity was the city-states of Italy. Genoa, Florence, Naples, Rome, and Venice were all small, rich, mercantile cities, many of them engaged in long-distance trade (or in the case of Rome, receiving and paying money from all over Christendom, through the Catholic Church). From the late medieval period onward, they developed a variety of banking institutions, mostly led by powerful families. The Medicis in Florence are the classic example. They were among the first to use double-entry bookkeeping, to conduct payments by making paper transfers between accounts, and to manage a network of branches abroad.[7] But their private familial wealth may have held back the creation of shared, public banking institutions, their banking activity became subsidiary to their political ambitions, and a single family firm remained fragile to surprising disasters. In 1407, Genoa created the Casa di San Giorgio to consolidate and manage the government debt, and it issued shares that were a favorite investment of the local merchant community. Naples developed a shared public banking system in the 1580s, and Venice established the Banco di Rialto in 1587. The Banco di Rialto was a 100 percent reserve bank, meaning it did not make loans for long periods of time from the money deposited in its vaults, and that model went on to be the template for the Bank of Amsterdam.[8] The others were what are known as *giro* banks, meaning merchants would deposit their various coins in the bank and be credited with a uniform bank money that would be used to settle payments among them.[9] The Genoese especially lent to the Hapsburgs and sometimes lost considerably in doing so. But these early banks were mostly intended to regularize and impose order on the chaos of coinage in each mercantile port city, to make trade and exchange easier.

Another mercantile and banking family was at the center of Hapsburg finance, and that was the Fuggers of Augsburg. (It's pronounced FOO-ger, I assure you.) Like many banking families, they began as merchants. Thanks to the scarcity of money, merchants were used to buying and selling on credit, as well as extending credit to one another. And merchants who were successful would build up capital from trade profits and loan interest, which they would then want to invest. There were many such banking families in late medieval and early modern Europe: the Welsers, the Medicis, the Strozzis, and the Höchstetters, to name just a few. The Fuggers began in the weaving and cloth trade. In the 1480s, they began to handle money transfers between Venice and Rome, via southern Germany.[10] Their big break came in 1485, when the brothers Ulrich, Georg, and Jakob Fugger made a loan of 3,000 florins to Archduke Sigismund of Tyrol, on the Austrian-Italian border.[11] The loan would be repaid not with interest but rather with access to silver. As Sigismund fought an ill-advised and unsuccessful war against Venice, he needed more and more money, which he borrowed from the Fuggers in exchange for the proceeds of his silver mines. By 1495, the Fuggers had acquired several mines outright, including a lead mine in Villach, in what is now central Austria, and some copper mines. They were soon supplying both Venice and several German princes (via Nuremburg) with copper and silver. As Mark Häberlein, the historian of the Fuggers, details: "From 1495 to 1504, the Fuggerau [one of their metalworks complexes] delivered about 50,000 hundredweight of copper and almost 22,000 Marks of silver to the Venetian market alone, while Hohenkirchen [their other complex] processed 54,000 hundredweight of copper and extracted more than 30,000 Marks of silver during the same time span."[12] The Fuggers were thus one of the merchants getting rich from the capitalist relations in mining and minting of the early Price Revolution. Marketing that much metal required creating a network of merchants and mint officials

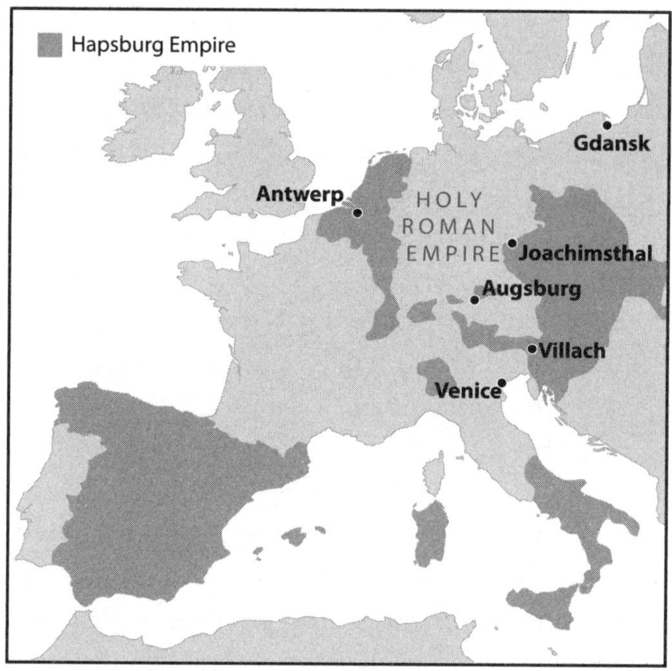

The Fugger network in Europe, circa 1550

all over Europe, especially in Venice, to access the Near Eastern and Mediterranean trades; in Lisbon, to connect to the Portuguese expeditions to Africa and India; and in Antwerp, the commercial nexus that linked the Baltic with the Rhine and the North Sea. The Fuggers set up a presence in all three places, but Antwerp emerged as the most important, because copper from Austria and Hungary could be transported on barges up the Vistula River from the Alps to Gdansk, then by ship to the Low Countries. "As early as 1503, forty-one ships laden with copper arrived in the port of Antwerp from Gdansk. Between 1507 and 1526, about half of the Hungarian copper was placed on the Antwerp market."[13]

The second turning point came in 1521, when the Fuggers provided copper, silver, and loans to Charles V, in exchange for future royal revenue from Spain. Since the Fuggers had a presence in Antwerp, they could also serve as a conduit for collecting Dutch credit (or indeed the credit of other merchants in the city) and lending it to Charles V, as well as selling *juros* to those same merchants after they were issued in 1524. By the 1540s, they had lent Charles something like half a million florins and were well established as international financiers. In that capacity they lent to the Dutch provincial governments, handled the pope's subsidies to the Hapsburgs, and in 1552, Anton Fugger personally marshaled 100,000 ducats and 300,000 Italian scudi for Charles's account.[14] By that point, the normal Spanish tax revenues were not enough to cover repayment for their loans, so the arriving silver fleets were paid directly into the Fugger accounts. In 1547, they were granted the contract to manage the Maestrazgos, a territory near Valencia, which brought both a substantial grain export business and more importantly, control over the mercury mines at Almadén.[15] That moment marked the peak of their power and wealth: Accounts for 1546 show that they had 7.1 million florins in assets with about 2 million florins in liabilities.[16]

But their power was short-lived: One problem with capital accumulation tied to individuals or family succession is that a single person or set of decisions can derail an otherwise continual expansion. By the 1560s, they had decided to restructure, abandoning their previous mining operations in Hungary and Austria. The Hapsburgs kept being late with their repayments, meaning the Fuggers had to take on debt of their own to cover their costs, and soon they were dependent on outside capital, especially from other Antwerp merchants. They did not spectacularly collapse, but their growth halted and they were soon overtaken by more permanent, institutionalized forms of capital and finance. For our purposes, they are a brief link between the processes of mining and money and the financial needs of the Hapsburgs. They could not fund the empire on their own, and by the 1540s and 1550s, the Hapsburgs were looking elsewhere for revenue. The Hapsburgs still controlled the Low Countries, one of the most prosperous places in Europe, and Antwerp was well established as a center for trade and finance. The problem was how to access those riches, given that their promises of repayment were no longer credible, and consequently lenders wanted high rates of interest on short-term loans.

Indeed, that dilemma confronted rulers all over Europe. As the financial historian James Tracy puts it:

> No government could do without the services of great financiers who were often agents of firms domiciled beyond its frontiers. Indeed, it was not unknown for financial brokers of this period surreptitiously to boost profits by lending to two hostile rulers at the same time. The only alternative to high rates charged by the bankers was long-term debt of one form or another. . . . [In the Netherlands] these common elements were blended together in a distinctive combination: as the government's borrowing needs on the Antwerp exchange expanded at an incredible rate, as much as seventyfold over the last thirty years of Charles V's reign, debt service costs were held to manageable limits only by paying off the bankers with funds raised through the sale of annuities—which in turn became more attractive to investors in proportion as the provincial parliaments, or States, assumed full responsibility for them.[17]

In other words, the Hapsburg Netherlands tested out several institutional innovations to solve the same problems faced elsewhere, and its solutions went on to become the general set of "best practices." Starting in 1542, it introduced some "novel expedients": province-wide excise and land taxes paid to the central government, and a new series of bonds (called *renten*) to be issued by the state governments and repaid by those new taxes.[18] Knowing the repayment funds were coming from a dedicated, predictable stream of income was reassuring to investors and administratively helpful. Importantly, since the states (meaning local governments, not the central, royal one) were providing this new flood of funds, they were able to demand that they would be in charge of collecting and disbursing the tax revenue. The state governments were more responsive to the preferences of wealthy locals (in part because wealthy locals comprised the governments), so they were more trustworthy to owners of capital, and since they both collected the taxes and repaid the debts, there was no principal-agent problem or conflict of interests. These new *renten* were therefore safe investments, which meant they attracted capital from the mighty Antwerp market, and even farther afield, especially other rich cities in the Netherlands. Successful repayment meant the states established a reputation for good credit, which in turn meant they could borrow more money at lower rates than the central government.

These successes had more than one unexpected consequence. Despite suddenly having access to more funds, the Hapsburgs lost control over issuing these *renten* and repaying them. The creditworthiness of the states increased but that of the central government did not.[19] And since Dutch merchants were paying taxes to repay debt held by other Dutch merchants, a political question began to simmer about why distant Spanish Hapsburgs should be involved at all.

And then in 1566, the Dutch provinces began to revolt against the Hapsburgs, with rebellion starting and stopping repeatedly until the 1580s, at which point sporadic rebellion became continual open war. By the 1560s, many Protestant groups, especially Calvinists (the followers of the Swiss priest John Calvin, another Reformer), had established substantial communities in the Netherlands, and seemed to be spreading rapidly.[20] For some historians, Dutch Protestantism was a serious moral force that opposed what was seen as corrupt, lax moral degeneration in the Italian and Spanish Catholic Church establishment. Many historians stress the ways that Protestant ethics around thrift, hard work, future-orientation, and a sense of salvation being demonstrated through material wealth all reinforced and were reinforced by emerging capitalist practices. Still others would more prosaically point out that nobody likes to be taxed by a distant authority that is indifferent to their preferences, especially if it seems that this authority is waging war against sympathetic coreligionists. Whether because of religion, capitalism, or taxes, the Dutch provinces went into open revolt, and took their creditworthiness and effective state-level tax-and-debt system along with them.

■ ■ ■

The Dutch Republic in the first half of the 17th century, if not sooner, was the first wholly capitalist society in the world, and for that reason it is useful to step back from finance for a moment to consider the components and importance of Dutch capitalism.[21]

By 1500, the northern Netherlands was already one of the richest and most commercialized places in the world, with one of the most literate and urbanized populations and the highest proportion of people working in wage labor.[22] The roots of its unusual growth, prominence of market relations, and relative social equality can be traced back to its recovery from the Black Death of 1348. Most of Europe experienced some form of economic growth after the plague, and wage workers especially seem to have done well, but in most cases by 1450 or 1500 that phase of growth came to an end in the face of rising population or extractive city elites. In the Netherlands it was maintained and expanded upon: Some economic historians would argue that the Netherlands was a capitalist society as early as 1400, almost certainly by 1500.[23]

As we have already seen, Antwerp emerged early on as a commercial center, tying together the Rhine corridor with the Baltic and North Seas. The Netherlands was also fortunate to not have much of a landed ruling class, meaning less of a parasitic edifice of surplus extraction and fewer entrenched interests protecting older forms of economic activity. Instead Dutch agriculture was dominated by a large class of free farmers, who could enjoy the benefits of surplus production and who had autonomy over what to grow and how to grow it.[24] For those reasons, Dutch agriculture oriented toward specialized market production very early, in the 16th century. By the 17th, instead of self-sufficient subsistence farmers who produced everything the household consumed, Dutch farms were highly capitalized and specialized enterprises producing cash crops like butter, cheese, and peat for distant markets, and the Netherlands as a whole depended on its mighty shipping fleet to deliver cheap food grains imported from the Baltic.[25] Shipping was especially important: The Dutch developed a new kind of ship called a "fluyt" that was especially efficient to crew and could carry a lot of cargo; they also developed a ship called a "herring buss," which was a kind of floating fish-processing factory. Already in 1560, the province of Holland had a fleet of some 1,800 vessels.[26] In the early 17th century, Holland had 500 herring busses in operation, and since each firm had only one or two, the total number of investors was huge and Dutch fishers exported salted herring all over northern Europe.[27]

Efficient, intense, capitalist agriculture in turn could support very large urban populations, and the Netherlands had an unusually dense network of unusually large cities.[28] Those cities were linked by a robust network of water transport, for both goods and people.[29] As Adam Smith would have said, the division of labor is limited by the extent of the market, and the Dutch Republic was probably the first integrated national market in the world, one that moreover connected to several overseas markets. Then, in 1585, mighty Antwerp was put under siege by Hapsburg forces, whose Dutch opponents cut off the Scheldt River, which connected Antwerp to the sea. Antwerp's fall to the Hapsburgs displaced its mercantile community to Amsterdam, which emerged as the new center of trade and finance.[30] Amsterdam merchants were already powerful in the Baltic trades, and its being a single place that combined centralized information sharing, low-cost transportation, a deep pool of buyers and sellers, and a relatively inclusive political environment yielded considerable wealth and advantages to the city.

With Amsterdam in the lead, the Netherlands then developed into an industrial powerhouse, driven by windmills and slow-burning peat fires, leading Europe in production of shipbuilding, brickworks, papermaking, book printing, and processing of tobacco and sugar.[31] The huge shipping fleet drew on hundreds of wind-mills and sawmills—in 1630, the Zaan region near Amsterdam had 191 sawmills toiling away.[32] By 1661, sugar imports from the col-onies were processed at 50 refineries in Amsterdam alone.[33] The workers in these industries, as well as the petty traders, shopkeep-ers, domestic servants, and unskilled workers of the urban econo-mies, were mostly free wage laborers, not guild members or serfs.[34]

The Dutch government, such as it was, emerged out of the older, creditworthy provincial states. The Dutch Republic as a pol-ity was in fact a federation of seven provinces formed in 1579 to finance and fight the war against Spain, with very little in the way of central government—indeed, the case can be made that the only unifying national institution was the East India Company, whose 17-member board of directors represented each of the provinces.[35] Representatives of the seven provinces also met at the States Gen-eral, the central federal assembly, but it often was a forum for dis-cussion, not a sovereign legislature. Amsterdam was always the first among equals, but the provinces preserved the majority of gover-nance for themselves, and were dominated by local urban mer-chant elites. For that reason, the Dutch historian Marjolein t'Hart characterizes the Republic as a "bourgeois state."[36] It was the first place that not only had capitalist economic structures in land, labor, and capital, as well as capitalist social mores and open-access mar-ket institutions, but, even further, was governed by a mercantile capitalist elite. City magistrates drawn from that elite ensured the courts treated merchants of different national and religious backgrounds equally, which incentivized everyone to do business in Amsterdam.[37] That, in turn, had an agglomeration effect: Knowing that buyers and sellers would be in Amsterdam ensured that trade concentrated there. In fact, the word "capitalist" itself was of 17th-century Dutch origin. As Tracy recounts, after a new graduated tax was introduced in 1650, "those in the top wealth category were known as *capitalisten*, and those in the next category down were called 'half capitalists.' "[38]

In 1595–97, a group of Dutch investors outfitted a voyage to the Spice Islands of Molucca, in what is now Indonesia, which upon its return delivered a profit of 500 percent. That was enough to launch several subsequent voyages: Between 1595 and 1602, seven fleets totaling 50 ships sailed from Amsterdam to Asia, with another 30 ships departing from other Dutch ports.[39] In 1603, the owners of these ventures merged to become the United East India Company, known as the VOC (which is the acronym of its Dutch name, the Vereenigde Oost-Indische Compagnie), holding a charter from the States General, but with autonomy to govern its own outposts, lands, and voyages.[40] It was immediately popular and profitable: Its initial share subscription attracted some 1,800 investors, who contributed 6.4 million guilders and included people with relatively little capital who invested as little as 20 guilders each.[41] Over the next 200 years of its existence, it delivered an average annual profit of 18 percent to its shareholders.[42] Over that same period, 978,000 people (not all of them Dutch) left the Netherlands in 4,700 ships on VOC voyages, and only 332,500 returned.[43] In the 1750s, the company employed 36,000 people worldwide.[44]

In 1609, the VOC took a radical step: It decided that investors could no longer withdraw their capital from the company. Instead, they had to sell their shares to someone else. That step created what is known as a "secondary market," where people buy and sell existing shares or securities from one another rather than from the entity or institution that issued them in the first place.[45] The creation of the secondary market in VOC shares marked the emergence of what became a stock exchange. Now investors could speculate, borrow against their shares, and contract for future deliveries. It also spread VOC shares and other financial instruments throughout the capital-owning economy. To take one example, by the early 18th century, the richest 5 percent of households in the city of Delft held 60 percent of their wealth in various bonds.[46] The VOC was so stable and successful that its shares held their value, meaning they were useful collateral for other financial activities and a favored investment for people with savings. Much like a modern US Treasury bill, VOC shares helped spread liquidity and capital accumulation through the Dutch economy, and created a new form of wealthy person: the city-dwelling owner of financial capital rather than land.

In this way, the rise of finance was tied from the beginning to the rise of long-distance trade. More capital tied up in trade meant more capital on the secondary market. The Baltic trade had already familiarized many Dutch investors with shareholding: In the 1560s, the Baltic fleet was probably 700 ships, each with partnership shares available down to one 128th of the ownership and the profit.[47] But a ship in the Baltic run could make two or three round-trip voyages in a single season, and could be small and not need much crew or much armament. The West Africa and Caribbean ships, which began slowly to depart around 1600, were much larger and more expensive, and took much longer to return. The huge, ponderous Asia ships cost as much as 100,000 guilders each, something like two or three times the amount even for an Africa or Caribbean ship, hence requiring new forms of business enterprise like the VOC.[48] That new form—the joint-stock corporation with alienable, transferrable shares—proved so successful that, with some modification, it became one of the archetypal organizational structures of modern capitalism. Profits from successful voyages brought more investment capital, and more capital allowed for more voyages. Access to liquid, transferrable, stable investment vehicles made credit cheaper throughout the Dutch economy, aided by the arrival of refugees from Antwerp, who brought both capital and business connections.

A large capital market incentivized the creation of a wide range of financial services at low costs. In 1609, the Bank of Amsterdam was established, at the initiative of the city government. Thanks to the many merchants and traders doing business in the city, there were something like 500 different coins in circulation, each with different weights and fineness of metal, each preferred for different trades and by different groups, each subject to manipulation by its issuing authority. To make sense of the chaos, the Bank accepted deposits in these coins and issued its own stable silver currency, the guilder, which was divided into smaller stuivers. Depositors had accounts at the bank, so exchanges between them could happen on the books in this common denominating bank currency, instead of through physical money changing hands and being laboriously weighed and assessed. In this way, the Bank of Amsterdam created its own internal fiat money, and one that people wanted to use instead of their various trade coins, because it was a safe and stable asset.[49] The Bank did not have macroeconomic policy goals, but it functioned much like a modern central bank: It managed a currency, settled payments, and engaged in quantitative and repurchase operations, meaning it bought and sold financial instruments like stocks or bonds.[50]

These corporate institutions were not long in existence before crises and disputes began. In 1610, one year after the VOC made its shares permanent, a major shareholder named Isaac Le Maire attempted the world's first bear speculator raid.[51] He had previously been governor of the VOC and its largest shareholder, before being embroiled in a corruption scandal. Driven by an admirable degree of spite, he set up a syndicate to short-sell VOC shares,

meaning he contracted to deliver shares he did not own at a specified price on a future date. If the market price on that date was
lower than his contract price, he would win: He would buy the
shares in the market at the low price and deliver them to his buyers at the higher contracted price. (This short-selling procedure
still takes place today.) Le Maire failed, because the States General
learned of his plan and made short-selling illegal, thus beginning
the long process of governments trying to tame financial markets.

Other crises and scandals followed. As the historian Anne
Goldgar has shown, the famous Dutch tulip bubble of 1634–
37 was not a major macroeconomic event, contrary to myth.[52] It
affected a small group of professional tulip dealers in the city of
Haarlem, but was blown out of proportion by English writers who
could not read Dutch and who had an interest in presenting rival
Dutch capitalism as irrational and unethical. But it does give an
impression of how deep marketization and commodification had
proceeded in the Dutch economy. The world's first stock market
manual, entitled *Confusión de confusiones*, was published in Spanish in Amsterdam in 1688, by the Sephardic Jewish financier Josef
de la Vega. It details the processes of short-selling, options in calls
and puts, margin buying, and futures contracts, much of the baf-
fling arcana that still characterizes financial markets. It is also the
origin of the terms "bull" and "bear" to describe market attitudes.

The VOC also began the institutionalized process of Dutch
imperialism in 1603–5, seizing and holding strongholds in the
Indian Ocean, as part of the process of fighting against and driving
out its Portuguese and Spanish rivals. In 1619, the VOC officer Jan
Pieterszoon Coen established a fortress at a place he called Batavia, now called Jakarta. It became the capital of the VOC in Asia,
and the base from which he conquered the Banda Islands, exterminating or enslaving the entire population, and in the process of
committing another of the genocides that litter the history of capitalism, he established control over the nutmeg production there.

Little wonder: The VOC was able to sell nutmeg in Amsterdam for 840 times its Indonesian price.[53] To the nutmeg monopoly he added a clove monopoly from the Molucca islands. From Batavia, the VOC constructed an Indian Ocean empire, with, as the historians Jan de Vries and Ad van der Woude put it, a "sales office in Europe."[54] Eventually they held a monopoly on the spice trade back to Europe, including pepper, and control of other luxury trades, like diamonds and coffee. Those trades were immensely lucrative, but also small in scale: Even in the 1780s, luxuries from the East probably averaged one pound per European per year, worth in sale price about one English shilling, and of course it was not actually evenly distributed, so many people had much less.[55] But it made the company and its shareholders very rich.

Inspired by the success of the VOC and a new phase in the long war against the Hapsburgs, in 1621 the States General chartered the West Indies Company, which went on to establish colonies in North America (in what is now New York), to access the fur trade. The WIC had both a trade monopoly in the Atlantic and territorial powers of governance, including making treaties and maintaining an army.[56] The WIC was enthusiastic in pursuing war and privateering against Spain and Portugal wherever possible, but it also was willing to trade with anyone, anywhere. It developed a salt trade from the islands of Tortuga and later from Curaçao, the latter of which becoming a vital Caribbean entrepôt.[57] Most significantly, in the 1630s, the Dutch invaded and occupied a huge portion of Brazil, as part of their global feasting on the hollow corpse of the Portuguese Empire. The main export crop of Brazil was sugar, but few people could be persuaded to migrate to South America from Europe, so the small group of Dutch colonists instead imported African slaves.

The Dutch had been sailing to Africa since at least the 1590s, trading from ships and small stations, getting into the ivory business and raiding Portuguese slavers.[58] The WIC formally established the slave trade at its second board meeting in 1623, but it took twelve years for it to begin shipping human captives on a large scale. Dutch colonists in Brazil took the lead, since they were the ones demanding captive labor: Between 1637 and 1641, they sent fleets to Africa (which included Indigenous Brazilian soldiers and sailors), conquering the Portuguese trading stations at Elmina, São Tomé, and Luanda.[59] It was in Dutch Brazil around Pernambuco in the 1630s that the Caribbean sugar–slave plantation system was born. When the Dutch were driven out of Brazil in the 1640s, they took that system with them, with world-altering consequences. For now, suffice it to say that the Dutch Atlantic empire reached its peak around 1642, and the total investment capital was about 22.1 million guilders in long-term WIC stock and bonds, as well as 10 million guilders in short-term commercial capital, far more than the capital tied up in the VOC trade to East Asia at the same time.[60]

By the middle of the 17th century, a Dutch capitalist system was fully established, and well known to writers and policymakers all over Europe. It combined wage labor with capitalist agriculture, an overseas trading empire run by joint-stock companies with transferrable shares, a proto–central bank, and stable government debt controlled by representative governments that also controlled a professional tax bureaucracy. The Dutch and the English fought three wars with each other between the 1650s and 1670s over markets, colonies, and commercial access. In 1688, the Netherlands was menaced by France under Louis XIV, and the Dutch leader William III crossed the Channel to become king of England, bringing along his Dutch advisers, financiers, and economic practices. In the Anglophone history, this is known as the Glorious Revolution, and William was "invited" by Parliament in a peaceful end of the long and ugly religious civil wars in England. In the Dutch story, it was more like a Glorious Invasion, since William crossed with a military fleet four times the size of the Spanish Armada, conducted a two-year military occupation of

London, and violently repressed several uprisings in Scotland and Ireland. In that sense, England may merely be the most successful Dutch colony, but whatever the case, 1688 marks another turning point in the rise of financial capitalism.[61]

■ ■ ■

As we have seen, the rise of finance was tied to the costs and profits of long-distance trade, and to the unending appetite of the Hapsburg state for money to run its world-spanning empire. Those specifics should not obscure the general point, which is that governments constantly needed money to fight wars, so it paid to innovate ways to safely profit from lending to governments. From about 1500 to about 1700, European governments in general vastly expanded the size of their armies and costs of their wars, in a process historians call the Military Revolution.[62] Over those two centuries, the number of troops involved in wars increased by a factor of 10.[63] The introduction of guns meant both that guns had to be bought, and that troops needed to be trained and organized so as not to shoot one another. Cannons were also expensive and required specialist training, but made fortresses obsolete, and that in turn put the military emphasis back onto winning battles with armies instead of building impregnable forts. More soldiers and more organization over time was expensive, so costs continued to balloon.

The Dutch and English maritime wars were even more expensive still. John Brewer, the historian of the English "fiscal-military state," provides some startling comparisons:

The capital assets of a large business in the early eighteenth century rarely exceeded £10,000. Ambrose Crowley's iron works, regarded as the wonder of their age, had a fixed capital of £12,000. A substantial multi-storey cotton spinning mill built at the end of the century cost a mere £5,000. By comparison naval vessels cost a small fortune. In the late seventeenth century the navy spent between £33,000 and £39,000 to build a first-rate ship, between £24,000 and £27,000 to build a second-rate, and between £15,000 and £17,000 to construct a third-rate vessel. By the second half of the eighteenth century the cost of constructing the largest ships had nearly doubled. . . . Even the smaller royal naval vessels were more expensive than most industrial plants.[64]

As he concludes, if there were about 180 ships in the English Royal Navy, then "the entire fleet amounted to a capital investment of nearly £2.25 million whose replacement cost was approximately 4 per cent of national income. This can be compared with the total fixed capital in the 243 mills in the West Riding woolen industry in 1800, which has been estimated at £402,651 with an average of £1657 per textile mill. The fixed capital in one of the largest sectors of the nation's most important industry was therefore a mere 18 per cent of the fixed capital required to launch the British navy."[65] This was a stunning amount of money, and it employed a huge number of people. The navy was one of the largest employers in the world, and in times of war there would be as many as 40,000 men afloat in the various ships, which was a population larger than any British city except London, all needing to be fed, paid, and provisioned.[66]

Although England did not have a robust financial system in the middle decades of the 17th century, it did have several of the elements of capitalist society. Like the Dutch, English agriculture oriented toward markets very early. From about 1500 onward, larger farms continually ate up smaller ones, producing a class of large landholders who employed landless agricultural labor (instead of family labor), producing for markets, including foreign exports.[67] More and more landlords shifted to monetary rents instead of payments in goods or days of labor, especially in the wake of the Price Revolution's general shift toward more money prices for exchange. Moreover, since the prices of some kinds of goods, like luxuries and agriculture, rose relatively quickly, that put pressure on the incomes of landlords, who responded by shifting rents to money payments, and then raised rents both to keep their incomes up and to reflect the greater value of their tenants' produce. This process was accentuated by enclosure, the privatization of public lands and consolidation of small landholdings, which forced many people onto wage labor by denying them access to their own means of shared subsistence.[68] By 1700 at the latest, capitalist agriculture prevailed in England. It enriched a small class of landowners, but it also was relatively productive, meaning more city dwellers could eat surplus food and more goods were exported to foreign markets. For many historians, this early agrarian capitalism was the key to England's "precocious" industrial development.[69]

The rise of capitalist agriculture has another dimension for the general rise of capitalism. For many talented scholars writing between the 1940s and 1980s, the civil wars that wracked England in the middle decades of the 17th century constituted a "bourgeois revolution."[70] Those scholars pointed to some striking evidence: In 1649, King Charles I was beheaded, the monarchy was abolished, and a republic was declared. Feudal tenures were abolished, as were nonparliamentary forms of taxation. Throughout the 1640s, radical sects like the Levellers and the Diggers preached an overthrow of the social order and the creation of a new one based on common land and social equality.[71] In the 1650s, the new republic fought commercial wars against the Dutch and implemented policies like the Navigation Acts, which were intended to produce a self-sufficient English imperial system by restricting trade to English colonies and requiring it to be conducted only in English ships. Imperial projects vastly expanded, including the introduction of sugar plantations to Barbados in the 1640s, the subjugation of Ireland between 1649 and 1653, and the capture of Jamaica in 1655. From the 1670s onward, the for-profit private tax collection system was canceled and a professionalized government tax bureaucracy was introduced, focusing on customs and excise taxes collected in port cities.[72] As with everywhere else, that tax revenue was nowhere near enough to cover the costs of wars, and the English financial system remained fragile, but it was a step toward a modern fiscal bureaucracy.

In 1672, King Charles II defaulted on his debt. At that time, 90 percent of the debt was held by a total of six goldsmith bankers.[73] Just as the Fuggers became bankers through managing payments in the cloth trade, so did many English goldsmiths become bankers because they had secure storage for precious metals. People would deposit their gold or silver with them for safekeeping, and they would issue receipts, which soon became an ability to grant credit based on the deposited collateral. But it was a small, thin, and insecure banking system, limited to a few known, trusted, and rich participants.[74]

In the "bourgeois revolution" view, these events constituted a kind of class struggle on two fronts. The rising capitalist middle classes overthrew the monarchy and instituted forms of representative government. But the threat of protocommunism from below pushed that same class to compromise with the landed gentry and the aristocracy, producing a relatively open, hybrid ruling class that consolidated a peculiar form of English capitalism that was finally completed and consummated by the Glorious Revolution of 1688, which established permanent parliamentary supremacy and paved the way for the subsequent Financial Revolution.

The "bourgeois revolution" explanation ran into difficulty for several reasons, and since the 1980s, scholars have mostly explained the English Civil Wars through religious and cultural forces.[75] Elites tend to hold diversified investment portfolios, so it is perennially difficult to find and identify a specific "bourgeois" class that lives on capitalist property alone, let alone a class that thinks of itself as a "bourgeoisie" and acts collectively with the intention of bringing about amenable capitalist legal and social relations. Moreover, painstaking research into local property has shown that the composition of the ruling class did not change substantially, nor was there a clear break between earlier monarchical oppression and later bourgeois market freedom, so the major sites of change were more in the social, cultural, and political realms than the economic.[76]

That may all be true, but it is still the case that by 1689, power in England had shifted from the monarchy to Parliament, comprised as it was of property owners.[77] In that year, Parliament issued the Bill of Rights, which restricted the power of the monarchy. It also assumed responsibility for the debt, moving it from the private possession of an individual to the permanent obligation of the nation as a whole. In 1694, Parliament granted a charter to the Bank of England.[78] The Bank emerged out of a loan for the new king to build a naval fleet: Over the course of 12 days, some 1,520 investors subscribed £1.2 million to lend to the government. In exchange, they were allowed to incorporate, with a charter for 11 years that granted them exclusive right to keep the government's balances and issue bank notes. The government would repay the loan at 8 percent interest.

The Bank was not the end of the Financial Revolution, not by a long shot. It was a political project, set up by prominent members of the Whig Party, the main supporters of the new constitutional monarchy. It faced resistance from rival joint-stock companies, which were also political projects and also focused on lending money to the hungry new government. The East India Company was split between Whig and Tory control and, after several failed attempts, lent £2 million to the government in 1698.[79] The Tories tried and failed to set up a rival Land Bank, and in 1711, succeeded at establishing the South Sea Company. The big joint-stock companies straddled the public-private financial divide. As the sociologist Bruce Carruthers writes, "Their corporate capital constituted a sizeable proportion of the national debt, and their shares dominated trading activity on the London stock exchange. Indeed, the success with which the government borrowed long term depended upon the liquidity that only an active stock market could offer."[80] They connected the capital-owning elite to the government, but with different factions of the elite supporting different projects.

The establishment of the Bank and the permanent national debt did not permanently settle the question of government finances, and the next decades saw a long learning process. In addition to using corporations for financing, the government raised money through lotteries and through selling varieties of annuities. In 1694, the government launched the Million Lottery, which tried to raise £1 million by selling 100,000 £10 tickets, each of which was a bond that would be repaid at £1 per year over the next 16 years, but 2,500 lucky winners would get an additional bond, paying an extra £10 to £1,000.[81] There were 37 further lottery loans between 1694 and 1776; the first Dutch lottery was conducted in 1709, and in 1757, France set up a larger and more complex version that continued through the French Revolution.[82] Lotteries are easy to understand and still exist as a method of state finance today, but they are also unpredictable: The state does not know how many winners there might be, or how attractive the odds are. The Million Lottery took three months to sell, and the drawing of the tickets took two further months. There were too many winners: In the end, despite raising £1 million, the lottery cost the government £2,375,000 in payouts between 1695 and 1711.[83] The second attempt, called the Malt Lottery because it would be repaid from the malt tax, did not offer good-enough odds, so its tickets failed to sell.

Annuities, on the other hand, offered predictability. Investors would lend the government a lump sum, and that sum would never be repaid—instead, the owner of the annuity would receive a payment every year (or twice a year) for a stipulated period of time. Some annuities were for the lifetime of the owner, others were for 99 years. Others were for the lifespan of some well-known person, like the Prince of Wales, because that person's death would be widely publicized and known to all. The most interesting version of an annuity was a "tontine," in which a pool of investors received back a fixed total annual payment, divided equally among them. As owners died, the survivors got a larger share of the total. I regret to report that I have never found evidence of any tontine owner killing off their fellow investors, but the final surviving owner of the 1693 tontine died in 1783, receiving the full £1,000-per-year payment, on an initial subscription of only £100.[84] Annuities also had disadvantages: Neither the government nor the investors knew how long payments would last, and they were difficult to sell to other people in a secondary market. But this thicket of strange forms of finance continued through the years of war against France. From 1694 to 1714, the English government raised £12,140,030 from selling annuities, and another £11,500,000 through lottery loans, while also borrowing £16,754,167 from the major joint-stock companies.[85]

As with VOC shares in the Dutch Republic, access to safe government bonds and company stock created a secondary market and a source of investment capital, as well as a form of collateral.[86] Trading in the secondary market was concentrated in a little street in London known as Exchange Alley, especially in two coffeehouses, called Jonathan's and Garroway's. Marine insurance was sold around the corner in Edward Lloyd's Coffeehouse, and fire insurance in Tom's and Causey's Coffeehouses.[87] With the presence of liquidity, collateral, and specialized traders, a stock market boom ensued. In 1691, the coffeehouse stock market consisted of about eight stocks, and a full day's trading might constitute about 13 trades, with ownership concentrated among at most a few hundred people.[88] By 1695, there were over 150 joint-stock companies in existence, and contemporaries wrote of Exchange Alley as a mad, carnivalesque place, where even Jews, Muslims, and *women* were active participants.[89] In 1697, John Castaing began publishing a twice-weekly newspaper called the *Course of the Exchange*, which carried stock prices over the past three days, the price of gold and silver, exchange rates, and quotations on various government bonds and annuities.[90] Weather and warfare permitting, the paper would be carried across the Channel on the daily postal-packet boat to Amsterdam. Some of the information from the *Course of the Exchange* would be reprinted in a "London paragraph" in the Dutch newspapers, which in turn were widely read in places like Paris and Hamburg. The regular, steady sharing of information allowed for market integration, and Larry Neal has shown persuasively that the London-Amsterdam capital markets reported the same prices for the same securities, starting with Bank of England stock in 1698, meaning there were international capital markets in existence at that date.[91]

In 1696–97, the new English government took another major step toward regularizing its financial situation: the Great Recoinage. By that time, the silver coins in circulation were old, worn, and sometimes clipped. What do I mean by "clipped"? Since there was never enough coinage, and since coins were large chunks of precious metal, people realized that they could cut off or shave off small pieces of several coins and melt the resulting shards down into a new coin, while still passing the old one off at face value. Of course this was illegal and harshly punished, but compliance was difficult to enforce, and by the 1690s, English coins in circulation were on average 30 percent lighter than their stated face value and about 10 percent of the coins were forged, which together meant that foreign merchants were often unwilling to accept them at full value. Problems with trade also meant problems with taxes, since so many taxes were collected as customs duties at the port cities. That, in turn, roused political complaint, given the power of merchants and traders. So the master of the Mint, one Isaac Newton, was tasked with melting down and reminting all of the coins in circulation. Holders of coins were required to deliver them to their tax collector, and after a lengthy public debate about the terms of the recoinage (should the government use it as an opportunity to devalue or debase the currency?) people were repaid by weight, not by the face value of the coins. That meant if you had turned in five guineas that were supposed to weigh one ounce each but were actually light, you did not receive back five full-weight guineas, you got back four or whatever number was equivalent to the weight of silver. In consequence, the government took in about £10 million in coin but only paid back out £6.8 million, creating deflation, scarcity, and an incentive to hoard money.

There was one other unexpected result. As the effects of the recoinage unwound, the mints made a historically significant math error. They underpriced silver relative to gold. That meant the same ounce of silver would be worth more elsewhere, so people gradually shipped their silver to Amsterdam or Paris, or used it as payment for foreign goods, given that it was worth more to merchants abroad. Slowly, over the course of decades, silver drained out of Britain, establishing a de facto gold standard. The consequences for the later history of global capitalism would be immense, and here again we have an example of a solution to a short-term problem having long-term consequences.

When the Tories founded the South Sea Company in 1711, they did so by conducting something known as a debt-for-equity swap. Since the government had continued to borrow to fight the War of the Spanish Succession against France, by 1711 there were huge amounts of government debt in private hands. The directors of the company offered an exchange: People could trade that outstanding debt for shares in the South Sea Company, which they promised would be profitable because it would conduct colonial trade with Spanish America. In 1714, the offer grew ever more appealing, because the company was awarded the *asiento*, the monopoly contract for delivering slaves to Spanish colonies. The plan worked: The South Sea Company exchanged £1,048,111 in lottery bonds for stock.[92] They received the interest payments on the bonds (at a lower rate than the original return) from the government, and the former holders of government debt now held their stock. In this way, when the War of the Spanish Succession ended in 1714, England possessed a regularized currency, a proto–central bank, a permanent national debt, a professional tax bureaucracy, a functioning stock market, access to international capital markets, and politically connected joint-stock companies with substantial reserves of capital. Financial capitalism had advanced by leaps and bounds. Conditions were perfect for a crisis.

■ ■ ■

The advantages that the new financial practices gave to England in terms of marshaling resources to fight great-power wars were not lost on its European rivals. In 1716, a Scottish gambler and convicted murderer by the name of John Law successfully established a new "General Bank" in Paris.[93] Law had been a monetary theorist since at least 1705, when he published a proposal for setting up a new kind of national bank in Scotland, as part of the debates over the terms of what became the 1707 Act of Union that brought England and Scotland together into the United Kingdom. Law's pamphlet, entitled *Money and Trade Considered*, argued that money was valuable not because of its precious metal content or because of government power but because of supply and demand. People demanded it to conduct trade and commerce, but its supply was limited, thanks to the absence of domestic mines and the continual problem of England running a trade deficit with Europe as a whole, and Europe with Asia. He thought that the supply could be increased by setting up a bank to issue paper money. In his 1705 proposal, the bank would own real estate assets, and the value of that land would impose a limit on how much paper money the bank could issue. This was a similar idea to the failed Tory Land Bank experiment, but Law genuinely had new ideas about why money was valuable, and how the addition of paper money could unlock national wealth that was held back by an insufficient supply of physical coins adequate to cover all of the potential demand for commerce.

Law did not successfully persuade the Scottish government, and he spent about a decade traveling among European cities, circulating in high society, ingratiating himself with powerful people, and proposing similar banking schemes in Turin and Paris. In 1715, Louis XIV died, leaving behind a power vacuum and a stupendous pile of debt. His great-nephew Phillippe, the Duke of Orleans, became regent, governing on behalf of the five-year-old Louis XV. In that moment of transition and fiscal crisis, Law set up his General Bank as a joint-stock company, a private institution backed by private funds (including his own fortune) that issued paper money backed by specie reserves. In 1717, Law helped the regent finance the purchase of a gigantic diamond, bought from Thomas Pitt Jr., the son of a former English East India Company governor who had bought the stone from an Indian merchant.[94] Law's bank made the payments every six months to Pitt, who in turn invested some of the proceeds in financial speculation. This whole affair established Law's connections with the London financial elite and with the new regent, who lent his public support to Law's bank.[95]

In September 1717, the General Bank conducted a debt-for-equity swap, much like the South Sea Company had done. Throughout that year and into 1718, Law began to buy out monopoly companies and tax farms throughout France, including the Mississippi Company, which owned the rights to colonization in Louisiana. As his company grew more successful, the price of its stock increased, and as the price increased, he had more capital available to buy up new assets. In 1718, the General Bank became the official national bank, now called the Royal Bank, and in 1719, conducted an even larger debt-for-equity swap. In that year, he consolidated all of his projects into one huge joint-stock company, usually called the Mississippi Company in English.[96] As Law's projects seemed to succeed and the value of shares in his company continued to rise, capital poured in from all over Europe to buy Mississippi stock, and in 1720, the regent named Law the controller general of the finances, essentially a mix of finance minister and foreign minister. Law claimed that his System (as he called the bank-money-company hybrid) would unleash French prosperity, and would lead to international peace, because if only England had reliable public credit, it would be a sole superpower, but if there was a general pattern of public credit, the different European states would balance one another, and would have an interest in supporting mutual trade and investment in one another's debt.[97] This was an early version of the idea that capitalism and trade would prevent wars.

But Law also had a problem. He needed the price of his shares to continue to rise, because that was the source of additional capital for his System. He also needed people to accept his paper money, which he was soon issuing in huge amounts. So as controller general, he took steps to force people to accept it: Government employees would be paid in his money, and taxes would be accepted in his money, and contracts would be denominated in his money. He also began printing money to buy up shares in his company, to support the stock price. By the summer of 1720 he tried to demonetize gold and silver and move France entirely to paper money, and that was a step too far. English and Dutch investors sold their stock and tried to pull their capital out of France, people in Paris ran on Law's bank to withdraw their specie deposits, and the whole System came crashing down. Law spent months trying to backtrack and salvage it and preserve his political position, but with no success. In December 1720 he fled France and his properties were confiscated. Billions of livres of his banknotes were burned, and his political enemies dismantled his System. His name was synonymous with financial fraud, and a central bank or paper money was politically impossible in France for the rest of the 18th century.[98]

But the crisis was not over. In 1719, the South Sea Company undertook another debt-for-equity swap, and its share prices rose accordingly. The flotation of new companies in Exchange Alley began to produce a stock market boom, as dozens of "projectors" advertised their new joint-stock endeavors to a public who had seen riches produced quickly for those who had bought into South Sea or Mississippi shares early. The company noisily advertised its expected profits from the slave trade and colonization and access to the New World market. It promised enormous dividends to its shareholders, which in turn attracted more investors. The company sold shares to important political figures, and was generous with the dispensation of bribes, and eventually began to invent fictitious people conducting fictitious trades in order to keep the price up. It was something close to a pyramid scheme: The high dividends to old shareholders were paid by selling stock at increasing prices to new shareholders. As capital began to flood out of the deflating bubble in Paris, some of it fed the new bubble in London, which kept the plan going for longer. Over the course of 1720, the price of South Sea shares rose from about £100 each to over £1,000.[99]

It couldn't last forever. In June 1720, Parliament passed the Bubble Act, which made it more difficult to start new joint-stock companies, and limited their size. The act was not a response to the bubble: In fact, it was pushed by the directors of the South Sea Company, who worried that the profusion of new start-up companies was diverting investment capital from their own shares.[100] But it prompted people to sell, which included selling South Sea shares. Some investors who had lost money in Paris sold their shares in a scramble for liquidity. And the MP Archibald Hutcheson began to produce a flood of pamphlets that showed that the company's promised dividends were mathematically impossible, eventually leading Parliament to convene a Secret Committee to investigate the company's finances.[101] Throughout the fall of 1720, the price of South Sea shares collapsed down to £150, and soon Parliament unearthed widespread fraud among the company's directors and their political supporters. John Aislabie, the chancellor of the exchequer, was investigated for corruption and imprisoned; James Craggs the Elder, the former postmaster general, killed himself; John Knight, the company's cashier, fled to Antwerp.

The crash in London cost many very rich English investors a lot of money, but it was not a major macroeconomic event.[102] The crash in Paris had much larger repercussions because of Law's paper money experiment. In Paris, the whole System was dismantled, but in London, the South Sea Company survived, the debt-for-equity swap remained, and the Financial Revolution was secure. Indeed, in 1723, half of the stock of the South Sea Company was converted into perpetual annuities, which were widely popular with both English and Dutch investors.[103] They were held by at least 35,000 people, which vastly expanded the reach of participation in financial markets, and provided liquidity and capital accumulation on a larger scale.[104] However, the Bubble Act restricted the creation of new corporations in England until it was repealed in 1825. That meant English banking remained small and insufficient: One of the big puzzles of financial history is why banks contributed so little to the Industrial Revolution of the late 18th and early 19th centuries, and the answer probably lies there. It also meant that more corporations were formed in the colonies, especially the American colonies, than in Britain, which would prove to have drastic consequences for the different trajectories of American versus British capitalism.[105] Likewise, the fallout of 1720 meant that the institutions of the Financial Revolution did not spread to France, which meant France continued to lose wars throughout the 18th century, and accumulated a huge amount of debt, ultimately producing a fiscal and political crisis in the 1780s that led to the French Revolution.[106]

■ ■ ■

In his 1930 essay "Economic Possibilities for Our Grandchildren," the British economist John Maynard Keynes claimed that he could trace "the beginnings of British foreign investment to the treasure which [Sir Francis] Drake stole from Spain in 1580."[107] According to Keynes, Queen Elizabeth used her share of the profits to pay off "the whole of England's foreign debt," and balanced the budget, and still had £40,000 left over to invest in the Levant Company, the profits of which founded the East India Company, and profits of that company went on to be "the foundation of England's subsequent foreign investment." He concludes this passage by exclaiming, "Thus, every £1 which Drake brought home in 1580 has now become £100,000. Such is the power of compound interest!"[108] Following Keynes, there is occasionally a similar instinct in the history of capitalism to attribute all existing wealth or capital or general economic activity in Britain or the United States or the global North to these past episodes of plunder.

But the great economist was wrong, in more than one way. Elizabeth did indeed pay off her Antwerp debt in 1574, but that was six years before Drake's plunder, and, as we have seen, a national debt is not actually a bad thing to have. A national debt provides a source of liquidity, investment capital, and collateral for other transactions, as well as a policy tool, since new debt can be issued when necessary, instead of having to establish creditworthiness from scratch. By 1589, Elizabeth was in dire financial straits and sent a representative of the Merchant Adventurers company to various financial centers in Germany to try to raise £100,000 at 10 percent interest, but found nobody willing to lend.[109] The 136 initial investors in the East India Company held a wide range of portfolio investments, including the Levant Company, but also the Barbary Company, the Spanish Company, the French Company, the Muscovy Company, and the Merchant Adventurers, most of which made their money through monopoly trade with continental Europe, not through plunder or colonialism.[110] Nor was even the largest share of plunder a significant amount by the scale of the flood of silver from Spanish America. In 1628, the Dutch West India Company managed to capture the entire annual Spanish silver fleet, which funded the Dutch war effort against Spain for eight months, and paid WIC shareholders a 50 percent dividend.[111] That was a lot, but a tiny fraction of the amount of silver Spain received in total and ultimately mortgaged to its creditors, military contractors, and trade deficits. And it seems that the WIC paid out too much, because it soon ran into fiscal problems and eventually went bankrupt.[112] Moreover, there were no banks or safe investment vehicles to pay Drake the 3 percent compound interest that Keynes estimates his plunder accumulated. Even if Drake had turned his plunder over to a goldsmith banker, his descendants would have likely lost it all in the Stop of the Exchequer of 1672, or speculated foolishly during the 1720 crisis.

The history of capital accumulation is littered with loss. Capital depreciates, governments default, business ventures fail, investments lose value, and stock markets crash. For those reasons, capital is trapped in a frantic search for temporary sources of gain, and has to constantly renew and reproduce itself, lest it be eroded away by the various forms of failure.

Drake's fortune provides an even sharper example: Starting in 1916 or 1917, an American con man named Oscar Hartzell swindled about $2 million from (allegedly) 70,000 people, mostly with the surname "Drake," by promising them that they stood to inherit Francis Drake's riches if they paid to join his lawsuit against the British government.[113] He employed some 11 agents in seven states to conduct his postal fraud over the course of more than a decade. There was no estate, but when Hartzell was arrested and put on trial for fraud in 1933, the people he had been scamming still put together $68,000 for his legal defense. He used Keynes's essay as part of his argument, a way of showing that fabulous riches had accumulated since the 1590s and must now be *somewhere*, owed to *someone*. He was judged to be insane, and died in a federal mental facility in 1943.

The point here is that plunder is nothing compared to profit.[114] Or as the communist poet and playwright Bertolt Brecht put it, "What is the robbing of a bank compared to the founding of a bank?"[115] The history of plunder is surely global, and traces back to antiquity. But neither the tribute paid to Roman legions nor the medieval Mongol seizure of cities all over Asia nor even Spanish and Portuguese conquests produced capitalism. Capitalism, and especially the steady accumulation of capital, requires a wide set of institutions, especially the institutions of finance, which were invented haphazardly not in order to create capitalism but in order to fight and win wars. As Charles V and Philip II discovered, even the continual plunder of an entire continent will not necessarily generate global power, because the plundered money will eventually be paid on to the bankers, creditors, stockholders, and investors who have durable vehicles for capital accumulation. In this way, what is special about capitalism is not plunder but banks, joint-stock companies, dividends, and permanent, alienable government bonds. Spain and Portugal received a tremendous amount of plunder, but both were in decline and utterly dependent on foreign creditors by the middle of the 17th century. France too received plunder from its overseas empire, but spent the 18th century trapped in a cycle of fiscal crisis and repeated "money famines" that ground commerce to a halt. Its overseas trade grew, and grew rapidly, but this did not translate into national wealth or government solvency. By the 1780s, the growing commercial interests and the frustrated holders of government debt crashed directly into the inability of the political class to conduct meaningful reform, ultimately unleashing the French Revolution.[116] But first the Dutch and then the English developed new institutions for capital accumulation, so by 1700 Amsterdam and London were the "capitals of capital," where wealthy people from all over Europe went to protect and invest their money.

None of this is to say that violence was irrelevant to the origins of capitalism. We have already seen in this book more than one genocide, and clearly the impetus of funding wars was at the heart of creating the Financial Revolution. Violence was also essential to the creation of capitalist labor, both in the sense of the enslavement of Africans and in the expulsion of European laborers and Indigenous societies from their land. But the violence was not enough in itself, and also was not unique to capitalism. Rather, capitalism emerged through violence that was committed in the context of monetized price relations, impersonal market forces, financial institutions, and governments composed of property owners.

Isaac Newton in 1717: Capitalism Under Construction

The year 1717 was a busy one for Isaac Newton, and especially for his contribution to the construction of global capitalism. He was 75 years old, famous across Europe for his scientific discoveries, and well into his second decade as master of the Royal Mint, which entailed overseeing and managing the production of coins in England. Newton is often thought of as a transitional figure. Using methods of experimentation and mathematical calculation, he discovered and theorized the concept of universal gravitation in his *Principia mathematica* of 1687, and simultaneously with Gottfried Leibniz, he developed the principles of calculus. In 1717, Newton produced the second edition of his book *Opticks*, which set out the results of his many experiments into the behavior of light and colors. In his methods and experiments Newton was one of the first modern scientists, and his discoveries ushered in the modern age of physics and mathematics.

But although Newton was one of the first modern physicists, he was also one of the last of the alchemists. Alchemy was not just a hobby for him but an integral part of his scientific agenda. He began his alchemical investigations while a student at Cambridge in the 1660s, publishing under the pseudonym "Jeova sanctus unus."[1] He compiled a vast personal list of over 5,000 references to writings on alchemy, kept a private library of alchemical texts and coded personal writings, and once he moved to London, he was an active participant in a circle of working alchemists.[2] His theory of universal gravitation and the behavior of light were part of his pursuits into unknown and unseen distant causal relations, and for him there was no clear separation between what today would be called chemistry and what was alchemy.

Like Luther had been 200 years before, and like Lenin would be 200 years later, Newton was an apocalyptic thinker.[3] As his biographer James Gleick puts it, "He read the Scriptures literally and indulged in a particular fascination with prophecy, which he saw as complex symbolism to be unraveled and interpreted."[4] He wrote many long letters to his friend the property theorist and slave trade investor John Locke, detailing what he thought were many "corruptions of the Scripture," especially his disagreements with the theory of the Trinity.[5] He wrote long private treatises on Revelation, and was fascinated by the problems of biblical chronology, which tried to reconcile the different (mutually exclusive) dating systems in various holy texts, especially the moment of Creation and the Flood. Toward the end of his life, he hypothesized that the comets he and his colleague Edmund Halley had observed would one day fall into the sun, creating an explosion that would annihilate the earth.[6]

But Newton's activities in 1717 were important for another reason: the establishment of the gold standard as the monetary system of England. After decades of study and seclusion, Newton was elected to represent Cambridge University in Parliament in 1689, immediately after the Glorious Revolution. In that capacity, he met and befriended Locke, and participated in some of the big public controversies of the day. His patron was Charles Montagu, whom he had known from Cambridge. In 1696, Montagu was chancellor of the exchequer, and arranged to have Newton named warden of the Mint, just at the start of the Great Recoinage. Newton was a logical choice, because the Mint needed to credibly demonstrate with exact mathematical precision the fineness of the precious metal in its coins. Newton's chemical (and alchemical) researches meant he plausibly knew more about the properties of precious metals than anyone. The recoinage was a profoundly unequal and controversial procedure, and although Newton himself did not agree with the government's policy, he was tasked with carrying it out. By 1700, he was promoted from warden to master, in which position he remained until the end of his life. As part of his duties, he prosecuted counterfeiters and clippers of coin, which he did with great energy, often denying requests for mercy or plea bargains.[7] He even paid £14, 10 shillings of his own money (which was a lot) to become a justice of the peace for the seven counties around London, so he could personally prosecute enemies of the coinage.[8]

Silver was underpriced at the Mint under the terms of the recoinage. That meant a given amount of silver could buy more goods or be exchanged for more gold if it was sent abroad, or sold as bullion instead of coin to silver merchants (meaning *not* sent to the Mint to be coined), who in turn would send it abroad. Newton realized the mistake by about 1700, and wrote a memo to the government arguing very reasonably that the cause of the outflow of silver was that it was in higher demand in India and China, so it was being sent abroad where it could command more goods.[9] To take only one example, the East India Company exported £5.7 million between 1700 and 1717, for use in their Asian empire.[10] Newton pointed out the problem more than once, but the government was unwilling to change the Mint ratios again, or the fineness of the metal content of the coins, so silver continued to slowly flow out. In September 1717, Newton wrote a report concluding that English monetary habits had fundamentally and irrevocably changed since 1702, such that silver was merely a commodity like any other, and the only money was gold.[11] For this reason, many economic historians today date the emergence of the gold standard to 1717. This change might not have had global significance or lasted very long, except that Britain would go on over the next century to become the trading and manufacturing behemoth of the world, and any country that wished to trade with Britain needed to be able to do business in gold, thereby creating a powerful incentive for other countries to adopt the gold standard. As more and more of them did so, pressure built on remaining countries to join so they too could trade with the growing gold bloc. The process was slow, and the gold-standard system only really came into operation in the 1870s, when Germany united and adopted gold and both France and the United States demonetized silver, but from 1717 onward, a single global monetary system gradually took shape, centered on London, and based on gold, or currencies that could easily be exchanged for gold.

Newton was often tasked with creating estimates of the value of the total currency in circulation in other countries, including Ireland in 1712, France in 1714, and Portugal right before his death in 1725.[12] In 1702, he produced a report for the Treasury that valued the metal content of 119 different coins in circulation in various countries in Europe.[13] These figures were used to make arguments in Parliament about trade policy and exchange rates, and Newton himself sometimes took part in public debates over the currency. These mathematized arguments were a new phenomenon after the 1680s, part of what the historian William Deringer calls a "quantitative civic episteme," meaning a new norm of using numbers and math to make public political arguments.[14] The big test case for this new civic episteme was the 1720 crisis. Newton made a lot of money as master of the Mint, and he invested heavily in the new joint-stock companies. He bought £2,500 of South Sea stock in 1713, and must have bought much more, because as the bubble was rising in April 1720 he authorized someone else to sell £3,500 of his stock, and he bought £1,000 more in June.[15] There is a legend that he lost a fortune in the crash and supposedly said that he could not calculate "the madness of men," but there is no direct evidence for either the loss or the remark. Instead, by August 1722, he owned over £21,000 in South Sea stock and in 1724 was one of the 48 largest owners of East India Company stock, with £11,000.[16]

By the standards of Luther's age, Newton lived in astonishing opulence. At his death, he owned a house on Jermyn Street in London, which he had filled with luxurious crimson furniture, a mechanical clock, and over 2,000 books.[17] He had a horse-drawn carriage and six servants, 16 paintings (four of them Dutch), dishes to serve 40 people, a coffee pot, and two silver chamber pots.[18] Of course, Newton was a famous, wealthy, and politically connected man. But his consumption habits tell us something about how the world of early capitalism had changed since Luther's time.

Laborers in Newton's London would have regularly consumed soft wheat bread, beef, and beer.[19] They would have sometimes consumed delicious tropical stimulants, like tobacco, coffee, tea, and especially sugar, most of which was produced by slaves in Atlantic colonies or imported from the East India Company. By 1717, London was an immense metropolis and growing rapidly, filling up with landless wage laborers who could no longer eke out a living in agriculture or afford to rent land. Many would sign indenture contracts to migrate to North America. Others would stay in or near London and work for wages in the growing protoindustrial sector. Their labor would produce manufactures to be exported to the colonies, and their wages would be spent in part on addictive luxuries imported from the colonies, so their economic lives were at least touched by, if not dependent on, the growing Atlantic capitalist system, and that system had African slavery at its heart. To be sure, even in England, in 1717 most people still lived in rural areas and worked in agriculture. Lives were still short, and often painful; plague swept through England in 1665, sending Newton home from Cambridge.[20] But there were far more people in England and the Netherlands working for wages and living in cities than had been the case in 1517, and far more people all over Europe enjoyed far greater consumption than nearly anyone had 200 years before. They had more books, more money, more commodities, and more colonies and wars. The reach of market activity was far greater, with English landlords, New England cod fishers, slaves on Barbados sugar plantations, African slave merchants, European slave-trading companies (and their shareholders), and European sugar eaters drawn together into a giant Atlantic-spanning system of capitalist production.

Indeed, there were few people in England or the Netherlands or the English Atlantic colonies whose economic lives were not oriented toward market production. The presence of capitalism in the world of 1717 was both more extensive and more intense than it had been in 1517, although it was not yet the dominant global economic system. But all the pieces were in place: corporations, wage labor, enclosed private landholding, consumer culture, monetized price exchange, and financial institutions. Those pieces forged the Atlantic system, and were forged by it. Capital made the Atlantic imperial economy, and the Atlantic imperial economy made capitalism.[21] It is to that wider Atlantic that we now turn.

CHAPTER 3

Land and Labor, 1640s–1800s

Whe most people think of capitalism, they think about work, and they are right to do so. Free wage labor is the most common form of work today, but it is a relatively recent and very unusual historical creation. Before the 18th century, very few people in the world worked for wages, and even in places like Amsterdam and London where many people were wage workers, they still were not "free" in the sense of being able to quit and leave if they chose. Many servants, contracted laborers, and even artisans were paid money wages to perform specific tasks or work for specified periods of time, but if they tried to leave, they could be fined or imprisoned.[1] Many of them could not choose their employer, or switch between jobs. Even many of those who earned wages were also partly paid in kind, either in room and board or in some share of the materials, or even in education and religious supervision. Modern free wage labor emerged between the late 17th century and the early 19th century, and then became the unique and fundamental labor relation that characterizes capitalism as a specific economic system unlike any other.

But the history of the emergence of free wage labor between about 1650 and 1800 cannot be told without the history of its opposite, which was the emergence of a new and especially virulent form of slavery. Over that same time period, the Dutch and then the English created an Atlantic trading system that depended on the enslavement and forced migration of Africans to Brazil, the Caribbean, and the Chesapeake, where they were made to work under the most unimaginably brutal conditions to produce cash crops, especially tobacco and sugar. This was a form of slavery unlike any other that had preceded it. Slavery had existed in some form or another almost everywhere in the world over almost all recorded history, but it was almost always a social status instead of the basis of the economic system. As far back as under Roman law, slaves were people who were spared from physical death, so their condition of slavery was a kind of *social* death, a death postponed under condition of their captor's total control.[2] Prisoners, debtors, and members of defeated armies or rival religions were often enslaved and forced to work as household servants or manual laborers, but not in plantation gangs.

The new form of slavery was also *racialized*, in the sense that Africans and only Africans could be enslaved, even if they were Christians, in sharp difference from earlier Spanish enslavement of Indigenous Americans. It was *permanent*, in the sense that it was not for a prison term or other specified period of time; it was *heritable*, in the sense that the children of slaves were automatically slaves; and slaves were *chattel*, in the sense that they were legally property, not persons with any form of rights. For that reason, it is imperative to tell the history of labor alongside the history of the emergence of modern capitalist property. Masters could murder their slaves with no repercussions; someone who murdered another person's slave would be prosecuted for property destruction, not murder. European gender norms were abandoned, such that women could be enslaved and worked in male-coded jobs, and were sexually abused at the whim of enslavers.[3] This form of slavery was new, and developed as a legal and economic institution across the 17th century; sugar and tobacco production was not new, but in Brazil and then in the Caribbean and the Chesapeake it was organized around slavery for the first time, creating a new kind of production system and a new kind of slave society.

The two labor regimes of wage work and enslavement, in turn, were connected through land and through consumption. Agricultural land in England was steadily being "enclosed," meaning consolidated and privatized, which deprived many poor people of the means to feed themselves. Between the 1620s and 1660s, many of them signed indenture contracts and migrated to the New World, working in the early stages of plantation agriculture, or soon acquiring their own land in the imperial conquest of North America. When there were not enough of them to continue to expand production at low costs, plantation owners switched to slave labor. The tropical goods that the slaves produced—especially sugar— helped create a modern consumer culture. Increasingly after the 1650s, European workers (especially wage workers in England and the Netherlands) worked more days and longer hours, and worked more often for money wages, so that they could buy more sugar, tea, tobacco, coffee, and chocolate. This "industrious revolution" led to the growth and expansion of American slavery to supply those tasty goods, as well as to the establishment of the Atlantic trade system, to the behaviors of modern consumption, and to the creation of the landless market-oriented wage labor force that would become the engine of the Industrial Revolution.[4]

The relationship between slavery and capitalism, or slavery and the Industrial Revolution (and thus modern economic growth), is probably the most hotly debated subject in the field of economic history. In 1944, Eric Williams, the future independence leader of

Trinidad and Tobago, published his PhD dissertation, *Capitalism and Slavery*, which argued that the "great wealth" of the triangular trade specifically went on to form the "huge outlay" that financed the specific inventions of the English Industrial Revolution.[5] After decades of debate, few scholars today would agree with that "narrow" version of the Williams thesis. However, nearly everyone would agree with a "broad" version, that slavery *in general* contributed to, and was part of, capitalism. But that leaves many questions still open to vibrant debate. The evidence presented here is the result of that debate, but this subject remains an open wound.

From about the 1640s through about 1800, capitalist forces moved Atlantic economic life from a profusion of unfree labor regimes like indenture, convict labor, redemptioner contracts, guild apprenticeship, service in husbandry, encomiendas, serfdom, and religious slavery to just two socially general forms: African slavery and free wage labor. To be sure, convict labor continued and continues today, as did encomienda labor until the late 18th century, but although both enriched some people, neither was the general form of labor in the wider economy. This consolidation process involved the enclosure and privatization of land, as well as the emergence of sustained intercontinental commodity trade, and all of it was paid for thanks to the new innovations in finance and backstopped by the monetization and unequal inflation of the Price Revolution.

■ ■ ■

For more than a century, the Atlantic economy was an Iberian imperial domain. Spain controlled most of the Caribbean and South America, while Portugal had its island outposts in the Atlantic and along the coast of Africa. Portugal also colonized Brazil as early as 1500, and divided it among various military-administrative captains, who tried (mostly unsuccessfully) to force the Indigenous people to farm and export red dye from brazilwood trees. In general, the Iberian colonizers struggled to find an export that was valuable enough to be worth the cost of shipping it across the ocean: Only silver and gold turned a profit. Various European goods flowed the opposite direction, exchanged for precious metals. Along with those goods came people: Some 450,000 migrated from Iberia during 1500–1650, as merchants in the new colonial ports, wage workers in the colonial provisioning system, or recipients of conquered land, which they governed as encomiendas with unfree, usually Indigenous, labor.[6]

Slavery also started early. African slaves were taken throughout the Portuguese Empire, from the sugar islands to Lisbon, and it was on a Portuguese ship that the first African slaves arrived in the New World in 1502.[7] The first slave revolt broke out in 1522, among Muslim Wolof people from Senegambia who were forced into sugar cultivation on Hispaniola, which alerts us to the fact that Muslims were in the New World not only before English Protestants but before the existence of Protestantism itself.[8] Charles V tried to encourage the slave trade by granting the *asiento* monopoly contract to Portuguese slavers in 1521, and Portugal continued to dominate the slave trade until the 1640s. But it was on a very small scale compared to what followed, and although many of the slaves were African, other slaves in the Portuguese Empire were former Iberian Muslims or captured Muslims from various ethnic groups in North Africa, and both the Spanish and Portuguese conquerors tried to enslave Indigenous peoples, without much success.[9] The first century of colonization was focused on the silver bonanza, and it was not until about 1600 that so many people had migrated and conquest had expanded over so much territory that colonists tried to establish viable economies in new areas. That brought demand for slaves. As one historian puts it: "The major demand for African slaves, after 1600, came from Portuguese America and the marginal lands that the Spaniards had previously neglected, above the lesser islands of the Caribbean. With no stable Indian peasant population to exploit, and few alternative exports in the form of precious metals, successful colonization in these zones required the export of products that Europe could consume."[10] And the solution to the export needs was sugar.

The only two economically successful captaincies in Brazil were Bahia and Pernambuco, and they began producing sugar on a small scale as early as the 1510s. Their sugar was on sale in Antwerp by the 1530s, and by the 1540s, sugar mills were constructed under the guidance of experts (probably enslaved) brought from the sugar-growing Canary Islands and Madeira.[11] By the 1570s, there were 60 sugar mills in Brazil, and in the 1610s, a technical improvement in the rolling process made mills cheaper to build, so they continued to proliferate.[12] This infant sugar industry was the first substantial destination for enslaved Africans, and it was also a fragile trade that was prone to failure through wartime disruption, or price changes in Europe.[13] In 1621, the Dutch war of independence spilled over into the Atlantic, and Dutch privateers began raiding towns, mills, and ships. In the 1630s, the Dutch West Indies Company (the WIC) captured Portuguese possessions on both sides of the Atlantic: Recife and Pernambuco in Brazil in 1630 and the slaving fortress of Elmina in 1638.[14] The Dutch brought capital, low shipping costs, and market access, so the Brazilian sugar industry boomed. The WIC captured the sugar mills and sold them to private investors, and indeed, although it was taxed and risky, the Dutch Brazilian sugar industry was characterized by individual private ownership and investment rather than government or even corporate possession.[15] By the 1640s, ships arrived not only from the Netherlands but from the Baltic and from Venice to buy Dutch-owned Brazilian sugar.[16]

Dutch Brazil was the proof of concept. By 1645, the Dutch were pushed out by rebellions in the interior, and the English Navigation Acts cut off access to London as a market for Dutch exports.[17] The epicenter of sugar production shifted to Barbados.

For decades, scholars believed that Dutch investors, owners, and shippers transplanted their slave-driven sugar production system to English-owned Barbados, but it appears that case is overstated. Dutch shipping was certainly important for (illicitly) moving goods to and from the English colonies, the Dutch were willing to sell slaves to anyone, and the Dutch supplied horses and oxen from Curaçao, but Barbados was owned and controlled by English colonists.[18] In the 1630s Barbados produced cotton and tobacco, and planters experimented with indigo and ginger but found them too expensive and difficult to produce. There was a tobacco glut in English markets in the 1630s, so profits dried up and planters looked for another cash crop.[19] Throughout the 1640s, Barbados was mostly a society of small owner-operator farms, often run by one or two unmarried men, and most of the agricultural work was done by white indentured servants.[20] In 1645, there were 5,680 African slaves on the island.[21]

All of that changed very rapidly between 1645 and the 1660s. With the introduction of sugar, land suddenly became more profitable and land prices boomed, which allowed the planters with the biggest property holdings to profit fastest and buy up the land of their competitors.[22] By 1680, 175 planters (which was 7 percent of landowners) owned more than 60 slaves each and together owned more than half of the land and half of the slaves.[23] They also utterly dominated the government and militia. By the 1660s, the land in Barbados had all been bought and concentrated and the need for labor to continue to produce sugar outstripped the supply of indentured workers, so planters switched to slaves. The number of servants continued to rise, but not nearly at the pace of the expansion of slavery.[24] Indentured servants who finished their terms of service could no longer find available or affordable land, so they began to leave: Between 1650 and 1680, between 12,000 and 30,000 English colonists (probably the lower end) migrated from Barbados to other English colonies.[25] More than half of the 1,300 European colonists who arrived in South Carolina in 1670–90 came from Barbados, and substantial numbers went to Antigua, Nevis, the Leeward Islands, and Jamaica.[26] These migrants brought techniques, commercial connections, and legal codes with them, spreading the slave plantation system and sugar monoculture across the English colonial possessions. This was not just a matter of economic know-how, but of laws producing the specific new form of slavery, codified in legal documents that established that slaves were chattel property and that only Africans could be enslaved. As the historian Russell Menard puts it, "The Barbados slave code of 1661 was the first comprehensive slave code created in British America and one of the most influential pieces of legislation passed by a colonial legislature. Four colonies—Antigua, Jamaica, South Carolina, and, indirectly, Georgia—adopted the entire code, while bits and pieces of it appear in the laws of many other colonies."[27]

The sugar boom was immense in scope. "By the mid-1660s sugar and its by-products accounted for 90 percent of the value of Barbadian exports, while the Barbadian sugar crop of 1665–66 was worth more than that of Bahia in 1700."[28] In the 1670s, Barbados produced 65 percent of the sugar consumed in England, and English people were eating more and more of it every year.[29] In 1670, English people consumed one pound of sugar per capita, but by the 1770s, it was 25 pounds per person per year.[30] By the 1680s, there were 38,000 slaves on the island, which constituted 70 percent of the population, and Barbados was the wealthiest and most populous English colony in the Western Hemisphere.[31] Sugar was so profitable that planters converted all land to agriculture and all agricultural land to sugar. They cut down all the trees on the island, forcing them to import wood to fuel their mills—and briefly generating a crop disaster as the monkeys and raccoons that had been driven out of the forests wreaked havoc on the sugarcane, until the planters instituted a bounty on them, leading to their extermination.[32] The slaves had to be fed somehow, so planters began to import slave-grown rice from South Carolina and salted cod from New England, boosting export industries in those places.

The Chesapeake tobacco plantations switched from servitude to slavery from the 1680s to 1720s, also drawing on cheap convict labor when economic diversification created demand for skilled nonagricultural work.[33] South Carolina made the switch between about 1700 and 1720.[34] Different forms of unfree labor produced different social and cultural patterns: Tobacco plantations had fewer slaves, each of whom did a variety of tasks, while sugar plantations had hundreds of slaves, who were specialized in work gangs.[35] Sugar had higher death rates, so depended more on continual imports of captives than on new births, so African traditions continued in sugar areas while new local traditions developed in tobacco areas.

Sugar was so central to the Barbadian economy that it even functioned as a method of payment. The planters invented a fictitious currency to serve as a unit of account, and they would buy slaves priced in that currency in exchange for an amount of sugar of equivalent value.[36] As early as 1648, sugar constituted the means of payment for more than half of all transactions on the island.[37] In 1706, the planters created a paper currency backed by a land bank, which provided owners of land on the island with credit up to one-quarter of the assessed value of their property, which meant the big landowners had access to even more resources.[38] Barbados was not the only colony to adopt these solutions to the perennial scarcity of money. Even in the rapidly monetizing, silver-based economic world of the 17th century, physical money was still always scarce in the colonies: Whenever some flowed in, it flowed right back out to buy supplies and manufactured imports. Other North American colonies adopted commodity units of account based on tobacco, beaver pelts, and grain, and in the early 18th century, many of them set up land banks to issue paper currency.

In this way, land seized from Native Americans and commodities grown by slaves were the basis for colonial monetary systems: another way that plunder was transformed into profit through the institutions of financial capitalism.

The slave–sugar plantation export system was pioneered in Dutch Brazil in the 1630s and 1640s, then was adopted, expanded, and, in its ugly way, perfected in English Barbados from the 1650s to the 1680s, then spread throughout the Caribbean. From the 1680s through the 1720s, the greater availability of enslaved Africans at lower prices relative to indentured Europeans meant that planters all over the English colonies switched from indenture to slavery. By that point, an entirely new form of social and economic organization had emerged: concentrated ownership of land, assets, enslaved human beings, and governmental power, specialized production of cash-crop monoculture for export, dependence on markets for imports including food, violently supervised gang-labor systems, and racialized chattel slavery as a means of social control. It was very possibly the most miserable social system yet devised on earth, and certainly the most unequal. Over the course of the 18th century, this system would become the norm in the European colonies in the Caribbean, as well as those in the southern half of what would become the United States, and in Brazil. These slave societies, in turn, were the engine that powered the entire Atlantic capitalist system.

■ ■ ■

A great deal of 20th-century thought on development economics focused on the problem of agricultural production.[39] The fundamental logic is this: Anyone who does not work in agriculture does not produce their own food, which means that people working in agriculture need to produce a surplus beyond their own consumption. The more productive agriculture can get, the fewer people it will require, and more and more people can move into cities to do other kinds of work, like services and manufacturing, which are more productive than farming. (It is essential to note here that when economists and economic historians use the word "productive," they do not mean it in the normal, colloquial sense of "being busy" or "getting a lot done." They mean the economic value of output, so a doctor who spends 30 seconds glancing at your chart and then bills you $500 before playing golf the rest of the day is a more "productive" worker than someone who works a backbreaking 12-hour shift in a sweatshop sewing clothes that will sell for less than $500.)

As in modern development, so too in history. Several prominent interpretations for the rise of capitalism have argued that it emerged in the English countryside, as landlords enclosed common fields and instituted high-investment, growth-oriented "rational" capitalist relations.[40] Indeed, for some scholars, this moment was the first "bourgeois revolution," and it coincided with the English Civil War of the 1640s–60s, supposedly overthrowing the old feudal aristocracy and replacing it with a class of landowning capitalists.

We have already seen that Dutch agriculture was privately owned and market-oriented very early. There was not much of a feudal elite to overthrow there, and the need to constantly reclaim land from the ocean and protect it from further flooding meant that Dutch farmers were unusually communal and collective. Some economic historians go so far as to argue for a "polder model" of society based on collective decision-making—a polder is the reclaimed land or flood plains enclosed by dams and embankments.[41] The story of English capitalist agriculture, however, was considerably less cheerful.

English land was transformed through a process called "enclosure," which meant the privatization of formerly open-access common land, and the consolidation of formerly dispersed small landholdings into fewer, large properties, thus replacing a society of small farmers with a society of a few large landowners and a lot of landless workers. There were two waves of enclosure in the English countryside. The first ran from about 1440 to about 1540, and consisted mainly of consolidating small, dispersed peasant landholdings into a few large ones, which were then encircled by hedgerows as a form of fencing.[42] This first round of enclosure was driven by landlords and happened on a private, individual basis: Landlords would raise rent or take advantage of insecure tenures to force small peasants off the land. Peasants were content with growing grain for their own consumption, but landlords wanted to convert the land from grain to sheep pasture, in order to profit from the rising price of wool.[43] The result was drastic: About 10 percent of villages in the English Midlands were destroyed and depopulated, and the inequality of both property and income rapidly increased.[44] This was entirely a response to market forces: The relative price of wool was higher and increasing faster than the relative price of grain, so land full of sheep was more valuable than land full of people.

The second wave of enclosures ran from 1600 to 1850, though most intensely after the early decades of the 18th century. As consumption prices increased during the Price Revolution, landlords were anxious to raise rents so their incomes could keep up with their expenditures, and were also eager to orient as much toward market production as possible to take advantage of rising prices for agricultural output. Many peasant land tenures were held for one or three lifetimes, so they could only infrequently be renegotiated.[45] Instead, landlords tried to clear or enclose new land or impose new kinds of fees. Fees and lordly interference effectively killed the peasant-to-peasant land market, meaning people who wanted to sell were strongly incentivized to sell only to landlords, not to one another.[46] But mostly, landlords raised rents over and over, exactly as (or even because) the price of output also increased. Agricultural employment declined, and specialized. From a rural world of family-operated farms, something new and profoundly unequal emerged. The concentration of land was not a vehicle for upward social mobility: Large estates were not the result of small landholders diligently saving and accumulating more small estates, let alone new people purchasing land and manors; they were the result of initially rich landlords getting richer at the expense of workers and smallholders.[47] Women disproportionately relied on the commons for their contribution to household income, so the loss of those resources pushed them out of agricultural work and drove down their wages.[48] Instead of a family handling all of the plowing, sowing, harvesting, threshing, digging, cleaning, and tending to animals, large landowners hired specialists to do those tasks, and the division of labor increased efficiency.[49] In the 17th century, agricultural employment for men declined 8 percent; for women, 12 percent; and for boys, 14 percent. In the century after that, employment for men declined by a further 24 percent, women by 29 percent, and boys by 36 percent.[50] These people lost access to the ability to feed themselves and to rural employment. Some became "paupers," living in poverty and dependent on charitable relief, and many moved to cities to become wage workers or emigrated to the colonies.

This second wave of enclosures were parliamentary enclosures, meaning the law recognized and enforced private acts, now with the considerable violence of a wide range of capital offenses against property that were created with the Black Acts of the 1720s.[51] These increased the number of capital crimes in England from about 50 in 1688 to over 200 by 1820, mostly between 1714 and 1725.[52] The key pieces of legislation were the Riot Act, Transportation Act, Combination Act, Workhouse Act, and the Criminal Law Act. As the labor historian Peter Linebaugh summarizes the consequences of these laws:

We can see that two of them affected the criminal sanction, making it at once more terrifying and more effective; two of them prohibited the most obvious means by which the collective power of the working class might manifest itself, in public assembly or in trade union; and one of them (the Workhouse Act) was a mixture of criminal policy and labour policy. The Workhouse Act, by generalizing the principle of incarceration, and the Transportation Act, by regularizing the supply of forced labour to the plantations, were bold attempts to find means of creating and encouraging new modes of production. The Combination Act and the Riot Act assured, in principle, that these could grow without countervailing organization.[53]

As church-based charity systems broke down, workhouses and debtors' prisons multiplied, increasingly moving toward penal-labor servitude for felons, at the same time that the number of possible felonies vastly increased.[54]

In between these two waves of enclosure were two other large-scale redistributions of land: In 1536–41, the newly Protestant Henry VIII dissolved the hundreds of monasteries, priories, and convents in England, Wales, and Ireland, and in the 1640s, the insurgent forces of the Commonwealth seized and redistributed Royalist lands. In both cases, the beneficiaries were the already-rich landlords who could afford to buy these new lands or had the political connections to do so.[55] Further, the period from 1600 to 1800 saw a wide range of projects to "improve" and expand agricultural land, including draining swamps and marshes, cutting down forests, and further privatizing common pastureland. These efforts probably increased the total area of English agricultural land by 25 percent.[56] They also increased land inequality, because they were expensive and capital-intensive projects, so they were undertaken only by landlords with money and secure land titles. Food prices rose and employment declined, which hurt poor people; rents rose, which hurt tenants and small farmers; and inequality increased. Figure 4 shows one measure of

Figure 4. **Rent in the South Midlands, 1450–1849, in shillings per acre**

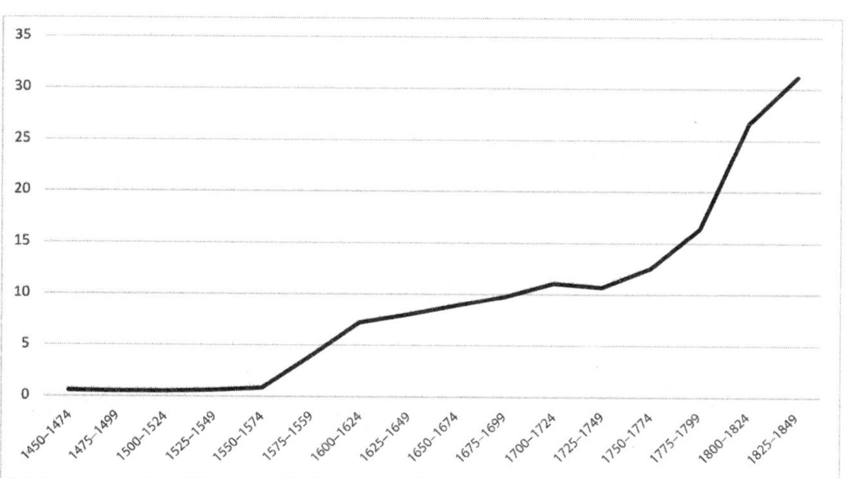

rents across the entire period of agricultural transformation.[57] As the economic historian Robert Allen puts it, landlords were "the *only* gainers of the agricultural revolution: real rents increased *sevenfold* from the middle of the fifteenth century to the middle of the nineteenth."[58]

The story of enclosure, as with the seizure and titling of colonial land in the Americas, was a central process to the production of capitalism. It is an example of one of capitalism's key features, which is the way that laws can turn *things* into *assets*—in this case, laws turned land into capital.[59] I have focused here on Britain, because it got a precocious start and because of its colonial reach. But capitalist property systems were made by law and enforced by violence across western Europe. Most notably, between 1791 and 1793, the revolutionaries in France abolished what they called "feudalism" and created a new, unified property system predicated on individual owners and the ability to buy and sell in markets.[60] Napoleon's armies later smashed the older, pre-capitalist property systems all over Europe, clearing the way for marketable property to follow.[61] Around the world, political and institutional changes reconfigured agricultural land, making it less like the environment a community lived in, and more like a factory or a machine.

We should absolutely view English imperialism in the 17th century as part of this profit-oriented, landlord-driven process of privatizing and consolidating land ownership. The English colonial occupation of Ireland began in the 1540s and vastly expanded after 1610, and it consisted of seizing Catholic Irish land and redistributing it to Protestant English landlords, who set about enclosing it, raising rents, and investing in "improvements." Some of these colonists went on to be founding members of English colonial ventures in North America, like Daniel Gookin, a colonist in the Irish county of Munster who went on to be a member of the Virginia Company.[62] The London Company financed both the Ulster Plantation of 1610 and the Virginia colony in 1607. In 1617, one colonial propagandist referred to Ireland as "this famous Island in the Virginian Sea."[63] In 1641, there was a large-scale rural rebellion in Ireland, which was ruthlessly defeated and suppressed by the Commonwealth army under Oliver Cromwell, again leading to large-scale redistribution of land to English colonists.

Both enclosure in England and colonialism in Ireland forced people off subsistence agriculture and into market labor, in a variety of ways. Small farmers had their rents raised or their tenures canceled or were bought out in the process of consolidating large estates. (Or in the case of Ireland, their land was simply seized.) Landless people who depended on common pasture or access to common forest land found it enclosed and that attempts to continue to hunt, fish, or graze on private land were punishable by death or forced transportation to the colonies. Between 1700 and 1750, 52,200 people who were convicted for the many new property crimes, or for rebellion in Ireland, were transported to the 13 North American colonies, amounting to about 17 percent of the total migrants.[64] Others migrated voluntarily as indentured labor.

Indenture was a specific form of unfree labor. People in England who wished to migrate but lacked the substantial funds to pay the cost of transit would sign agreements with an employer: In exchange for the employer paying the costs of transport, the migrant would agree to work for that employer for a set number of years, usually four to seven. Early on, indentured servants would receive land at the end of their term of service, but that was increasingly phased out and instead they got a set of tools and clothes and sometimes some money.[65] Indentured servants were mostly young male adults, mostly from lower-middle-class backgrounds (meaning yeomen farmers, artisans, skilled laborers), and most historians agree that they saw indenture as a way of aspiring to land ownership in the colonies while escaping the harsh governance of landless wage laborers in England.[66] As one historian puts it, "Seventeenth-century England may not have had slavery but it did give masters large powers to enforce contracts. Those who would not enter such contracts and who did not own sufficient land to support themselves faced severe laws against vagrancy and idleness, the aim of which was the extraction of labor from those unwilling to volunteer it for wages."[67]

People migrated through indenture in large numbers, especially to the mid-Atlantic. From about the 1630s to about the 1660s, many people who migrated from England to the New World did so as indentured servants. In the entire 17th century, about 60 percent of the 200,000 English people who crossed the Atlantic went to Virginia and Maryland, with the Caribbean in second place, and New England well behind.[68]

Indentured servants were not free, but they also were not slaves. They could not work for anyone other than their masters, and they could not leave: A law in Maryland in 1641 made running away, or helping a runaway, a capital crime. That was later reduced to what was a colonial norm of 10 extra days' service time for every one day spent escaped.[69] However, indentured servants could not be sold and did have some contractual rights. Masters had to provide living quarters and food, and although they had a legal right to administer corporal punishment, they could not arbitrarily harm or assault their servants. Rather than thinking of indentured servants as a permanent alienated underclass, it is more accurate to think of them as temporary adjuncts to what were fundamentally household economies, although they were subject to more coercion than would have been tolerated toward servants or family members in England.[70] Servants, wives, and children were all household dependents, legally entitled to be maintained by the head of the household, but also subject to his governance.[71]

There were other forms of unfree labor. German migrants often used a system called "redemption," which was similar to indenture, except for a flexible period of time depending on the cost of transport and the kind of work done, and the migrant could negotiate the form of repayment. Upwards of 80,000 German-speaking immigrants moved to Pennsylvania between 1683 and 1775, many of them redemptioners departing from the port of Rotterdam.[72] There were also nonindentured servants. In fact, "servant" was the most common occupational category in early modern England, and it took in a wide variety of experiences, usually young people who worked for room and board and sometimes wages, either in agriculture or in households, and who could not quit or work for someone else.[73] Servants usually served by the year and could be renewed, and were paid wages, while apprentices served longer terms and were given education instead of money.[74] When indentured and nonindentured servants are lumped together, they probably constituted half of the European migrants to the colonies before 1775. Indenture ended abruptly between 1815 and 1820, when migrants shifted to financing their transit by borrowing from relatives already in the Americas.[75]

From the beginnings of English colonization until the early 18th century, these various forms of unfree white labor were the main labor relation everywhere except New England. The New England colonies essentially never produced an export commodity valuable enough to make sufficient profit to be able to afford indentured workers or slaves. Instead, New England depended on nonindentured servants, debtors, household labor, and occasionally cheap convict labor.[76]

When various unfree white workers in the colonies finished their tenures or sentences, they mostly did not convert to becoming free wage laborers. Instead, whenever possible, they obtained land. Throughout the colonial era, English governments were consistently willing to grant small parcels of land to petitioners who could claim the ability to cultivate or "improve" it, and they established relatively cheap, easy, and transparent methods of land titling and registration.[77] Colonial Virginia (which was a vast territory much larger than the current state of Virginia) regularly granted 100 to 1,000 acres to individuals, but without any required spatial framework.[78] Individuals could go claim whatever land they chose, wherever they chose, without any need for it to be cleared, contiguous, or spatially regular. A 1705 law in Virginia allotted 50 acres for every individual person who arrived, regardless of whether the individual was in fact allowed to own it, so a petitioner would get 50 additional acres for every slave, indentured servant, or family member they could claim would work the land.[79] Some of those people (family members and servants) might one day get their share of the land, but slaves never would. Land at the frontier was so cheap that most people could buy it outright after a few years as a servant, and this continual migration to new land seized from Native Americans was the core dynamic of colonial American politics, economics, and violence.[80]

Different European empires took different legal approaches to land ownership. In New Spain, Indigenous land was meant to be under Crown jurisdiction, including when it was "empty," but the Crown had limited abilities to survey land or enforce its claims. In the 1640s it introduced surveyors, and allowed local landowners to pay lump sums to register their land titles, which effectively meant legitimating the land they had previously expropriated from Indigenous people.[81] The French colonies tried to invent forms of feudal systems, claiming political loyalty and tribute rather than taxable landed wealth and capital assets. An effort in the 1720s to create a full colonial property inventory with annual rents had the effect of institutionalizing European-owned land and leaving Indigenous land in a separate, ambiguous legal state.[82] In the 1680s, the New England colonies tried a surveying and registration system similar to New Spain's, but it failed in the face of colonist resistance. The New Englanders claimed they had legitimately bought land from Indigenous people, and owned it by virtue of working it, while the Crown claimed that Indigenous people had no concept of land ownership and no legal standing, so they could not legitimately sell land—only the colonial monopoly company could.[83] There were continual conflicts between the Crown and the colonists over legitimate land claims throughout the 18th century, and they increasingly focused on the frontier. The Proclamation of 1763 was an attempt to settle the problem, ruling that Indigenous people *did* own land, but that they could sell it only to the Crown, not to individual colonists (or land speculators, like George Washington), and that decision produced a political conflict that contributed to the outbreak of the American Revolution.[84]

The colonial creation of private property was not limited to the New World. In 1793, the English East India Company issued a policy known as the Permanent Settlement, which applied to the vast territory under its control in Bengal and Bihar and later spread across northern India and even to other colonies, like Kenya. The company had established its first trading posts in India in 1611, but by 1757, it had become the revenue collector and de facto ruler of large swaths of what today is Bengal.[85] With the Permanent Settlement, the company was responding to the devastating famine of 1770, which it thought was the result of insufficient incentives for land improvement and a corrupt revenue-collecting class.[86] The Permanent Settlement created a system of property rights held by local landlords called *zamindars*, and fixed the rent obligations they had to pay to the company in perpetuity.[87] The company believed this would incentivize investment in increasing production (because the landlords would get to keep the surplus) and would create a class of tax-collecting officials with loyalty to the colonial government. It did not solve the famine problem, to say the least: During the period of East India Company rule, from 1765 to 1857, Bengal had at least 12 famines. Instead, the Permanent Settlement created a consolidation of landholding and power, as marginal or unproductive *zamindars* had their land seized and auctioned off to others who could afford to expand, and also incentivized forcing tenants to shift from food production to cash crops. The power of the new, conservative, extractive landlord class persisted in India until land-reform efforts after independence, if not longer. The Permanent Settlement was also only one of many attempts by the British Empire to impose its ideas of how property, tenancy, and legal frameworks should work in rural areas.[88]

The policy of colonial land ownership and the spread of enclosure in England both proceeded from the same political philosophy, which scholars today call "possessive individualism." John Locke, who among other things was an investor in the slave-trading Royal African Company, was the key theorist of this idea. In brief, it proceeds from the assumption that all people naturally own themselves, so ownership and property are at the core of all social relations. People who retained independent ownership of themselves could be full participants in civil society, but people who did not (or could not, either because of their own mistakes or misfortunes or because of some inherent inferiority) were dependents and did not have full access to political and civil rights.[89] Anything that is property and can be owned can also be bought and sold, or lost through legal means. Thus, as David Eltis, the historian of Atlantic slavery, puts it: "If, in the Western world, possessive individualism meant a recognition that one owns full rights in oneself and that one has the right in a market society to bargain away such rights, it might also mean the accumulation of rights in others in the hands of a few, as indeed happened in the slave societies of the European Atlantic."[90]

This ideology underpinned the system of unfree servant labor, because masters viewed themselves as having legitimately bought exclusive legal right to their servants' labor time, so their servants were not free to sell that labor to someone else or use it for themselves. It also underpinned slavery, since English slave owners argued that they did not *themselves* enslave anyone (a more objectionable act, in their view) but instead legally bought ownership of an already-enslaved person. In the case of property in land, possessive individualism hinged on the idea of "improvement."[91] Legitimate ownership to land was based on "improving" it, which meant converting it to market-oriented production that maximized output. In the minds of English colonists, no land in the Americas was improved, so the Native people on it did not "really" own it. The same went for the English commons. Peasants and small farmers who were producing only for their own subsistence also had not "improved" their land. Colonies granted land in amounts that individuals claimed they could improve, and individuals who claimed to have already begun improving land would often find that colonial governments were willing to recognize their seizure of it. As one historian of land tenure writes, "Improvement or betterment lies at the heart of Locke's notion of property rights. It is linked to landhunting, squatting, and speculation; often it was also the basis for government acquisition of land from indigenous peoples and a principle guiding how governments reallocated it. . . . To improve the land meant to apply labour and capital, so as to boost the land's carrying capacity and hence its market value."[92]

In this way, a specifically capitalist political ideology underpinned the legal changes that ratified and violently enforced enclosure and land consolidation in England, seizure and land redistribution in Ireland, colonization and Native expropriation in North America, a colonial company-state in Bengal, and slavery in Barbados. Doing so generated and legally enforced a flood of indentured servants, redemptioners, convicts, and other forms of unfree labor, then when that supply of workers was insufficient, underpinned the separate creation of slaves as a distinct legal category.

At the same time that new land tenures were being established in England and land was being distributed in the Americas, slave codes were being written to create the new and unusual form of heritable, permanent, racialized chattel slavery in the Atlantic. In 1660, a report of the English Council of Foreign Plantations declared that Black people in the colonies were "perpetuall servants."[93] A Virginia statute of 1661 also declared that Black people were permanent servants, and another in 1669 designated them as chattel instead of people whose labor alone was property of someone else.[94] The Barbados slave code of 1661 also designated them as chattel, and created a comprehensive code for governing them as property. From there it spread throughout the Caribbean.

In Virginia in 1676–77, a group of white settlers, indentured servants, and both enslaved and free Africans together launched what is known as Bacon's Rebellion against the colonial government, including setting Jamestown on fire. (Among other things, they objected to the governor's reluctance to continue driving Native Americans off the land, and his willingness to recognize them as legal subjects—the multiracial solidarity still had sharp boundaries.)[95] They were eventually defeated, and in the wake of the rebellion Virginia passed more slave codes in 1705, which created more separations between white indentured servants and Black slaves. The new slave laws and the simultaneous extension of granting new land were both solutions to the threat of cross-racial solidarity.[96] For this reason, some scholars argue that capitalism itself invented modern racism.[97]

■ ■ ■

Between 1600 and 1800, the processes of enclosure, conquest, colonialism, slavery, and indenture unleashed a tremendous flood of capital, land, and labor into the capitalist world. More so land and labor than capital, which remained relatively scarce, especially compared to the movement of millions of people and the colonial occupation of two entire continents. Together these newly accessed resources were combined to generate a system of commodity production that circled the Atlantic Ocean. The scale of Atlantic trade dwarfed the traffic in luxury goods from East Asia to Europe, and European economies increasingly Atlanticized, as overseas trade emerged as the most dynamic and rapidly growing sector in an otherwise not-very-dynamic economy.[98] Europe dominated British trade in 1700, but "by 1772–3, North America and the West Indies took 38 per cent of exports and provided 39 per cent of imports. By 1797–8, North America and the West Indies received 57 per cent of British exports and supplied 32 per cent of imports."[99] By the 1790s, 20 times as much tonnage of merchandise was imported from the Americas to Europe as from Asia to Europe.[100] Table 1 breaks down the contributions of different world markets to British, French, and Dutch imports in the 1770s.

The historian Kenneth Morgan provides a useful summary of the extent of this Atlantic economy: "Geographically, this trading complex embraced 2,000 miles of the west African coast, a free trading zone open to all the European powers; the Atlantic wine islands (Madeira, the Azores, the Canaries); ports in continental Europe such as Lisbon, Malaga, Amsterdam and Hamburg;

Table 1. **Geographical Structure of Imports to Britain, France, Netherlands, 1770s**[101]

Source of imports	Britain, 1772–73	France, 1772–76	Netherlands, 1770s
Europe	45%	53%	75%
Western Hemisphere	38%	42%	11%
Asia	16%	5%	14%
Total Value (millions)	£13.6	369.6 *livres tournois*	143 florins

the thirteen mainland North American colonies that became the United States plus Florida; the Canadian maritime provinces; the Caribbean islands, the Bay of Honduras and the Mosquito Shore in central America; and ports in Britain and Ireland."[102]

Sugar was the core of the system. From the Dutch in Brazil to the British in Barbados, sugar production then spread across the Caribbean. French colonists began slave-plantation sugar production in San Domingue (what is now Haiti) in the late 1660s, Portugal continued sugar production in Brazil after pushing out the Dutch, and the Dutch themselves produced sugar on Sint Maarten and in Guiana and Suriname. The VOC also imported up to a million pounds of sugar every year from its plantations in Java.[103] Following the template of Barbados, these places were settled, organized into large-scale plantations, stripped of their indigenous ecosystems in favor of sugar monoculture, presided over by a white planter elite, and worked by African slaves in a violent gang-labor system. From the 1670s to 1820s, sugar was the most lucrative commodity imported to Britain, after which it was overtaken by slave-grown cotton.[104]

The Dutch seizure of Portuguese assets on both sides of the ocean meant they controlled the start and the end of the slave trade, so the second half of the 17th century saw a phase of Atlantic slavery in which the Dutch, English, and Portuguese competed. England established the London-based Company of Royal Adventurers to Africa in 1660, ostensibly to export gold from Africa, but the company soon found slaves more profitable.[105] It was promptly ruined by wartime disruption, and replaced by the Royal African Company (the RAC) in 1672, which held a monopoly on trade to Africa. The RAC built forts in Africa, maintained troops, owned ships, and was a giant bureaucratic undertaking intended to deliver a set number of slaves to the New World on a predictable basis. It too largely failed: The fixed costs were too high, the slave trade too unpredictable, and its monopoly too difficult to enforce.[106] Its monopoly was revoked in 1698, and from that point onward, the slave trade was in private hands. Bristol dominated from about 1720 to 1740, then Liverpool after that, while London slavers continued to participate, and another slave-trading community grew up in Newport, Rhode Island.[107]

Rather than thinking of the slave trade as something at the core of the richest and most powerful segment of British society, it is more accurate to think of it as a gruesome mechanism for the social mobility of marginal groups. After the failure of the RAC, the slave trade was dominated by smaller outports like Bristol and Liverpool, and even in those ports, it was known as a risky and dangerous activity mostly undertaken by young men newly arrived in town who were otherwise locked out of established lines of trade. These outport merchants, often the sons of petty tradespeople like barbers or brewers, forced their way into the Atlantic trading system by aggressively seeking out new, marginal markets.[108] If Barbados or Jamaica was already controlled by established traders, they would sell to newly cleared plantations in the Chesapeake or on other, more remote Caribbean islands. If the three big African slave ports (Old Calabar, Bonny, and Anomabu) were already dominated by well-capitalized competitors, they would proceed down the coast to find new sellers. The same logic held within Africa: Selling captives was an effective route to wealth, prestige, and guns.[109]

Slavery had long existed in Africa as a social status, either for men defeated in wars, as punishment for debt or crimes, or as household labor, or for women as concubines in a specific category of Islamic slavery. Children of slaves could inherit enslaved status, and people of low social status could be taken as domestic slaves by people of higher social status. There was a long-standing trans-Saharan slave trade to supply labor for salt mines, well digging, or date harvesting in the desert. Slaves were transported to more urbanized Ottoman North Africa via a 40-day route from Darfur to Egypt, another route from Chad to Libya, and others from Timbuktu to Tripoli. In the 18th century a French slave trade developed from East Africa to France's Indian Ocean sugar islands of Mauritius and Réunion, and in the early 19th century, after the closure of the transatlantic slave trade, slave raiding and trading continued throughout West Africa, sometimes dedicated to the production of new export commodities.[110] Each of these slave trades affected, and was affected by, the considerably larger and distinct Atlantic slave trade.

Focusing for a moment on the Gold Coast (in modern Ghana) illustrates how the internal African slave trade was intensified by the Atlantic slave trade, and vice versa. Before the arrival of European guns, it was difficult for any African polity to win a total, conquering victory over any other, so slave raids tended to be sporadic and on a small scale. Then in the course of the 17th century, the Akwamu and Denkyira states in northwest Fanteland used newly acquired guns to crush their neighbors and sell enormous numbers of people into slavery, thus beginning the establishment of the Gold Coast slave trade.[111] The presence of domestic gold allowed powerful people to purchase slaves—including from the Portuguese at Elmina—who could be put to work clearing the rainforest to establish settled agriculture, one of the key steps in centralized state-building in West Africa. The Asante, who were one of the vassal states of Denkyira, resented their subject status and began a successful war of independence in 1701, followed by a series of expansionary wars through the 1750s, the result of which was a consolidation of political power and the capture of half a million slaves.[112] Asante demand was so great that neighboring rulers instituted legal codes that featured enslavement as a punishment, or undertook their own expansionary raids on neighbors in order to obtain slaves to sell to them, thereby encircling the frontiers of the Asante Empire in a growing ring of violence. In 1728, the Asante built a Great Road from their capital at Kumasi to Elmina, complete with rest stops and markets on the way. More roads followed, to the Danish fort at Accra and the Dutch at Cape Lahou. The Portuguese had brought maize from the New World, and by the 18th century it was at the core of the slave economy. Slaves worked the maize crop in the spring and fall before they were sold in the summer or winter, and the proceeds of the maize fields were sold to slave ship captains as cheap sources of food.[113]

Following the Asante were the Aro, a multiethnic trading diaspora in what is now southeastern Nigeria. They functioned as something like middlemen, setting up permanent coastal fairs in the Niger Delta to buy, sell, and consolidate slaves from various intermediaries, especially the Igbo, who were a populous ethnic group farther inland.[114] After the 1720s, the Kingdom of Bonny gradually crushed its local competitors, secured a supply of yams from inland, and formed a partnership with the Aro, thus moving from being one small player among many to operating one of the three largest markets for slaves.[115]

Over time, the main areas for slave exports shifted and spread, not necessarily sequentially, decade by decade along the great arc of coastline that ran from the Gold Coast to the Bights of Benin and Biafra, and all the way to Angola, as slaves became more difficult to obtain or as individual kingdoms refused to participate.[116] The

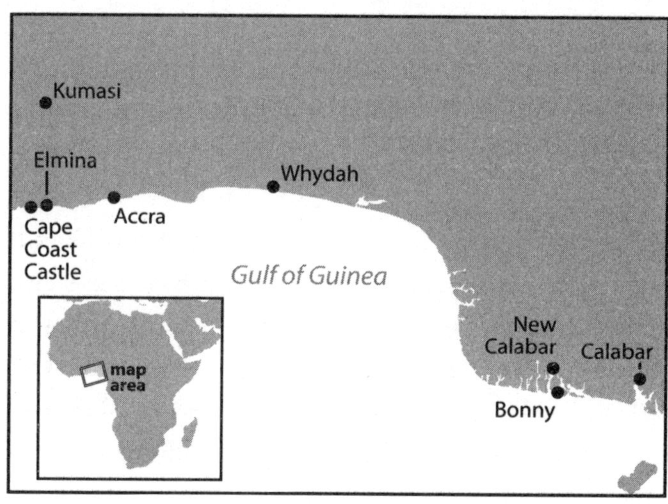

The slave ports of West Africa, circa 1700

main determinant of the supply and location of slaves was wars, though there are records of African kings denying that they went to war specifically to obtain slaves.[117] In the 16th and 17th centuries, kings in Wolof, Benin, and Kongo sometimes opposed the slave trade, which meant in practice that they would not supply slaves, but their rivals and neighbors took the opportunity to supply captured people from their own kingdoms instead.[118] In the 18th century, the Asante and the Oyo kingdoms refused to supply their own people, but would supply others.[119] In Senegambia, Maraka merchants would supply first Wolof captives, then later Bambara captives, as they moved farther inland in search of new people to enslave.[120] In the 17th and 18th centuries, there were at least 61 recorded instances of shore-based African attacks on slave ships, especially in Senegambia and the Windward Coast, but these mostly had the effect of sending Europeans to more friendly locations. Revolt was persistent, but among the enslaved, not among African rulers, who derived power, prestige, and profit from the slave trade.[121] As the historian David Eltis puts it, "These findings should force us to see the slave trade as a product of bargaining between equals as far as African and European elites are concerned, but as the evidence of shipboard resistance suggests, and ignoring for the moment the activities of European consumers of plantation produce, there was far more shaping the transatlantic slave trade than just negotiation between elites."[122]

Along the African coast, the capture, transport, and sale of slaves was mostly in private hands, although under state protection. Kings taxed and protected the slave trade, and sometimes kept slaves for themselves, perhaps as many as one-third of all captives until the mid-19th century. In some regions, like Asante and Dahomey, kings exercised rights and responsibilities over all slaves, though they struggled to hold a durable monopoly on the trade, while in Angola and the Niger valley, slave caravans were owned and controlled by a few large-scale merchants.[123] In those places, the imported luxuries, especially guns, were concentrated among the elite; elsewhere, like in the Igbo kingdoms where individuals sold one or two people who had been enslaved as a result of debt or crime instead of warfare, the proceeds of Atlantic luxuries were more widely dispersed.[124] In most slave ports, prices were set by negotiating with the local leader (especially distributing gifts, tributes, and bribes) to decide on the price of a prime male slave in the local unit of account. All prime males would be bought at that price, and all others at settled fractions of it.[125]

The Atlantic slave trade was predominantly young and male: 64.5 percent male, according to the Slave Trade Database.[126] And it emerged as the solution to the colonial labor-supply problem after the 1660s because slaves were relatively cheap. In fact, the price of a slave at the point of purchase in Africa fell from about £14 in the 1630s to below £5 in the 1670s, before rising to about £25 in the 1730s, where it fluctuated for the next several decades.[127] Before the 1770s, human life was cheap, for several reasons. First and most obviously, because capturing someone meant that the cost of social reproduction—raising them from birth—fell on their families. In grotesque economic terms, transforming someone from being a captive to being a slave turned them into an asset.[128] Second, the process of that transformation, in which they were desocialized and depersonalized, was physically carried out by marching them to the coast, first an average of 100 kilometers but later farther and farther, up to 600 kilometers by the 18th century.[129] They could be forced to transport goods at essentially no extra cost, adding profit to the caravan owners. And finally, agriculture in sub-Saharan Africa was relatively unproductive. People were vulnerable to tsetse flies, which transmitted sleeping sickness and are endemic in the wet tropical soils. The soil also responded badly to plowing, limiting economies of scale. Most agriculture was done by women, by hand, which increased the African demand for female slaves, but meant that there were economically superfluous young men, who might furthermore pose a rebellious danger to elites. In the most appalling possible form, the Atlantic slave trade was another method for wringing profit out of unproductive agricultural labor.

By the 1730s, the demand for enslaved people began to outstrip the enslavers' ability to capture people, so prices in Africa began to rise. From 1775 to 1791, prices rose to £19 per person, then to £33 by the time of the English abolition of the slave trade in 1807.[130] Prices on the other side of the Atlantic also continually increased across the 18th century, as shown in Figure 5 below.[131] Those average increases conceal substantial regional variation. The sale price for the same person in Barbados was £38 in 1765, but £42 in the more distant Windward Islands and £47 in Jamaica.[132]

What did these prices actually mean? In the 1680s, £5 in Africa would have bought 17 muskets or 200 liters of brandy, or the amount of cheap food that a slave would have consumed over the course of about six years.[133] As prices rose across the century, so too did African sellers demand a wider variety of goods, and they were notoriously picky about the quality. Higher sale prices in more remote places were a matter of hideous calculation for ship

Figure 5. Real slave prices in the western Caribbean, 1674–1804 (indexed percentage change, 1674 = 100)

captains, because some number of captives were sure to die on the longer voyage. Higher prices in places like Jamaica might also entail a longer delay in actually getting paid, depending on the availability of credit and of goods for return voyages. Higher prices, bigger ships, and more difficult terms of credit incentivized consolidation in the slave trade. Early on, marginal investors would contribute as little as £300 to buy a 16th share in a voyage, thus risking relatively little capital.[134] By the 1790s, the ships were more expensive, the capital needs greater, and there were fewer and fewer participants as moral disgust discouraged new entrants, so higher costs fell on fewer slave traders. That made them extremely prone to financial crises, as with the credit crisis of 1793 that deranged the Bristol slave-merchant community.

The slave trade was the knot that tied together Asian luxury exports to European manufacture and American colonization. British ships carried colorful cotton textiles made in India and imported by the East India Company to Britain.[135] These were the preferred commodity for traders in Africa, followed by guns, alcohol, metal manufactures, and eventually English-manufactured cotton. Cotton textiles from India constituted 27 percent of all goods shipped from England to Africa in 1699–1800.[136] After the 1740s, English-produced cotton textiles came to predominate, which would ultimately have implications for the scale of the Industrial Revolution.

Under British control, the 18th century was the peak of slave trading in the Atlantic: From 1698 to 1807, at least 2,672,763 people were forcibly transported from Africa to the New World, mostly to the Caribbean sugar colonies, and probably 398,000 died en route.[137] Figure 6 below illustrates the total number of enslaved people transported by English ships. Many more people died awaiting embarkation in Africa, as well as after arrival in the Americas awaiting transshipment to local markets, both surely enormous magnitudes of human suffering that left few reliable numbers behind.

The number of slaves leaving Africa doubled from 1640 to 1690, probably reflecting an increase in warfare, and consequently, prices in English colonies declined.[138] The number of slaves shipped increased even more in the 18th century, even as the price rose, meaning the profit for African slavers must have increased. The export of at least 100,000 people, predominantly young men, every year for a century had a profound social impact. Population growth was either stagnant or even negative along the western coast, and the gendered division of agricultural labor intensified, as did the norms of elite polygamy. As one historian puts it, "The effect of the slave trade on African politics was to build up the power and wealth of kings and warlords in the short run, but to create conditions of instability and collapse in many African polities over the longer run."[139]

Slaves were not the only African export: Gold still predominated until the 18th century, and from 1675 to 1731 the Dutch WIC

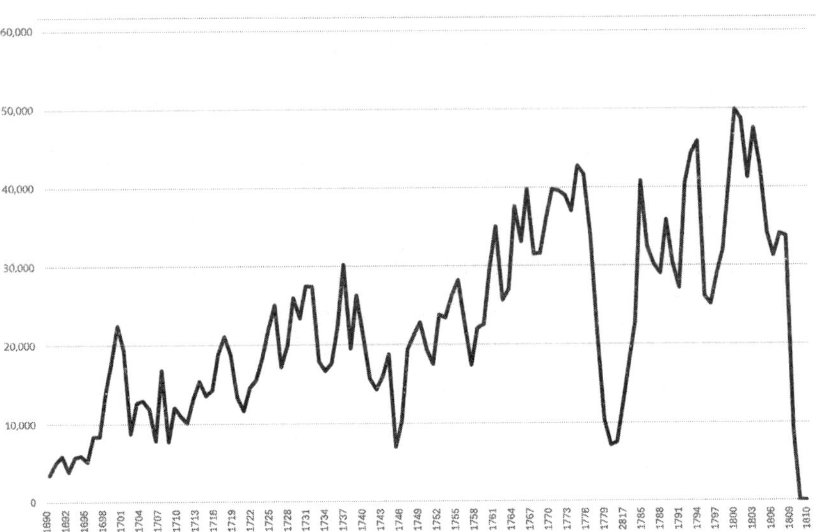

Figure 6. **Number of slaves transported by British ships, 1690–1810**

carried more gold than slaves.[140] Senegambia exported a greater monetary value of cowhides to Europe than slaves to the Atlantic until the 1680s.[141] But for the most part, the export of slaves enriched kings and large merchants to such an extent that they put little effort into other kinds of exports. On the other side, Europeans died at such a velocity on the African coast that they did not try to expand beyond their forts and islands to establish colonies with their own export crops. Instead, the coast remained a free-trade zone of contact between African elites and European slavers.

A ship crossing the Atlantic took about 60 to 70 days, and before the 1750s, about 20 percent of slaves died in the Middle Passage, mostly of enteric disease, and still about 10 percent after the 1750s.[142] In the New World, the slaves would be sold for sugar or for bills of exchange to be returned to England. In the Caribbean, the slaves would probably be worked to death within five years. The low price of human life, the relative lack of women, and the brutality of the work meant that slave populations in the Caribbean did not grow on their own until the end of the 18th century, and until then planters relied on a continual inflow of new captives. In 1700, most slaves in the Caribbean colonies were imported, but by 1776, only about 20 percent were African-born.[143] The aggregate figures give an indication of the horrifying mortality: "By 1820, some 10 million Africans had migrated to the New World as compared to some 2 million Europeans. But in 1820, the New World white population of some 12 million was roughly twice as great as the black population."[144]

The Caribbean sugar–slave plantation system was the source of stimulus that boosted economic activity around the Atlantic. The slaves would be fed with rice grown on slave plantations in South Carolina, and with salted cod caught in the North Atlantic. Unlike absentee Caribbean planters, the South Carolina slave-owning aristocracy remained on their plantations, creating a distinctive society of oppression, and rice accounted for 60 percent of their exports by the 1740s.[145] The New England fishing industry was immense very early: In 1618 it employed roughly 250 ships and 2,000 men and grossed £135,000 yearly.[146] Salt fish was mostly exported to Iberia, but formed a common consumer good around the Atlantic basin, and the needs of the fishing industry sustained a shipbuilding industry in New England, employing at least as many as 1 in 10 men by the 1770s.[147] The sugar produced by the slaves would be refined in England: In the mid-18th century, Bristol had 20 sugar refineries and London had 140.[148] Since they were huge wooden buildings full of hot copper, they were also a stimulus to the fire-insurance industry, just as slavery was to marine insurance.

Second to sugar was tobacco from the Chesapeake. Tobacco exhausts the soil in about three years, so a huge amount of slave labor was oriented toward clearing and converting land, spreading the colonial territory farther inland.[149] Cities like Bristol and London set up snuff mills to process the tobacco and reexport it; Glasgow and Whitehaven especially thrived on the tobacco trade.[150]

Manufactures from both old England and New England produced everything that plantations needed: beds, nails, tools, guns, cutlery, glassware, saddles, mirrors, clocks, and before the 1750s, wool clothing, with cotton after.[151] The Atlantic shipping industry in turn stimulated demand for hemp, flax, timber, and naval stores from the Baltic, wine from the Atlantic islands like Madeira, and linen from Ireland.[152] Sugar mills burned a continual flow of wood, which had to be imported to places that had been deforested for sugar monoculture. In each case, economic activity was oriented toward figuring out what sorts of local products were worth the high shipping costs and could be exchanged for access to slave-grown sugar and tobacco. New Englanders could sell hardware and salt cod to Barbadian sugar planters; Swedes could sell lumber to English shipbuilders in exchange for reexported sugar; English landlords could export wool grown on their enclosed pastures to Chesapeake tobacco growers; English slavers could export Indian cotton to Africa to buy slaves to sell for sugar. And so on. Here is the economic historian Philip Curtin with an example of the full system at work:

> Or a French ship might make the outward voyage to Africa, pick up a cargo of slaves, but sell it in Spanish America for bullion. The bullion, in turn, found its way to the Compagnie des Indes for shipment to southern India in return for indigo-dyed cloths of a kind much in demand in Senegal. These cloths might be sold in Senegal—not for slaves, but for gum and for Senegalese cloths in demand farther down the coast in Dahomey. The Dahomean slaves would be sold, in turn, in the New World, and variants of the same cycle could be played out again.[153]

In this way, the famous "triangular trade" was only a subset of the broader Atlantic commodity system. The commodity trades depended on the new supplies of land and labor produced by enclosure and colonization, as well as indenture and slavery. They also depended on forms of credit and finance produced by the Financial Revolution, and eventually benefited from the fiscal-military state in the form of the English navy sweeping the seas of pirates. At this point it should be clear that this Atlantic economy was hugely profitable for an international class of merchant elites, and for their creditors, and it should also be clear that this system depended on varieties of unfree labor, especially the distinctive form of racialized, permanent, heritable chattel slavery, but also, in early stages, on indenture and servitude. It remains to explain how this system also contributed to the rise of free wage labor.

■ ■ ■

At the beginning of the 17th century, wage labor was unusual everywhere in the world, but there were substantial wage-earning sectors in the English and Dutch economies (perhaps 30 to 40 percent of workers in England in 1600), as well as in most cities around Europe and in China.[154] The colonies were characterized by unfree labor, and most free people moved to the frontier and obtained land rather than working for wages. Even in England, most wage labor was not entirely free, and wages were often only part of the laborers' payment, which might also take the form of room, board, or some amount of the work materials. Food made up about half of the value of wages between 1650 and 1750, and also crucially meant that rising food prices were borne by employers instead of workers.[155] Most workers were not free to quit or to choose their employers, and they were often paid infrequently because of the "big problem of small change." Workers who were paid money once or twice a year were especially dependent on employers for room and board or customary rights to various scraps and extras. Workers were also mostly paid by the task, and they often had substantial control and autonomy over the pace and intensity of their work. Laborers, artisans, apprentices, and other workers customarily observed "Saint Monday," still a common practice among undergraduates, which consisted of being too hungover on Mondays to do much work.[156] They might straggle in and work slowly on Tuesday and Wednesday, then work long hours with a lot of intensity at the end of the week before spending the weekend getting wrecked and starting the process all over again. Added to Saint Monday were the very many religious holidays, and the seasonal pattern of work in agriculture, under which a great deal of labor was performed at planting and harvest but which left many workers (including landless wage workers) underemployed most of the rest of the year.

From about the 1650s onward, more and more people in England and the Netherlands oriented more and more of their time to wage work in the market. Both elements are important: They worked longer hours and more days each year, but also allocated more of their work activity toward market production, either goods they could sell for money or work they could do for money wages. In the medieval period the average worker probably worked 150 days a year, but by 1800 it had risen to over 300 days per year.[157] Even with higher initial estimates of 250 workdays, the time of supplied labor probably increased by 20 to 25 percent in the second half of the 18th century.[158] People laboring in low-intensity nonmechanized agriculture probably could get by on 4 to 6 hours of work a day outside of harvest and planting seasons, but industrial work by the late 18th and early 19th centuries averaged 10 to 12 hours a day, six days a week.[159] Estimates of the exact number of working days differ, but it is clear that after decades of steady increase between about 1790 and 1830, English people worked more hours and more days than any wage workers before or since. Scholars refer to this shift as the "industrious revolution."[160]

It is difficult to discern the main driving motivation for workers to do this. For Jan de Vries, the historian of the industrious revolution, the goal was to maximize consumer aspirations.[161] After 1650, more and more delicious and addictive tropical products became available to European consumers, at lower and lower prices. Sugar prices alone declined by more than half after 1650.[162] Consumers loved (and still love) sugar, tobacco, coffee, tea, and chocolate, but it is climatically impossible to grow those things in northwestern Europe, so they had to be purchased with money from importers. That need for money incentivized working for money, so some workers supplemented their agricultural duties with protoindustrial handicrafts in their downtime, or by hiring themselves out as wage workers a few days a week. But consumer aspirations have not yet ever been completely satisfied. The only thing better than some sugar is *more* sugar. Further, consumption tends to require other consumption: Tea alone is not satisfying in a way that tea and sugar and milk and a kettle and porcelain cups and dishes all are together. Consumption has a component of cultural emulation: As norms of respectability and luxury developed, they brought demands of new kinds of consumer habits. At first, these habits encouraged an "industrious household" in which every member worked more for the market, but later households opted to specialize in a "breadwinner-homemaker" model. Across the entire span of cultural change, women played a vital role in shaping consumer aspirations. (Indeed, it is not safe to assume that any reference here to consumers, workers, households, and people is implicitly male.)[163] These consumer aspirations, in turn, are another way that slavery and empire contributed to the rise of capitalism: The availability of slave-grown tropical goods encouraged a shift to market-oriented wage labor and modern consumer habits.

However, there is another explanation for the industrious revolution, which was force and coercion. Through the process of enclosure, people whose livelihoods depended on access to common fishing, forestry, and grazing rights had to turn elsewhere. Women and children especially lost their source of contribution to household income.[164] Consolidation and specialization in agriculture reduced male employment, and moved many small landholders off the land and into wage work. Some of them migrated as indentures, but some stayed and became landless wage workers—what Marxist scholarship would call the proletariat. These poor people were increasingly subject to violent governance in the 18th century, like the Black Acts and vagrancy laws. Customary rights to scraps and extras were increasingly criminalized, especially in the sugar and silk industries.[165] Restrictions on workers leaving their jobs actually grew stricter in the early 18th century: In 1720, "An Act for Regulating the Journeymen Taylors" (meaning tailors) made leaving a job before it was finished an offense punishable by two months of hard labor in the House of Correction. There was another, similar law in 1740 for the leather trade, and another in 1766 stipulated one to three months' hard labor for artificers of various kinds.[166] As with the way that law turned land into capital, here the law turned some people into employees and others into servants, and criminalized both the attempts to avoid these relations and attempts to secure autonomy once in work.[167] In this way, clearly many people had little choice but to work for employers and work longer and with more intensity than they would have otherwise chosen.

By the middle decades of the 18th century, a new form of labor relation had emerged and become the norm among most types of industry and manufacture.[168] Known as the "putting-out system," it consisted of a merchant obtaining raw materials and handing them off to individual workers for each stage of the production process. If we take the example of the cotton industry, the putting-out process went as follows. A merchant would buy raw cotton imported from the colonies, probably in Liverpool (from Egypt, Cyprus, or India in the 18th century, and by the early 19th century, certainly grown by American slaves). The merchant would then "put out" the raw cotton to a group of spinners, mostly women and children dispersed in rural areas, very often spinning at night or in slack agricultural times to supplement their incomes. They would use their own small spinning machines at home and would deliver the raw cotton transformed into spun thread at some stipulated future date. One 17th-century observer estimated that a single woman could spin about a pound of wool (not cotton) per day, and a married woman about 2.5 pounds per week, because she would be otherwise occupied with housework.[169] Children spun more slowly, but often helped with cleaning the raw material. The spinners would be paid for the task, and the merchant would then take the thread and "put it out" to a weaver, probably a skilled adult man who worked full-time as a weaver with his own handloom. The weaver would transform the thread into woven cloth, again by some stipulated delivery date, and would be paid for the task. The merchant would then pick up the cloth and either pay to have it bleached and dyed, or sell it as a finished product, worth much more than it had been as raw cotton at the beginning of the process.

The cotton remained the property (indeed, the *capital*) of the merchant through the entire process, and the workers were paid wages by the task, not by the hour.[170] The merchant bore the costs of transport and coordination, and since he (probably a he) might put out batches of cotton to a large number of people over a wide area, supervision was essentially impossible, so the workers controlled most of their own work. As one historian writes, "By the middle of the 18th century the 'plan of giving out material for wages' was characteristic of every important industry and was especially noticeable in textiles, clothing, metal goods manufacture (nailing and cutlery), watches, straw hats, and articles of wood and light leather. Clapham [the economic historian], describing Britain in the 1820s, suggested that out-work was probably still the predominant form of capitalistic industrial organization."[171]

Throughout the 18th century, more workers spent more and more time supplementing their income with this kind of protoindustry, or by day labor in spot-labor markets, or moved into retailing and shopkeeping.[172] By 1800, more than half of English workers worked for wages.[173] People worked longer hours and more days and women and children worked more for wages instead of contributing to household subsistence. More people were paid in wages and only wages, and a proliferation of lower-denomination cash meant more regular payment and more frequent purchasing of tropical commodities. By the time the new technological changes of the Industrial Revolution began to take hold after the 1760s, an "industrious" labor force dependent on wages for subsistence and willing to work for more consumption had been created in England and the Netherlands. It was a fundamentally different form of labor relation than the forms of unfree labor or servitude that had existed before or that still existed elsewhere in the world. The capitalist labor force was born.

■ ■ ■

In his classic book *Capitalism and Slavery*, Eric Williams made two arguments that have shaped the scholarship ever since: first, that the super-profits of the slave trade funded the Industrial Revolution, and second, that England abolished the slave trade not out of humanitarian sentiment, but because the profits of the plantation lobby were declining and no longer worth the protection costs to the government. Many scholars today disagree with the strong version of the first thesis. Profits are extremely difficult to calculate, but it is clear that the slave trade involved some risks and expenses that other trades didn't: the costs of food, water, and guards, the risk of rebellion, the deaths of enslaved people on the voyage. Most recent estimates for the height of the slave trade put profits around 7 percent for 1785–1807, while earlier estimates put the overall average in 1760–1807 at 9 to 10 percent.[174] To be sure, 7 to 10 percent is a lot, but not unprecedented for other trades. The risks of the slave trade made it highly volatile from voyage to voyage, hence the preference for upstarts seeking their fortunes. Those who failed were replaced by new aspiringly upwardly mobile arrivals, but that means our surviving records reflect the successes more than the failures.

If we move from the slave trade specifically to slavery more generally, the profit numbers remain high, but that does not quite translate into significant volumes of national investment. According to one historian, "Sugar plantations as a whole probably made about 7.5 percent on capital (when realistically computed) in 1790, at least 10 percent between 1750 and 1775, and perhaps as much as 20 percent in the halcyon days before 1700."[175] Another estimate puts Jamaica plantation profits at 13.5 percent in the mid-1760s, falling to about 6 percent thereafter.[176] These are also formidable numbers, especially at the early end. But profits before 1700 are a bit early to fund industrial transformations after 1760, and they were concentrated among a very small group of powerful plantation owners.

The aggregate size of the sugar economy and its profits were just not that big. As Eltis puts it, in 1700, the British Caribbean colonies were about the size of a smaller English county, and by 1800 they had grown to be more like a large English county.[177] Attempts to figure out the size of investment from sugar profits run into a fraction-of-a-fraction problem: The sugar economy was a subset of the imperial economy, and profits were a subset of that, and the amount invested rather than spent on consumption or politics or lost gambling was a subset of *that*. As Morgan estimates, "If all slave trading profits [for the second half of the 18th century] were invested, their contribution to total national investment would amount to 1.59 per cent."[178] The historians Maxine Berg and Pat Hudson are keen to show the importance of slavery, but their estimates are full of qualifiers: "The potential contribution of the slave trade alone to *industrial and commercial investment* rather than to total investment, in 1750 and 1770, may have amounted to almost 40 percent."[179] "Potential," "may have," and "almost" are not going to resolve this argument.

There is another objection. If the Atlantic slave-sugar complex had some direct causal impact on economic growth and industrial-ization, we should expect to have seen the effects in Portugal. Portugal was the first mover, and the slave system of Portuguese Brazil (both before and after the Dutch interruption) was a much larger segment of the Portuguese imperial system than the Caribbean was of the British Empire.[180] The evidence for a *necessary* causal relation between slavery and industrial capitalism is not strong, whether through the investment of profits or not. To make matters even more complicated, although it is difficult to conclude that slavery *caused* capitalism, most scholars also have abandoned the earlier (mainly Marxist) idea that slavery was a kind of primitive precapitalist economic system.[181] Instead, most scholars today, especially those in the "new history of capitalism" school of thought, argue that slavery *was* capitalist, so the causal argument is misplaced. One didn't cause the other; they were the same thing. These scholars, who mostly study the slave-cotton complex in the 19th-century Southern United States, point to the ways that plantations were run along the lines of managerial calculation, how enslaved lives were financialized, and how slave markets followed recognizable capitalist procedures.[182] These arguments are especially concerned to show how American capitalism today, and American racism today, are one and the same, sharing the same origin.

The evidence in this chapter points to a somewhat different and more complex story. The connection between slavery and capitalism was forged in the 17th- and 18th-century sugar and tobacco colonies, not the cotton South in the 19th century. Slavery and the slave trade were clearly things done by capitalists: private actors with private property, responding to price incentives, motivated by profit. That point holds for every step of the slave system, from the African slave merchants to the European slave traders to the American colonial plantation owners. Indeed, slave plantations were probably among the largest economic units of their day: The median sugar plantation in Jamaica in 1774 comprised 600 acres and 200 slaves, plus livestock and a sugar-processing plant, with total equity over £19,000, which was a size of labor force and fixed capital investment that most industrial employers in Europe would not reach until well into the next century.[183]

Slavery was one of many vile things—almost certainly *the* most vile thing—that the early modern capitalist elite did to other people. It made many of them very rich, and especially in colonial contexts, their wealth made them politically powerful. They used that wealth and power mostly to set back other forms of economic activity. Rather than investing in the general creation of capitalism, they were focused on protecting themselves at the expense of everyone else. With some exceptions, the recipients of the profits of slavery mostly did what rich people often do: They spent it on themselves, on amassing power and displaying their appalling aesthetic taste, not on funneling their proceeds into industrialization. As in Europe and the New World, so too in Africa: In the vast swath of West Africa from the edge of the Sahara to what is now Angola, the demand of European slavers produced a society of centralized gunpowder empires continually engaged in expansionary warfare, ruling territories of extractive middlemen with little incentive for investment, depopulated for generations.

However, as Berg and Hudson argue, the consequences of these elite depredations contributed to the more general rise of capitalism in several ways. The heart of the Atlantic trade system consisted of supplying or buying from the sugar and tobacco plantations, so land, labor, and capital were reconfigured, physically moved, and redirected toward that purpose everywhere from Angola to Newfoundland to Pernambuco. Thus, the profits of the sugar planters mattered, but so did the profits of the New England cod fishers, Baltic hemp growers, Carolina rice planters, Glasgow tobacco processors, and Madeira vintners. We can add to that the financial sphere, both for funding the trade and because enslaved people were capital assets that could be used as collateral, so the profits of "discount houses, commission agents, bankers, mortgagees, brokers, [and] underwriters" were likewise boosted by slavery.[184] Sugar and tobacco stimulated the industrious revolution in England and the Netherlands, which increased the total supply of labor, and created a new, permanently higher level of aggregate consumer demand. Could that have happened without slavery? Perhaps: The VOC imported huge amounts of sugar from Indonesia—though that too was grown by slaves of a different sort. The shift from indenture to slavery suggests that it would have been impossible to grow that much sugar that quickly and sell it at such a low price to so many European consumers without the slave system. But we cannot know what might have happened, only what *did* happen, and that was a transformation of labor and consumption, as well as an oceanic division of labor and production that all centered around slavery.[185] As any good arsonist will tell you, a great conflagration depends not just on a spark but on an accelerant; the imperial Atlantic slave system was the accelerant for propagating the flames of global capitalism.

Nevertheless, although I think this evidence shows that slavery was done by capitalists, within a capitalist Atlantic trading system, and contributed to a more general rise of capitalism, I remain reluctant to conclude that 17th-century Barbados was a capitalist place. Barbados still grows and exports sugar today, though it is much less important to its economy than it used to be. It seems impossible to assert that Barbadian sugar production in 1680 and today are the same capitalist economic system, and the most obvious difference is that in the former, sugar was grown by slaves, and in the latter, it is grown by free wage workers. The difference between slavery and emancipation should not be elided, especially given the suffering and sacrifice that went into fighting for emancipation, and for that reason, it seems necessary to preserve a distinction between slave societies run by and for capitalists and *capitalist societies*, or, for that matter, slave societies run by and for noncapitalists. Likewise, when we ascribe the profits of those cod fishers, rice growers, and bankers to slavery, we are ignoring an important counterfactual. Free people would probably also have bought cod and rice, maybe more of each than the amount they got as slaves. Bankers and underwriters would no doubt have still earned profits without the slave trade, as indeed they have continued to do. For these reasons, capitalism probably *could* have happened without slavery. But it didn't. And likewise, although capitalism may have "depended" on slavery, capitalism was perfectly able to survive and even expand after slavery's abolition.

What of abolition, the second part of Williams's argument? His focus was on the 1807 British abolition of the slave trade. But abolition took more than a century, and happened in many different forms. Vermont abolished slavery by legislative vote in 1777. In 1794, the Jacobin-led National Convention abolished slavery in the French Empire. The Haitians abolished slavery in 1804 by leading the first successful slave rebellion in history. Their self-emancipation terrified the remaining enslavers, which encouraged Napoleon to sell the Louisiana Territory to the United States, and served as inspiration for more slave revolts across the Caribbean and American South. It also came with a terrible cost: In 1825, a French naval fleet imposed an indemnity on Haiti, forcing the former slaves to pay for the cost of their own freedom. Under continual violent coercion, Haiti continued to pay this indemnity— sometimes constituting 40 percent of its government revenue—for decades. The Haitian government eventually took out loans to cover the costs of the indemnity. In 1915, the United States invaded Haiti and took control of its treasury to ensure continued repayment to American banks (one of which later became Citibank), and the Haitians continued to pay for their freedom until 1947.[186]

It's true that in 1807, the British Empire abolished the slave trade, and went on to abolish slavery in general in 1833, and its ships patrolled the Atlantic, intercepting other slave traders.[187] But its abolition involved paying an indemnity to former slave owners, and its ostensible efforts to stop the slave trade eventually led to its invasions and colonization of the African continent.[188] Abolition in the United States required a bloody civil war that ended in 1865, part of which very much included former slaves emancipating themselves.

When the Atlantic slave trade ended, the price of African slaves fell, and suppliers reoriented.[189] Some redirected toward North Africa and the Middle East, while slavery expanded in the Sokoto Caliphate and in Zanzibar. Slavery also remained a central part of the Brazilian economy until it was abolished in 1888. With the exception of Brazil, in the latter half of the 19th century, slavery became an intra-African phenomenon, driven in no small part by the need to supply export commodities to the global market. The palm oil, peanuts, cloves, cocoa, and coffee that Africans supplied to the market were often, though not always, grown by slaves, and robust international demand meant a continual incentive for slavery. In this way, slavery died a very slow death, and its end involved the heroism of slaves emancipating themselves, religious crusades of abolitionists, economic calculation of imperial parliaments, and the use of abolition as a pretext for further brutal colonialism.

Other forms of unfree labor also died lingering deaths. In North America, the supply of indentured workers declined as fewer people were willing to migrate on indentured terms, both because the cost of migration fell and because English wages rose, and the colonial labor system bifurcated between a small landowning and wage-working North and a slave-society South. With the end of slavery in the British colonies, many Caribbean plantations switched back to indenture, but drew on migrants from South Asia instead of Europe. Indenture was only formally abolished in the British Empire in 1917. The American Revolution cut off the flow of convict labor, and some state constitutions made all forced labor illegal, slavery and indenture alike. Most famously, the Indiana state constitution did so, resulting in a Supreme Court case in which a formerly enslaved woman named Mary Clark won her freedom in 1821 on the basis that she had been forced to agree to a term of 30 years of indenture. At that point, legally speaking, in the United States "labor became involuntary the moment a laborer decided to depart and was not permitted to do so—whatever previous agreement she may have made."[190] Debtors' prisons were subsequently banned in most American states in the 1830s.

The story of unfree labor of course continued, and people still labor in slavery or slave-like conditions around the world, including in American prisons. For our purposes, though, free wage labor—the new and unusual form of capitalist labor—was fully formed by the 1830s, and its construction coincided with at least a century of slave labor. Wage labor was a weird thing to invent, but it became the global norm, as it still is today. And that fundamentally altered people's relation to the market, and to one another. From then till now, people in wage work are both free—free to choose their jobs, and free to quit—but also not free, in that most workplaces are run like little dictatorships, not democracies, and unless someone can live comfortably on passive capital income, they are not free to *not* sell their labor for wages, which puts them in a structurally vulnerable position relative to employers. That strange and anxious condition of being both free and not is the distinctive experience of life under capitalism.

CHAPTER 4

Industry, 1710–1830

When many people think of capitalism, they think of factories, industry, and machines. Many others think of climate change. And they are right to do so. Along with the inventions of settled agriculture and the atomic bomb, the Industrial Revolution is one of the most significant turning points in the history of the human species, and of the planet we inhabit. The communist historian Eric Hobsbawm once described it as "the most fundamental transformation of human life in the history of the world recorded in written documents."[1] Between about the 1770s and about the 1830s, Britain transitioned into something now called "modern economic growth," which has continued (with interruptions) ever since. No economy anywhere had ever managed to sustain growth for that long, and especially not growth of that speed and scale, spread over that much territory, affecting that many people. It was also a new kind of growth. Previous economic growth was mostly what is known as *extensive*, or "Smithian," growth, from Adam Smith's argument that economic activity was limited by "the extent of the market."[2] Extensive growth happens when more outputs are produced by adding new inputs or, in other words, by extending the market. If one shoemaker can make one pair of shoes in a day, then adding another shoemaker will mean more shoes get produced. That's extensive growth: Add more land and you will get more agricultural produce; add more workers, and more work will get done. Industrialization was a technological shift to *intensive* growth, or what economists call "productivity growth." Instead of adding another shoemaker, add a machine that helps the single original shoemaker produce two pairs a day. Or, eventually, instead of a skilled shoemaker, an underpaid teenager runs a conveyer belt powered by fossil fuels, continually producing thousands of shoes every day. That's the difference.

At the onset of the Industrial Revolution, there were about one billion people in the world, and nearly everyone everywhere took for granted that average standards of living could not rise significantly, because the population would increase and the surplus would be consumed by those new people, driving living standards back down. Today the global population is more than eight billion, and although it is a world of profound inequality and hundreds of millions of people live in poverty, those eight billion people on average live longer, healthier, richer lives than the one billion did in the 18th century. That is, in many ways, a miraculous outcome, a truly spectacular change in the character of human life. For these reasons, uncovering the causes of the Industrial Revolution has been one of the holy grails of economic history. Most economists and economic historians look at the immense improvement in lifespans, infant mortality, and living standards, and conclude that the Industrial Revolution was an excellent thing, and that if we can learn how it happened, we can spread that knowledge to poor parts of the world today, which will unlock their own transitions to modern economic growth, and thus, to longer, happier, richer lives. Indeed, there is no clear path to modern economic growth that does not run through industrialization.

The Industrial Revolution was also a "metabolic rift" in the history of the human relationship to the planet.[3] British industrialization was driven by the cotton textile industry, which itself combined the modern workforce, slavery, and modern consumer culture. But there already were cotton-textile-producing places all over the world, in Europe and in India. The British case was special because of coal, and the wave of inventions in coal, iron, steam engines, and metallurgy that went in parallel with the inventions in the cotton sector. Prior to industrialization, all economic activity on earth depended on a flow of solar energy, moving through renewable photosynthetic sources. The addition of coal and fossil fuels meant also drawing down a finite but tremendously powerful stock of energy, producing waste and emissions in the process.[4] The new productivity unlocked by industrialization meant two things: cheaper and easier transport (on railways and eventually steamships), and immensely more demand for inputs to nonstop mechanized industrial processes. Together, those changes meant more of the world could profitably be harvested for human use, and there was more demand to consume more of it. Suddenly it was physically possible and economically profitable to deforest North America for cotton monoculture, or to grow hay to feed millions of horses who worked in industrial contexts, or to move hundreds of thousands of Asian workers to Peru and Chile to mine hundreds of millions of tons of nitrogen-rich guano to ship to Europe and North America for fertilizer, or to hunt and kill thousands of whales to produce oil for industrial lighting.

For decades, if not more than a century, nearly everyone considered the Industrial Revolution to be a good thing, even if living through it was a miserable experience.[5] The association with modernity, growth, technological change, higher incomes, longer lives, and more surviving babies is too strong not to think it constituted an immense improvement for the human species. From our perspective, in the face of looming climate catastrophe, the environmental costs and intergenerational inequalities are more stark. Noting those costs, and telling the story of the Industrial Revolution through the environment, does not mean that the benefits were not real, nor that life before industrialization was pleasant and desirable. Instead, the goal is to tell a more complete story, and to recognize that the meaning and impact of industrialization has changed over time, and that some of the costs are only now becoming clear. To be sure, many 19th-century commentators observed with alarm the degradation of the natural world, and the environmental damage of the "dark Satanic mills," but they did so without a knowledge of the biosphere, anthropogenic climate change, or the outcomes in terms of either the extent or intensity of subsequent economic growth and environmental costs. The bulk of global warming has happened since the scientific discovery of global warming in the late 20th century, and although by the late 19th century there were some attempts to regulate or reduce industrial pollution and preserve parts of the natural world, people then had no idea of the coming magnitude of the "Great Acceleration" after the Second World War.[6]

A final point is in order. The British Industrial Revolution was a profoundly capitalist process, driven by business owners seeking profits and lower costs. It was often opposed by traditions, guilds, and ideas of justice and fairness, sometimes in the form of organized workers who destroyed machines and burned down factories. Wage labor and price relations changed social life in England, where pre-industrial life was dissolved, and in India, where older hand-driven forms of industrialization were wiped out, and in the American South, where a new, expanded, and especially vicious form of slavery became entrenched. And the British Industrial Revolution was environmentally destructive, since the "negative externalities" of waste, extinction, deforestation, and pollution were not paid by the capitalists who profited from these new commodities and markets.

But industrialization is *in general* environmentally destructive and socially deranging. It was at least as calamitous in the Soviet Union in the first half of the 20th century, and in communist China since the 1980s. The first industrialization happened in already existing conditions of capitalism, so its environmental consequences took on a specifically capitalist character, and it probably would not have happened at all without the profit and price incentives of capitalism, but the environmental destruction was due to industry in general, not capitalism in particular. I am not arguing that capitalism is uniquely environmentally destructive.[7] Rather, it makes certain forms of environmental destruction possible, others invisible, and others profitable, while also undermining the capacity for collective action to address social problems like climate change.

■ ■ ■

Cotton clothing may not seem like an especially high-tech commodity today, but it was the bleeding edge of technological and industrial innovation in the 18th century. The cotton textile production process has several steps: raw cotton first, then spinning into thread (confusingly, usually called "yarn"), then weaving into cloth, then bleaching and dyeing to be colorful and desirable. Until the invention of the Singer sewing machine in the 1850s, cloth was the final good, and was transformed into clothing or household goods by shopkeepers, or by people at home. From the 1730s through about 1800, technological changes at each step of the process transformed who did the work, where they did it, and how much they produced. Any given technology increased the productivity of its own step in the process, which moved the bottleneck to another step, and that incentivized finding a technological solution to the new bottleneck. In this way, these inventions were not random outcomes of some general passion for science, let alone the product of a special British genius, but rather were what is known as induced innovation. It paid to invent these things, so people did.

The revolutionary transformation of economic life began with the flying shuttle, a relatively minor process improvement in an important piece of a weaving loom. It was patented by John Kay in 1733: He had been a weaver's apprentice, and spent much of his life tinkering with improvements to textile machines. The flying shuttle was cheap and easy for weavers to buy and use. You can think of it as a kind of machine part that you might buy at the hardware store. Thanks to the ongoing industrious revolution, there was plenty of thread being spun by women and children working extra hours for extra cash. The flying shuttle probably doubled the speed at which weavers could weave, and meant that one person could work a loom alone, without need for an assistant or a second weaver. It was not an immediate success: Annoyed weavers petitioned the king to outlaw Kay's invention, and he was consistently unable to enforce his patent rights or profit from his device. But the technology spread, and weavers could weave twice as fast as before, moving the bottleneck to spinning.

In 1764, James Hargreaves invented the spinning jenny.[8] Instead of one person spinning one spool of thread on one wheel, with his machine, one person could spin *eight* spools at once. But that was only the beginning. Hargreaves kept the machine secret for a while, and at first only used it in his own production or to sell to his neighbors. In 1768, angry spinners broke into his house and smashed his machines, and he fled to Nottingham, where he continued to improve his invention, and got a patent in 1770—which he was also unable to enforce. Over time, the number of spindles in the machine increased from 8 to 120, but the thread remained fragile and prone to breaking. The machine was small enough to be purchasable and operable by people at home, so spinning productivity increased, but the organization of work remained unchanged.

At the same time, Sir Richard Arkwright (employing John Kay) invented what he called a "spinning frame," or a "water frame," a machine that spun thread using metal cylinders instead of human fingers, and that could be powered by falling water. In 1771, Arkwright built the first water-powered textile mill at a place called Cromford, which is between Sheffield and Nottingham in northern England. His mill employed 200 people, mostly women and children, and since it had to be located next to the water supply, he had to build a village to house his workers. He kept building mills throughout the 1770s, and spent the 1780s engaged in protracted disputes over his patents. In 1779, Samuel Crompton invented the "spinning mule," which was a hybrid (hence a mule) between the spinning jenny and the water frame. The mule was unpatented, so it was widely produced and copied and improved upon, and it was made out of metal, so eventually it was able to be run by furious steam engines instead of falling water. Like the water frame, it was a huge machine, so it was something installed in factories owned by capitalists, not by spinners working at home. It was also astonishingly productive, running hundreds or thousands of spindles continuously, driven by inanimate energy, supervised by women or children employees. The social transformation was well underway.

By the time the spinning mills were operational in the 1770s and 1780s, more thread was being produced than weavers could possibly weave. One response was extensive growth: Hundreds of thousands of people became independent handloom weavers, working at home to weave this huge flood of cheap thread. But another response was a further invention: the power loom, patented by Edmund Cartwright in 1785, though it took several more improvements and patents through 1792 to finish his machine, and even then, it remained difficult to use and prone to breaking thread until William Radcliffe invented a complementary "dressing machine" in 1803. Cartwright's own factory in Doncaster failed after two years, and another one in Manchester that contained 24 of his looms was burned down by furious weavers in 1792.[9] As with other inventions, it took years of experimentation and improvement for the power loom to be really functional, and it was expensive and slow to catch on, so first there was a great influx of new handloom weavers, but by the 1820s and 1830s, power looms began to dominate, with socially cataclysmic consequences.

So by the 1790s, spinning mills could spin more thread than anyone could previously have imagined, and hundreds of thousands of handloom weavers plus an increasing number of power looms stood ready to weave that thread. The bottleneck moved to raw cotton production. In 1793, an American inventor named Eli Whitney invented the cotton gin, a machine that cleaned and removed the seeds from raw cotton. Previously a slave would spend all day cleaning a single pound of raw cotton, but with Whitney's invention the same person could now clean 50 pounds a day.[10] It was also well suited to a new variety of cotton, the Upland variety, which was slowly crossbred from Mexican and Guatemalan stock to suit the climate of the American South.[11] With infinite demand from the English mills, new productivity from the cotton gin, and a new variety of cotton, American slavery expanded rapidly and focused increasingly on cotton production. In 1790, more than half of all American slaves were in Maryland and Virginia, mostly in tobacco production.[12] The state of Mississippi was founded in 1817 and Alabama in 1819, each on the basis of enslaved cotton production, which followed an earlier phase of forced dispossession and extermination of the Native population, then widespread deforestation to clear the land. As the historian Giorgio Riello writes, "In 1791, US cotton production was practically non-existent. Ten years later, in 1801, the US exported as much cotton to England as the entire British West Indies. In 1811, the US sold 43.9 thousand tons of cotton to England, 56 percent of all cotton used by British mills."[13]

Running in parallel with the cotton inventions were coal and steam technologies. By 1700, Britain was already an unusually intense user of coal, but mostly for household heating and some specific industrial activities, like brick and glass making, brewing, forging, and soap boiling.[14] In the north of England, Tyneside salt boilers used 80,000 to 100,000 tons of coal per year by the mid-17th century, at a rate of six to eight metric tons of coal to boil one ton of salt.[15] Coal mining was good business, but one of its main problems was that coal mines tend to fill up with water. In 1712, Thomas Newcomen patented an engine that burned coal in order to produce steam, and used the steam vacuum to run a piston, thereby making the first steam engine. But it was incredibly inefficient, needing something like 45 pounds of coal to produce one horsepower, so it made sense to use it only right next to a coal mine, where it was useful for powering a pump to get the water out.[16] At about the same time, a Bristol Quaker named Abraham Darby figured out a way to turn coal into coke, through what is essentially a very destructive distilling process. Coke burns hotter than regular coal, so Darby could run a hotter blast furnace and thus produce a new, strong, cheap type of iron. That process too was improved and changed many times over the subsequent decades, by which point Darby's firm was controlled by his major investor, Thomas Goldney, who made his fortune in Caribbean slave ships.[17]

The new ability to mine coal more cheaply (thanks to having the water pumped out) and a new source of demand to fuel the new blast furnaces meant more coal for industrial processes. Cheaper, stronger iron was used in more things, like construction and machinery. The next big breakthrough came with James Watt's steam engine. Watt had worked at the University of Glasgow making and repairing scientific instruments, and eventually formed a partnership with Birmingham manufacturer Matthew Boulton. Boulton provided the money and business know-how, and Watt the technology, and they got a patent on their steam engine in 1775. The machine needed the new, stronger iron from the blast furnaces, and the cheap coal, and the precedent of the Newcomen engine. The Watt engine also managed to convert the movement of a piston into rotary motion, meaning it could run a drive shaft or turn a crank or a propellor or a wheel. Their first market was mines in Cornwall, but those soon began to exhaust themselves, so in 1786, Boulton sold the first engine to the Papplewick mill on the River Leen in Nottinghamshire.[18] By 1790, they had sold a dozen engines to textile mills, and 84 by the year 1800.[19] Boulton and Watt ruthlessly protected their patent for 25 years, which prevented the generalization of the technology for other purposes, but it also allowed them to successfully improve and sell their machine, especially to cotton mill owners. (Boulton also invested in 65 slave voyages between 1792 and 1807, which transported 21,213 captives from Africa. Upon abolition, he received £27,836 from Parliament as compensation for the freedom of the 642 human beings he owned in plantations on Saint Vincent and in Demerara.)[20]

Finally, in the 1780s and 1790s, Henry Cort patented the "puddling and rolling" process to make wrought iron, which was far stronger and more versatile than previous forms of iron. Some recent research suggests he may have learned of this technique from a community of enslaved metallurgists in Jamaica, who may have brought the knowledge from West Africa.[21] Either way, his partner was a sinister Royal Navy clerk named Adam Jellicoe, who turned out to have embezzled £39,676 in Royal Navy funds and died bankrupt, which also destroyed Cort's business and reputation.[22] Richard Crawshay (one of only 10 known British millionaires in 1799) realized that Cort's iron both could replace Swedish iron in supplying the Royal Navy *and* could undercut the power of skilled metallurgy workers, so he licensed the technology and set about improving it and applying it to his furnaces.[23] So the invention survived, and Cort's wrought iron was the basis for essentially all metal in industrial and military uses through the 1860s. Cheaper metal meant cheaper fixed capital, cheaper industries, and cheaper empires.

This brief and somewhat bloodless list of inventions reveals two things. First, there was an internal logic to the series of technologies: They were not random or spontaneous, nor were they centrally planned and directed by the state or some kind of scientific authority. Inventors responded to bottlenecks in production and cheap materials to take advantage of gains from specific improvements in a known production process. Many of these technologies were invented by people with work experience in the relevant industry, mostly trying to solve practical, immediate problems. Second, the cotton textile sector needed the coal and steam energy system, and that addition of inanimate energy not only had environmental consequences but also marked a shift in labor organization, away from independent household manufacture to centralized factories owned by a capitalist, employing laborers for wages.

■ ■ ■

England faced an energy crisis as early as the 17th century due to the extent of deforestation.[24] Early modern forestry conservation laws were focused on local self-sufficiency, especially hunting, not trade or commerce or industry. Wood was an essential part of early modern life, forming the basis of not only industrial heating but domestic heating and essentially all construction. There was no single obvious alternative, and indeed, the later industrial replacements turned out to be both coal and iron for different uses. Coal and iron themselves are wood-intensive to produce, so there was no energy transition either in the 18th century or since.[25] When 17th-century English writers began to notice the wood shortage and predict political consequences, the first solutions were imperial, drawing on the forests of either Ireland or Virginia, depending on the writers' specific dreams of empire.[26] Both proved difficult: Virginia forests were too diverse and diffuse for efficient large-scale lumber production, Irish colonists were interested in other crops, and wood was too bulky to profitably ship long distances until it met the voracious demand of the sugar colonies. By the 1670s–1680s, an intercolonial wood trade developed, with Virginia shipping wood to Barbados, and New England specializing in supply for the Royal Navy.[27] One large navy ship required the timber of several thousand mature trees, and the masts of large ships especially needed to be cut from huge trees that were hundreds of years old, so all the domestic English options were depleted before the series of commercial wars with the Dutch after the 1650s.[28]

Specialty wood and colonial wood were profitable to ship, but regular fuelwood was not, and it was increasingly scarce and expensive. From 1501 to 1601, timber prices in England more than tripled, then from 1601 to 1649 almost doubled again.[29] Scattered English woodlands could profitably produce 2.5 metric tons of fuelwood per hectare, but took 25 years to renew; some land underwent "disafforestation," when the legal category of land was changed from regulated forest to waste so the wood on it could be commercialized and sold.[30] But by the 1770s, English forests were exhausted. The historian E. A. Wrigley states the problem clearly:

But on a sustained-yield basis an acre of woodland could normally produce only 1–2 tons of dry wood per annum. Two tons of dry wood produces the same amount of heat as one ton of coal. To produce a ton of bar iron in seventeenth-century England involved consuming about 30 tons of dry wood. If half the land surface of Britain had been covered with woodland, it would only have sufficed to produce perhaps 1¼ million tons of bar iron on a sustained-yield basis. . . . It was physically impossible to produce iron and steel on the scale needed to create a modern railway system, or to construct large fleets of steel ships, or to enable each family to have a car, if the heat energy needed to smelt and process the iron and steel came from wood and charcoal.[31]

There was simply not enough wood in England for its demand, even without full-scale industrialization, hence the use of coal in domestic heating and some specific heat-intensive industrial applications by the late 17th and early 18th centuries. Observers were already satirizing London's dense coal smoke by the late 17th century. Soon the city depended on a continual inflow of coal. In the icy winter of 1739–40, canals froze and coal could not be delivered to London for weeks, producing a social catastrophe.[32] Depending on the local climate and standard of living, most 18th-century Europeans consumed about two tons of wood per year, which works out to about five kilograms per day (or about 11 American pounds), and at that rate, the 150 million Europeans in 1750 would need to consume 160 million hectares of forest, or one-third of the continent, to sustain themselves if all of their energy came from burning wood.[33] That situation was impossible even then, and would have left no room for substantial growth in either population or living standards.

The use of coal gave Europeans access to what economic historians call "ghost acres." As Wrigley puts it, "In 1700, when the English coal output was estimated at about 2.2 million tons, to have provided the same heat energy from wood on a sustained-yield basis would have required devoting 2 or 3 million acres to woodland. . . . By 1800, on the same assumption, 11 million acres of woodland would have been needed. This would have meant devoting more than a third of the surface area of the country to provide the quantity of energy in question."[34] By 1850, the ghost acres from coal were twice the size of the entire island of Britain.[35] Or, put differently, thanks to coal, British industry burned two entire Britains every year: Little wonder that Britain accounted for more than half of global carbon emissions until late into the 19th century.[36] These ghost acres were supplemented by actual acres. The entire cotton-production chain included both coal-burning engines in the factories and deforestation in the American South.

All actions are transformations of energy, and all economies are uses of energy, transforming the natural world into things for human consumption. As the environmental historians Astrid Kander, Paolo Malanima, and Paul Warde put it, "Investment in fixed capital was also largely aimed at providing the means to make possible the exploitation of energy and then was indirectly aimed at procuring energy."[37] Many economists and economic-growth models have ignored the role of energy in production (let alone waste and emissions and finite fuels) but they have done so erroneously. Technological change has focused mostly on energy-intensive replacements for labor, and since the Industrial Revolution, both the total amount of energy used and its efficiency have increased enormously. To take only one example, an animate source of energy like a horse can deliver, well, 1 horsepower of energy. A water mill delivered 3 to 5 horsepower per hour, though with unpredictable variability due to climatic conditions. A single steam engine in the late 19th century could deliver 8,000 to 12,000 horsepower.[38] Modern economic growth has meant a continual increase in energy consumption through a steady addition of new sources of energy used in new ways. Figure 7 shows the per capita growth in energy consumption from before the time of industrialization until it was well underway.[39]

The environmental historian John Richards summarizes the historical impact of coal like this: "Lacking coal as a fuel, British industry could not have grown as it did. Lacking coal, the general population would have been distinctly more uncomfortable in the winter and subject to much-lowered standard of living as fuel prices soared. Lacking coal, the need to grow trees for fuel might have superseded agriculture near the cities. Certainly, cheap, reliable supplies of coal stimulated the growth of cities in this period. Lacking coal, domestic wood production for fuel could not possibly have been an adequate substitute."[40] None of this should be taken to imply that the use of wood ended. In fact, it is more accu-

Figure 7. **Annual per capita energy consumption in England and Wales, in megajoules, 1561 to 1859**

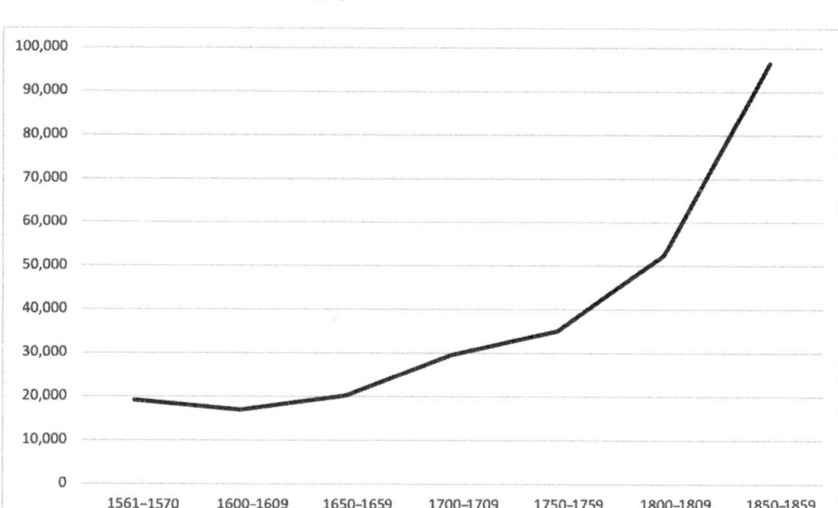

rate to think of energy accumulation rather than energy transition: Coal added to wood, just as oil eventually added to coal, and all of them are still in use today.[41] As of the writing of this book, every year has set a new record for the most use of wood and coal in the global economy.

Coal did two other things. It produced carbon emissions and other forms of toxic waste on an unprecedented scale, which has only continued to increase and ramify until today. The combined steam-coal production complex also completed the historical separation between employers and employed, owners and workers. With coal, mill owners did not have to build their factories near reliable running water and build towns to house the workers, who then became expensive and difficult to replace. Coal meant that mills could be located next to cities, which could provide a deep reservoir of cheap, replaceable labor. Underground coal meant less competition for land use, and more agglomeration effects from concentrating industry and employment and transport linkages all together. And coal meant that the insatiable machines never had to stop. Climate change and modern class conflict were born together.

. . .

Before returning to the wider environmental consequences of the Industrial Revolution, we first need to pause to consider the effects on the workers who lived through it, not just in Britain but in America, Africa, and India too.

The new factory system meant a transformation of the experience of work in Britain. It began in a small sector and gradually generalized across the industrial economy. Mechanization, standardization, and inanimate energy demanded continuous work at a continuous pace. Instead of working at their own speed, starting and stopping when they chose, exercising some autonomy over the final products of their labor, and using skills accumulated through years of training and apprenticeship, industrial workers were now subject to factory discipline. They started work when a bell rang or a whistle blew, and stopped only when it told them to, regardless of exhaustion, hunger, thirst, or the need for a bathroom. (Most American workers got the right to bathroom breaks only in the 1990s.) Arkwright's mill at Cromford ran two 12-hour shifts, from 6 a.m. to 6 p.m.: The gates opened at those two times and closed immediately, and any worker who was not inside lost that day's wages, plus one more day as a fine. Workers were intended to be interchangeable and easily replaced, so they did the same menial, easily trained jobs over and over, at the machine's pace. In many cases they were prohibited from talking to one another, and they were under constant supervision. The Round Mill in the Strutt factory complex at Belper was even designed on the basis of a panopticon prison, so that workers could always be observed but never knew whether they actually were or not.[42]

People *hated* it. They hated the machine pace, the supervision, the lack of control, the various methods of discipline. Employers complained constantly that their workers were unreliable and migratory. To take one example, the McConnel and Kennedy spinning firm in Manchester had 100 percent annual labor turnover.[43] Early on, many firms tried to preserve old models of unfree labor and tried to use various forms of bondage or indenture, but they soon found that to be undesirable, because they wanted the ability to costlessly fire a worker and replace them.[44] Instead, employers wrote up factory codes, starting with Josiah Wedgwood's porcelain factories in 1780, then Boulton's Soho Foundry in 1796, then spreading throughout the industrial world. These codes dictated all manner of worker conduct, and in the case of factory towns like Wedgwood's or New Lanark, Deanston, or Blantyre in Scotland, the rules of conduct applied outside of work, stipulating church attendance, morality, and acceptable leisure time, while banning drunkenness or promiscuity.[45] The most common punishment was fines, and since employers got to keep the proceeds, they issued them with great enthusiasm. The few skilled adult male workers were exclusively fined (replacing them could be expensive), while children were more likely to be beaten, including by their adult coworkers and supervisors.[46]

Unskilled mass employment reduced the incentive to send children to be apprenticed to a craft, and the collapse of craft handwork also reduced the set of people hiring apprentices. Without farms to supply both tasks and subsistence, many families had nowhere to send their children. The new factories were happy to employ them as young as 9 or 10 years old—children began work younger in the peak years of the Industrial Revolution than in the decades either before or after.[47] Cumberland mine workers would sometimes begin as young as 5. Silk mills were heavily dependent on child labor, typically with two-thirds to three-quarters of workers in a given mill under the age of 18, though in some cases it was even higher. Wool spinning tended to average more like half of the workers being under 18, and in the cotton industry, the average was around 40 to 45 percent. In 1816, 30 percent of Wedgwood's employees were under 18, and about 3 percent were under 10.[48] Optimistic assessments of the experience of industrialization tend to point out that there was a wage premium for factory work over other kinds of unskilled labor, and that mills always had more willing workers than they had jobs. The preponderance of child labor is difficult to reconcile with that view. If 40 to 75 percent of the workers are coerced children, then it is difficult to reasonably assess how freely the labor force chose to work in the factories; likewise, while it is true that the children got a small money wage and probably would have gotten none while working as apprentices or on farms, they did not control the spending of their wages. And probably few people today would prefer that their children work 12-hour shifts in textile mills instead of going to school and not getting a wage. There were no health and safety standards before the Factory Act of 1833 established a rudimentary inspectorate, and those early attempts at factory regulation were exactly in response to the concerns of doctors in Manchester over the health and welfare of child workers. It is possible that a generation of workers sent their children into the mills in order to fulfill their consumer aspirations, but desperation seems to me a more likely explanation, especially given how often children were sent to work in response to declining adult wages.[49] There were additional consequences: What began as a temporary expedient to make up for lower wages in turn became a social norm, and a generation of children didn't go to school or accumulate skills and education, which in turn made it difficult for them to acquire jobs with higher wages to keep their own children out of work.[50]

People resisted factory discipline in various ways. The most dramatic was machine-breaking. Britain had already seen recurrent machine-breaking, like the textile riots in Melksham in 1738 and the Northumberland coal miners' riots in the 1740s. The Spitalfields weavers rioted and smashed machines in 1675, and again rioted against printed imported Indian cloth in 1719, and *again* against cheaper immigrant labor in 1736, and yet again against rate cutting for loom work in the 1760s. Each of these was a case of what Eric Hobsbawm called "collective bargaining by riot."[51] They were specific attacks on specific employers carried out by specific groups of workers, aiming to achieve specific demands, either wage increases or the freedom to choose between employers, or blocking threats to employment. We have already seen several cases of workers smashing or burning factories or machines in the new textile sector. There were many more: riots against flying shuttles in the Trowbridge wool manufacturing area in 1785, 1792, and 1810–13; one of Arkwright's factories in Chorley was destroyed in 1779.[52] These were class-conscious attacks, not opposition to all new technologies in general: In 1778–80, the Lancashire machine-wreckers broke only large factory spinning jennies, not the small kind that people could use at home.[53] As the economic historian Jeff Horn puts it, "The labouring classes were not necessarily opposed to all innovation, rather they wrecked machines in order to maintain control over the labour process and resist the imposition of the factory system."[54]

The most dramatic wave of machine-breaking was the Luddite rebellion of 1811–13. The term "Luddite" survives today as an all-purpose accusation that someone is superstitiously or obstinately backward and afraid of technology. The machine-breakers of 1811 were not like that at all. They were weavers and their families who correctly perceived that their livelihoods were under threat from the new machines, and they conducted over 100 attacks, destroying over 1,000 machines, for a cost of over £100,000. They claimed to be the followers of a legendary folk figure called Ned Ludd, hence the name. They were met with overwhelming violence: Parliament made machine-breaking a capital crime, and deployed 12,000 troops against the Luddites, which was more than were sent for the Duke of Wellington to fight Napoleon in Spain at the same time.[55]

Despite substantial support from the general population (not a single person was denounced to the government for machine-breaking), dozens of people were hanged, hundreds were shot, and thousands were transported to prison colonies in Australia.[56]

But the resistance went on. There was another extensive wave of machine-breaking in Lancashire in 1826, with attacks on at least 21 factories.[57] As agriculture also began to mechanize, rural workers attacked threshing machines, following their own folk hero they called Captain Swing.[58] In 1830, the Swing Riots probably constituted more than 1,500 attacks across Southern England, again met with violent repression. But by then, an entire generation had been raised with the experience of factory discipline. Between 1793 and 1820, more than 60 acts were passed in Parliament to prohibit working-class collective action, and many civil liberties were suspended during the Napoleonic Wars.[59] When the Poor Laws were amended in 1832, and the voting franchise (barely) extended in that same year, it was not a hard-won victory for the working class but rather an expression of their violent defeat.[60] As the economic historian Sidney Pollard puts it:

> The acclimatization of new workers to factory discipline is a task different in kind, at once more subtle and more violent, from that of maintaining discipline among a proletarian population of long standing. Employers in the British Industrial Revolution therefore used not only industrial means but a whole battery of extra-mural powers, including their control over the courts, their powers as landlords, and their own ideology, to impose the control they required.[61]

Nowhere was the consequence of the industrialization of labor clearer than in the fate of the handloom weavers. The vast increases in spinning productivity led hundreds of thousands of people to become handloom weavers: a solid, respectable, male breadwinner occupation. From the 1780s to the early decades of the 19th century, their numbers increased enormously, until by about 1820, they numbered close to a quarter-million workers, with perhaps twice that many family members also in some way engaged in their work, making them the largest group of workers in any British industry.[62] But the effect of the power looms began to appear at the same time, and their wages started to fall after about 1805. At first they responded by working harder, but all of them doing so together only exacerbated the downward trajectory of their output prices. From an average weekly wage of 23 shillings in 1805, they got 8 shillings a week in 1820, and 6 shillings in 1830.[63] Many tried to hang on, to ride out market turbulence, or find new markets, but the rise of power looms was inexorable, and more and more handloom weavers were forced to give up and find work in factories.[64] Figure 8 shows the peak and fall of the weavers across two generations.[65]

The British handloom weavers were not the only large occupational group annihilated by their inability to compete with factory

Figure 8. **Number of handloom weavers in Britain, 1806–62, in thousands**

production. On the other side of the world, the same process happened in India. At the start of the 18th century, India had been the world's center of cotton textile manufacture, mainly produced by skilled handloom weavers, in relatively small quantities, but with a very high standard of quality. (Indeed, the historian Prasannan Parthasarathi maintains that the "induced innovation" cycle in cotton was due not to supply but to attempts to match the high quality of Indian cottons.)[66] Indian cottons were the source of the initial demand boom in Europe, highly desired by people across the social spectrum. Chances are good that the crimson interior decoration in Isaac Newton's house was at least partly high-quality Indian textiles, and his crimson dye was probably made from cochineal, an insect native to Mexico. Indian cottons were also a useful imperial mechanism: Members of the East India Company who decided to cash out their plunder and extraction could buy them and export them back to Europe to sell for even more money, so they functioned as a kind of imperial capital-mobility mechanism.[67] In the early 18th century, India probably had a technology advantage over England in spinning and weaving, as well as lower wages and access to the Indian Ocean trading zone, so southern India especially hosted a vibrant textile-manufacturing sector, and as late as 1750, India probably accounted for about a quarter of global manufacturing exports, a larger share than any other single place.[68]

British manufacturers objected to the imports of high-quality Indian cotton (usually called "calico," but there was a wide range of varieties of textiles). After several failed attempts from the 1670s onward, Parliament passed the first Calico Act in 1700, which banned the import of printed cottons, but kept white cotton (so printers could keep working) and created a system of bonded government warehouses for taxation and supervision.[69] France did the same between 1686 and 1691, with the exception of the port of Nantes, where Indian cottons arrived to be reexported to Africa in exchange for slaves.[70] Then, in 1721, a more comprehensive British Calico Act kept out imported cottons in general, again with some exceptions, subject to taxes. These import laws were a classic example of what today is known as "infant industry protection." By keeping out high-quality rivals, British cotton producers had the time and space to develop their technologies, and they had a captive home market to sell their goods to. Today such policies are banned under the TRIMS (Trade-Related Investment Measures) agreement of the World Trade Organization, and are widely considered to be economic nonsense by economists and development professionals. The economist Ha-Joon Chang has spent years pointing out that Britain, Germany, the United States, Japan, and China all developed their industries behind protective tariffs and import restrictions, and indeed, essentially no country has ever successfully industrialized without such policies, but the policy consensus has persisted.[71]

Sheltered behind their protections, the British experimented with, developed, and industrialized cottons until they could produce an immense amount of cheap manufactured textiles for export. And export they did. English exports (including reexports) to Africa and the Americas increased by a factor of 6 between 1700 and 1772–74, and the manufacturing share of exports increased by a factor of 8.4.[72] By the end of the century, the Americas took up about 60 percent of British exports, and they were by far the leading market for fabrics.[73] After them was Africa, where a great many of the slaves discussed in the previous chapter were bought with cotton textiles. The slaves in the American South who grew raw cotton were also clothed in cheap British manufactured cottons. By 1800 more than 40 percent of all British exports was cotton, and its dominance continued for decades.[74] As late as the 1880s, Lancashire accounted for 80 percent of global cotton-goods exports.[75]

Britain first sheltered its cotton industry behind protections, then once it had gained a technological advantage, dominated the global export trade. After about 1810, newly independent countries in the Americas raised tariffs, which made Indian textiles even more unaffordable, while cheap British ones were still in demand, even with the tariff costs.[76] The half century after 1810 saw the deindustrialization of India, and the collapse of the old hand-powered manufacturing economy. To be sure, part of the process was internal: The successors to the Mughal political hegemony were more extractive, raising rents and taxes; wars disrupted commerce and cash advances; there were several years of bad droughts caused by El Niño, which raised agricultural prices. Some people switched into agriculture to take advantage of those high prices, while others demanded higher wages, which made their outputs more expensive.[77] Many of these processes were exacerbated by British colonialism, but some were not. Still, after taking over export markets, British cottons eventually took over the domestic Indian market, probably cutting the manufacturing share of the Indian labor force in half over the 19th century.[78] Under colonial administration, India shifted to commodity agricultural exports like sugar, raw silk, and, of course, opium.

This detour into labor history is important in its own right but is also not separate from the environmental story. The coal-powered factories were built near cities in order to access their large labor forces, and as the factory complexes grew and demand for factory workers increased (and as alternative forms of employment evaporated) more and more people moved into cities, so first Britain and then the rest of Europe urbanized at a rapid pace. These newly immense cities were swathed in dense coal smoke from the factories and from domestic heating, and generated an enormous amount of waste and effluent, including from the thousands of horses who were needed for transport and work in urban contexts. The city of Manchester, the epicenter of the Industrial Revolution, grew from a population of 93,000 in 1801 to over 500,000 by 1881, at which time each person consumed an average of six tons of coal per year.[79]

The meteorologist R. A. Smith first used the term "acid rain" in 1872, and people from northern Britain to Scandinavia reported black snow. In 1900, Manchester's rain had a pH value of 3.5, which is somewhere between Coca-Cola and tomato juice, and it began to dissolve the brick buildings of the city.[80] In 1889, one social reformer estimated an annual cost of £5 million in London alone due to 24 different kinds of harms caused by coal smoke, including workdays lost due to sickness.[81] The early study of industrial pollution led to the development of the concept of "externalities," now at the core of economic thinking about climate change. In this way, the problems first posed by Manchester's black snow were at the beginning of a line of failures that has led us to the current world, where every human body contains "forever chemicals" and every human brain and human testicle contains microplastics.

Factory workers had to be fed, so commercial agriculture both mechanized and relied on intense fertilizers, at first using nitrogen-rich guano mined from islands off the coast of South America.[82] Farmers increasingly relied on monocrop culture, and urban, industrial Britain relied on food imports, especially of a new dietary norm focused on animal proteins and refined carbohydrates, which made people both stronger and more susceptible to new kinds of chronic health problems.[83] The metabolic rift of industrialization extended from the digestion of Peruvian birds to British child workers.

*   *   *

The most important environmental impact of the Industrial Revolution was the adoption of fossil-fuel energy and the production of carbon emissions in the economic process. But beyond that epochal, world-altering event, the demands of industry and industrial workers on the one hand and the lower costs of transport and mechanized destruction on the other fundamentally reorganized the biosphere toward less natural habitat, less biodiversity, and more land and biomass controlled by and oriented toward human use, especially uses intended to turn a profit. As the environmental historian John Richards puts it, "In region after region, pioneers cleared land, drained wetlands, irrigated dry lands, killed off wildlife, and expelled indigenous peoples in order to reduce biodiversity and biomass and thereby expand output."[84]

The expansion of slave-grown cotton monoculture across the American South can be envisioned as a hard edge of fire and blood, moving steadily westward from the coastal Carolinas to the Mississippi River. First came violence, as Indigenous people were dispossessed, expropriated, and expelled, through either concerted military violence or more sporadic violence from white settlers. Slaves followed, cutting, clearing, and burning the forests. Without an efficient transportation network for bulky goods, timber cut from cleared agricultural land was too expensive to ship and sell, so, as one forestry official later estimated, three-quarters of it was burned on the spot.[85] Once cleared, the land was tilled and planted with new hybrid cotton varieties. The cotton plantation owners adopted the new methods of standardization, mechanization, quantification, and factory discipline learned from industrialists, with the result that between 1801 and 1861, the average amount of cotton picked per slave per day quadrupled, which was an increase substantially faster than the best measures of average labor productivity in the overall economy.[86] But cotton exhausts the soil, so the bleeding edge of the cotton kingdom kept moving west from the 1830s through the 1860s past the Mississippi, spurring, among other things, the political conflicts that precipitated the outbreak of the American Civil War.

The cotton South was not the only place where capital incentivized a large-scale shift to monoculture. In Brazil, the area around São Paolo switched from sugar to coffee in the 1830s.[87] Coffee soon proved profitable enough to incentivize railroad construction and steamship ports. The pattern would repeat with Argentine beef, Russian and American grain, West African palm oil and cocoa. Again and again, from about the 1830s or 1840s, all around the world, people shifted to cash-crop monoculture, and large-scale capital-intensive industrial transport infrastructure followed, which lowered prices, and lower prices incentivized expansion.

Another significant example of the consequences of monoculture was potatoes in Ireland. Swaths of Ireland had been deforested from the 17th century onward, both to try to alleviate the English energy crisis and to clear land for plantation agriculture under the control of English Protestant landlords. Potatoes generate more calories of output per acre than most other forms of agriculture, and by the late 18th century, much of Ireland had switched to potato cultivation, mostly consumed locally, because potatoes are more difficult to transport than grain is. There is some debate over whether population grew first and potatoes were a solution, or the switch to potatoes allowed for population growth; likewise, there is some argument over whether Irish people ate a lot of potatoes out of necessity or because they liked them.[88] Whatever the case, after 1800, at least a third of the population was dependent on potatoes, and other forms of food were exported to feed industrial Britain.[89] In 1845, an outbreak of a water-based mold called *Phytophthora infestans* swept through Europe, probably emerging from the Toluca Valley in Mexico, then destroying potato crops in the Eastern United States, before traveling on ships to Ireland. It killed one-third to one-half of the crop in 1845, then three-quarters in 1846, leaving few remaining potatoes to plant a new crop in 1847, and even the 1848 crop was only two-thirds the normal amount. The Tory British government first tried to enact some relief laws, but also incoherently repealed the Corn Laws that had protected British grain farming, intending to make food cheaper and more market dependent. Controversy over it led to the fall of the government, and the fragile Whig replacement, having drunk deeply of the doctrine of laissez-faire and already committed to other economic policies that left them unable to borrow, decided to let the free market sort out the problem.[90] About a million people died in Ireland, both from starvation and from typhus preying on their weakened immune systems, and over two million people fled between 1845 and 1855, producing both a catastrophic century-long population collapse at home and an influx of new workers in the Americas. At least 100,000 people died across the rest of Europe, but nowhere else was as dependent on a single crop, nor governed so ruthlessly by the strictures of the capitalist market.

Deforestation and monoculture went hand in hand with the extermination of animals on a previously impossible scale. Early modern travel writing is full of accounts of incredible animal abundance. Writers describe shoals of fish so thick that fishers struggled to row through them, flocks of millions of birds that darkened the sky and took days to pass over, or herds of millions of bison, in addition to forests so dense that a squirrel could cross entire American states without touching the ground. To be sure, we should greet these claims with some skepticism: Many of the writers were keen to emphasize the abundance and riches of the frontier, to induce migration and investment. Early modern writings are full of exaggerations in general, and the culture of scientific quantification was not what it is today. However, these descriptions are so common that they are difficult to ignore. Moreover, as ecologists have noted, "there are dozens of places in the Caribbean named after large sea turtles whose adult populations now number in the tens of thousands rather than the tens of millions of a few centuries ago. . . . Place names for oysters, pearls and conches conjure up other ecological ghosts of marine invertebrates that were once so abundant as to pose hazards to navigation but are witnessed now only by massive garbage heaps of empty shells."[91] And not only marine life: Britain is full of medieval towns and villages named for bird species that were once plentiful and are now rare or extinct. The Carolina parakeet, once abundant in the Ohio and Mississippi

River Valleys, was annihilated when its habitat was deforested.[92] Exterminating beavers for fur also meant destroying the habitats they created with their dams, which led to collapses in populations of ducks, osprey, otters, and other animals.[93] From the 1810s through the 1840s, North American settlers and planters organized large-scale "circle drives," in which hundreds of hunters formed county-sized loops and worked inward, exterminating all large animals along the way.[94] The metabolization of North America's biomass has been an ongoing process, accelerating after the full-scale industrialization of the United States in the latter half of the 19th century, and especially after the introduction of railroads from the 1840s onward. In 1820, Ohio was still a mostly forested frontier state, and the near extinction of the bison took until the 1880s.[95]

Reports of early modern abundance were themselves probably the result of what ecologists call a "trophic cascade." This idea describes the unpredictable consequences when a food web is radically altered in a short time, as with the extermination of an apex predator. Once gone, the animals they consumed will be free of predation and will vastly expand in number, until they in turn consume too much of their own food and their numbers crash—and the intense consumption of their food might mean whatever thing further down the chain becomes superabundant, and so on. In the case of the early modern superabundance of fish, birds, bison, and other large animals, chances are good that the trophic cascade began when Europeans exterminated or expelled the Indigenous people at the top of the ecological system. Industrial technology and industrial demand then consumed the resulting superabundance.

Whales are another powerful example of the violent interaction of industry and the natural world. Starting in the 1660s, the Dutch dominated the early whaling industry, as might be expected from their early market dominance and maritime reach. In 1733, the British Parliament offered a bounty to whalers, then increased it in 1740 and again in 1749.[96] From 1733 to 1800, a little over 4,000

British whaling voyages killed upwards of 12,000 whales, for a harvest of 1.4 million hectoliters of whale oil (about 37 million gallons, which I regret to report would fill 56 Olympic swimming pools) and 5,300 metric tons of whalebone.[97] The whalebone (which is actually baleen, not bone at all) was used in a variety of things that required flexibility and strength: whips, baskets, ribs for umbrellas and corsets. There was no comparable product until the arrival of synthetic plastics in the late 19th century. The oil was used in artificial lighting, in cities and factories. The growth of artificial lighting is another of the dramatic transformations of industrialization: In the preindustrial world, artificial light was scarce and expensive, and agricultural workers labored according to the rising and falling of the sun. Factories running 24 hours a day required light, as did the cities that housed their workers, and whale oil was a cheap initial solution.

Whale oil was delivered in sufficiently abundant quantities to be price competitive with vegetable oil, and much like coal, it provided Europeans with "ghost acres," since thousands of acres did not have to be devoted to fuel-oil production. From the 1660s to 1800, Dutch and German whalers harvested enough blubber to produce five million barrels of oil, refined in dozens of refineries and factories near Amsterdam and Rotterdam, much of it exported to France.[98] By the end of the 18th century, British whalers had exterminated Atlantic bowhead whales, so they moved farther and farther out to sea. Between 1500 and 1800, more than 162,500 Greenland whales were killed, then in the first four decades of the 19th century, at least 60,000 right whales in the southern Pacific, and probably 15,000 bowhead whales in the northern Pacific throughout the century.[99]

As a case of metabolic rift, it is difficult to beat hunting whales to extinction in order to generate cheap industrial lighting. Whales were an energy link between tiny phytoplankton and human industry, vast and ancient creatures that transformed sunlight into scarce warmth, until they were processed into fuels to be burned down over the course of a few nights.[100] Lighting running on coal gas was pioneered in 1814 by a former employee of Boulton and Watt but required a huge infrastructural investment, so became ubiquitous only after the 1860s.[101]

Another significant animal linked ecology to industry, and that was the horse. The onset of industrialization, especially in the United States, did not render horses obsolete, but rather created for them a wide range of new employment. The number of horses employed in short-distance hauling vastly increased, even as steam engines were used for long-distance transport in the form of railroads and steamships. Cities relied on horses for deliveries, but also to power mass transit (they pulled streetcars and omnibuses) and for communication through stagecoaches and mail delivery.[102] Indeed, from 1840 to 1910, the number of horses in the United States increased at about twice the rate of human population growth, even given the rapid rates of immigration after the 1840s, and horses *urbanized* about 50 percent faster than humans did.[103] Horses were also used in a variety of industrial contexts, for motive power and haulage, because they could learn routines and execute them without much supervision. The capital-intensive canal boom of the 1820s–30s in the northeastern United States depended on horses, because they pulled the canal barges: Two canal horses could tow 50 to 80 tons of freight, and a barge would cover 40 miles a day, changing horses at towns and rest stops every 15 to 20 miles.[104] The same went for railroads: Horses were widely used in construction of new track (since it, by definition, was not yet on a railway line), and people taking trains or moving goods from one train line to another would connect in a city through a variety of short-range horse transports, and many river or lake crossings happened on ferries powered by horse treadmills.[105] Until the advent of the automobile, any trip or haulage of more than 15 miles, or over rough terrain, or undertaken by someone who wanted autonomy of timing and pace, was undertaken by horse. Railroads connected cities, but within them, horses were the main source of power for the circulation of urban life and commerce.[106]

Horses made possible more efficient bison extermination, and in their place, the vast cattle ranges of the American West, which in turn produced meat that was carried by railroad to industrial meat-packing plants in cities like Chicago, all of which was bankrolled by large-scale capital investment.[107] But horses also have to be fed, and they mostly eat hay. Hay is bulky and cheap, so mostly consumed locally instead of exported, which means it is easily overlooked and does not readily show up in customs accounts. One ton of hay requires about one acre of land, so the increase in the number of horses meant the expansion of cleared land for their food production.[108] By the 1850s, hay production accounted for about 23 to 24 percent of farm area in the American Northeast, where it was most concentrated, and about 10 to 11 percent nationally.[109] It was lowest in the South, where cotton had the primary claim to land, so Southerners imported Northern hay in large quantities. From the 1840s onward, farmers developed a variety of technologies and techniques to increase hay production: It was well suited to mechanization and monoculture, and the horses it fed were important to powering machines as well as to hauling and delivering other crops to the growing global commodity markets.[110] According to some contemporary estimates (and a later scholar's attempts to reproduce them), by the 1850s, the total value of the annual hay crop might have roughly equaled the total value of the cotton crop, which is widely taken by historians of capitalism to be the central commodity in the making of the modern industrial capitalist economy.

The commodification, capitalization, and consumption of the natural world is an important corrective to our usual understanding of capitalism. Many historians and analysts of capitalism, especially those who admire it, tend to focus on technology and innovation as its distinctive advantages. They often tell stories about progress and obsolescence, moving toward greater efficiency. But if we look instead at what things actually happened most commonly instead of what was new, we find something surprising: New technologies tend not to replace older ones but rather to reconfigure how they are used, or to use them with greater intensity.[111] Steam engines did not replace horses; they actually increased their economic importance. Coal did not mean the end of deforestation but rather its intensification. The labor that was replaced by machines was well-paid and autonomous adult male labor—child labor increased. Enthusiasts of technology also tend to imagine the natural world as inexhaustible, which itself was an idea formulated in the 19th century, and which has been at the basis of economic reasoning ever since. But the world is not inexhaustible, and the efficiency gains of technology have in part meant an increase in the efficiency with which nature has been metabolized into human consumption. To be sure, that has meant a great increase in human living standards, which is arguably the overriding ethical imperative. But it has been predicated on a view of the relationship between technology and nature that was never sustainable and which in our current historical moment is breaking down. Technology harnessed to the imperative to earn profits under capitalist competition has not freed us from our place in nature; rather, by consuming nature faster, it has made our dependence on nature both more obvious and more vulnerable.

▪ ▪ ▪

The Industrial Revolution was an epochal rupture in the history of the human species, and the planet we live on. It was also an acceleration in the intensity and extent of the capitalist system. Although industrialization, modern economic growth, and capitalism are sometimes taken as synonymous, capitalism long predated the Industrial Revolution, and it is more accurate to say that capitalism caused industrialization rather than followed it or was identical to it.

The Industrial Revolution happened because owners of capital could make investments, because of the creation of an industrious wage labor force, an existing consumer culture governed by prices instead of tradition, and a world-spanning network of commerce. The British state certainly helped, with its import restrictions, subsidies, and violent repression of worker resistance. And there certainly were imperial linkages, with the cotton, the slave trade, the East India Company, and the export markets. But there had been violent states and empires before the Industrial Revolution, and after it too. Instead, states and empires were some of the tools that capital owners used to protect their property, expand their markets, and deliver their rates of return.

But to say that the Industrial Revolution was primarily driven by private capital owners is not to imply that all industrializations happen through market processes, or even that markets exist without state structures. The British Industrial Revolution cannot be repeated, because it was first: All subsequent industrializations have had to happen against the competition of an already-industrial Britain, and with the existing knowledge that industrialization is possible. Indeed, it is striking how unintentional British industrialization was, at the level of scientific knowledge. Thermodynamics was mostly not scientifically explored until the latter half of the 19th century, partly because Isaac Newton disliked the word "energy," so the inventors of steam engines and fossil-fuel use were not thinking about the economic system as an energy system.[112] As with energy, so too with the environment. The concept of "extinction" was only first developed in the 1790s, and was subject to a heated debate that mostly ended with its defeat.[113] William Stanley Jevons, one of the founders of mathematical utility theory in economics, wrote a book worrying about the sustainability of finite coal in 1865, and in 1896 the Swedish chemist Svante Arrhenius hypothesized that carbon dioxide emissions could warm the earth's atmosphere.[114] Industrialization and its environmental consequences were not the outcome of a plan, a state strategy, or a scientific vision: They were unintended results from a large number of people making immediate decisions to solve either technical problems at work or profitability problems in business.

The scale of the transformation cannot be overstated. By the 1830s, a single spinning mill could run 50,000 spindles powered by a central drive shaft with a steam engine and, in a 12-hour shift, could spin enough thread to circumnavigate the globe *twice*.[115] From 1780 to 1830, the production cost of a yard of cotton fabric fell by between 76 and 83 percent.[116] In the late 18th century, a skilled handloom weaver could produce 48 yards of cotton fabric in a week, but by 1833, a single teenager supervising a power loom could produce 432 yards per week.[117] This gargantuan flood of cheap cotton remade the Atlantic trading system, and the economic position of Britain in the world. After 1820, the "British model of energy consumption" spread across Europe, transforming the entire world economy, social system, and climate.[118]

The model was also tremendously wasteful. As late as the 1870s, cotton production in Britain took 10 pounds of coal, a nonrenewable mineral resource, to process one pound of raw cotton, a renewable vegetable resource, into a consumer good.[119] The system converted that intense use of dense energy into products and jobs. In the 1850s, say, about 1.8 million enslaved workers planted and picked raw cotton on millions of acres of deforested land in the American South, violently seized from Indigenous people and cleared of all large animals. The cotton was a hybrid from Mexico, and it received additional productivity from nitrogen fertilizer mined by indentured Asian workers from islands of bird guano off the coast of South America. The cotton was carried by horses fed on Northern hay to ports, where it was shipped in steamships made of iron, running on coal mined by some 17,000 mineworkers mostly in the north of England. It arrived in Liverpool, where it again was carried by horse to railroads that took it to the spinning factories around Manchester, where some 360,000 people worked for wages, running the coal-powered machines nonstop. The finished cotton was then carried again by horse to railroads and back to ports to be exported around the world, including to India, where the descendants of skilled weavers, now landless agricultural workers, bought it, and paid taxes to the East India Company. More people in the world wore cotton than ever before: It was cheaper, and by the 1850s, wages had begun to rise for the British people who earned them.

From the 1830s onward, industrialization spread across the continent of Europe, followed by the United States, and then Japan. Steamships and railroads lowered transport costs enormously, creating global commodity markets in a wide variety of goods that previously would have been too bulky or expensive to ship long distances. Around the world, country after country specialized in specific commodity exports in what is sometimes known as the new "global division of labor." But they mostly did not do so of their own volition: They were forced, either by economic incentives or by violent imperial coercion. Industrialization also meant cheaper and more reliable guns, faster imperial communication, and the faster movement of soldiers. In the second half of the 19th century, the price of imperialism fell, and Europeans bought more of it.

They also created a globalized capitalist economy, with Britain at the center. Under British leadership, the world coalesced on a single monetary system—the classical gold standard—and the proceeds of commerce and empire flowed through European and American banks. The processes of extinction, monoculture, and environmental degradation set in motion by industrialization expanded and intensified and spread around the world. By the second half of the 19th century, capitalism ceased to be an unusual subset of economic activity and became the dominant form of economic life on the planet.

CHAPTER 5

Empire, 1840s–1914

When many people think of capitalism, they think of corporations and globalization. Other people think of class conflict and imperialism. And all of them are right to do so, because each of those things was a constitutive element of the world of full-fledged global capitalism that characterized the second half of the 19th century. The years after about 1850 and, especially, *definitely* after 1870, were the first time that it is not only possible but unarguable to speak of capitalism being the dominant economic system in the world. As we have seen, capitalism began in small communities of traders, mostly in cities but also in colonial mines and ports, conducting unusual trades. By the middle of the 17th century, it was the dominant economic system in an entire country, the Dutch Republic. By the 18th, it was dominant in Britain and the British Empire, which underwent the Industrial Revolution, thereby changing forever the intensity of capitalist production and the ease with which it could be extended around the world.

The first half of the 19th century witnessed a kind of global crisis of long-standing territorial empires. The Qing dynasty in China, established in the 1640s thanks partly to the monetary chaos of their Ming predecessors, ran into fiscal, monetary, and political crises. The Mughal Empire in India was massively reduced by the East India Company's imperial projects, and ultimately dissolved following the Indian Mutiny (or the First War of Indian Independence) in 1857. The Spanish Empire, long a moribund and ossified shambles, finally collapsed when Spain was conquered by another territorial empire, the Napoleonic one, and when wars of liberation in Latin America between 1810 and 1825 dismantled its colonies. The Napoleonic Empire, in turn, was defeated by Britain and its allies, but not before helping to destabilize both the Ottoman Empire in the Middle East and the Romanovs in Russia. Each of those latter empires lingered on, trying to modernize their economies, militaries, and political systems, each struggling to fund and fight wars, each dealing with internal revolts. In the ashes of these vast multiethnic territorial dynastic empires arose new nationalist political movements, which in some cases succeeded in establishing a new political form: the nation-state that would characterize the 20th century. That is an important and compelling history, but it is to the side of our story: For our purposes, Britain emerged as the global hegemon by the middle of the 19th century, both as a result of its revolutionary industrial transformation and because of the crises and exhaustion of its rivals. For these reasons, the global capitalism of the 19th century was a specifically *British* global capitalism.

More and more parts of the world shifted (or were shifted) to production for the market, allocating resources based on prices instead of customs, and using money instead of other forms of exchange. The old silver flows from Latin America were profoundly disrupted by Simón Bolívar's wars of independence in 1810–25, which contributed to the destabilization of the silver-standard empires in China and India, and to the rise of a new gold standard under British control. More and more states and empires developed central banks and fiscal-military apparatuses, and they engaged in international capital markets that centered on London. Those capital markets turned out to be an excellent mechanism for enacting imperial control, and a conduit for channeling British investment to the entire world. Slavery persisted, only being abolished in the United States in 1865, Brazil in 1888, and continental Africa through the intervention of British imperialism in the 1880s and 1890s. Serfdom was abolished in Russia in 1861. Free wage labor was on the rise around the world, and truly stupendous numbers of people voluntarily migrated long distances to try to access higher wages. But unfree labor did not go away, and new systems of bonded labor, especially from India and China, involuntarily moved millions of people into horrifying working conditions with little to no pay. Industrialization also continued, spreading from Britain to the European continent, and then to the United States and Japan.[1] The hunger for industrial production continued and intensified the metabolization of the world, as species continued to be hunted to extinction and forests destroyed. The move to a fossil-fuel economy was permanent: First coal and iron, then by the end of the century, oil, steel, and electricity formed the basis of industrial production. Money, finance, wage labor, and industry: All persisted and intensified and combined together to form a full global capitalist system.

But the late 19th century also saw the emergence of new elements. Industrial technologies allowed for an astonishingly rapid spread of European empire after mid-century, violently producing what is sometimes known as a "global division of labor," in which countries or colonies specialized (or were made to specialize) in the export of individual commodities to the global market. Capitalist interests and empire were fundamentally linked, as were empire and the process of globalization. New industrial businesses, especially railroads and certain types of American manufacturing or sources of industrial inputs like steel and oil, developed a new system of organization. Management was increasingly separated from ownership, huge complex organizations created professional internal bureaucracies, and businesses attempted to create vertical or horizontal monopolies.[2] This was the birth of the modern corporation, which was an especially American contribution to the shape of modern capitalism. At the same time, inequality, instability, and the new pattern of recurrent financial crises led to organized opposition, both at the level of shop-floor antagonism against specific bosses and working conditions and at the level of international or national political organizations based on ideological opposition to capitalism. Trade unions, strike waves, and socialist parties were all products of the late 19th century.

By the latter half of the 19th century, capitalists assembled a coherent economic system from the existing components of money, finance, trade, and industry, and they added new elements of empire, globalization, and class conflict. Global capitalism took perhaps 300 years to emerge; it then lasted about 50 years before blundering spectacularly into decades of bloody calamity. The years 1870–1914 were the era of the most untrammeled imposition of capitalist logic on the lives, bodies, environments, ideas, and activities of people around the world, matched only by the era from roughly 1990 to the present. For that reason, the patterns of that era are of particular importance to us today, because they are the best example we have of how an unrivaled global capitalist system works, and what kind of results it produces. The image is not an encouraging one.

■ ■ ■

This book began with European empires, when Spanish and Portuguese conquistadores crossed into North Africa, and then continued into the Atlantic. We have seen several empires since then, and with good reason, because empires have probably been the most common form of political organization in human history. But by the early decades of the 19th century, it was by no means clear that formal overseas empires would continue, let alone expand. Part of the problem was ideological: The new doctrine of free-trade liberalism argued that empires were inefficient, corrupt, and antiquated. Adam Smith spent hundreds of pages of his *Wealth of Nations*, published in 1776, conducting a thorough demolition of the economic rationale for the East India Company, and the company itself had a high-profile corruption scandal with the impeachment of Governor General Warren Hastings between 1787 and 1795. Part of it was material: With the loss of the American colonies in 1783 and the abolition of the slave trade in 1807, much of the formal machinery of the old Atlantic imperial system broke down. The wars against the Napoleonic Empire left Britain with a huge amount of debt and no clear rival to justify imperial expansion. And finally, although Europeans had been very successful at subjugating the relatively centralized, relatively urbanized societies they found around the world, from the Aztecs to the Incas to the Mughals, it was more expensive and difficult to dominate sparse or nomadic people, especially in remote places with dangerous disease environments and unfavorable geography. As the historian Daniel Headrick puts it, "By the mid-nineteenth century, Western imperialism seemed to have reached its limits. Three centuries after Cortés, over half of the Americas were still Indian territory. In Asia, the British advance was stopped by the Afghans. Sub-Saharan Africa, the Middle East, and East Asia were off-limits to Europeans. The French conquest of Algeria required as many years as Napoleon's conquest of Europe, as did Russia's conquest of the Caucasus."[3]

New industrial technologies changed all of that. European empires expanded rapidly in the second half of the 19th century, especially in the so-called Scramble for Africa between roughly 1884 and 1914, when the entire continent was divided up into colonies, possessions, and zones of control.[4] The most notorious example was of course the Belgian Congo, a vast territory populated by tens of millions of people, which was granted as the personal possession of the Belgian King Leopold II at the Berlin Conference of 1884, partly as a neutral buffer zone between other imperial spheres, and partly because he claimed he would end slavery and deliver humanitarian benefits like education and Christianity. That was all lies. He delivered some of the most brutal and horrifying exploitation in the dismal annals of European imperialism, creating a vast zone for private corporate exploitation of resources, mainly ivory, rubber, and minerals, using forced labor and prodigious violence.[5] The social dislocation of people fleeing violence produced famine, Europeans arriving in new places transmitted diseases, and villages would be destroyed and their inhabitants massacred for resisting forced-labor quotas. Many histories estimate up to 10 million deaths, but there were no reliable statistics and the murderous colonial authorities did not keep very accurate figures. No matter the case, the atrocities of the Belgian Congo became public in 1904, and horrified even other European imperialists, to the degree that the Belgian government took over the colony in 1908.

The Belgian Congo was the limit case of imperial violence for the purposes of extracting capital and resources. Europeans at the time would have claimed it was not typical, so I will mostly turn here to the "normal" mechanisms of capitalist empire, as made possible by the technologies of the Industrial Revolution. The proliferation of steamships after the 1820s made river travel deep into continental interiors into a cheap, fast, and reliable endeavor. Already in 1820, there were 69 steamboats on the Ohio and Mississippi Rivers; by 1850, there were 740, and their combined engines probably accounted for the majority of steam power in the American economy.[6] Steam made passenger travel and communication faster, but also made the shipment of low-value bulk goods more profitable. White American settlers flooded into the continental interior, annihilating the forests (in part to fuel steamships: One estimate suggests that the 740 Midwestern steamships alone consumed 70 square miles of forest every day), and often bringing Black slaves to grow food, hay, and cotton for export to the East Coast.[7] In this way, the American economy reoriented from a coastal Atlantic system to an interior continental one, which only intensified as railroad construction began in the 1840s.

The North American interior was not the only place drawn into global capitalism by steamships. From the 1830s onward, the British government subsidized a lengthy effort to create a steamship route to India. In 1837, the Peninsular and Oriental Steam Navigation Company (which eventually was sold to Carnival Cruise Line in the year 2000) won a contract from the British navy to deliver mail to Spain and Portugal, and then, in 1840, got the contract to take mail to Egypt. By 1845 it was shipping mail to India, and in 1847, it got involved in opium shipping to China. By the 1860s, the British government was spending about one million pounds per year on steamship subsidies.[8] Steamships must be refueled, so longer lines also incentivized territorial expansion. In 1839, the British annexed Aden, in what is now Yemen, to secure a refueling station on the way to India, which began the long British involvement in the Middle East.[9] In 1840, an expedition of missionaries and merchants steamed up the Niger Delta. Out of 150 Europeans, 130 contracted some form of fever, and about a third of them died, but their surgeon began to experiment with quinine as a prophylactic against malaria. It took years of trial and error, but quinine eventually made the tropics habitable for Europeans, thereby enabling a permanent imperial presence, and far longer expeditions. But first there were supply problems, the story of which neatly illustrates some of the patterns of 19th-century imperial capitalism.

Quinine was extracted from the bark of cinchona trees, which were indigenous to the tropical Andean forests along the northern rim of South America, from Peru to Colombia. Once it was discovered, bark hunters rapidly depleted the forests, leading to swings in prices and unpredictable supply through the 1860s. European governments employed new scientific experts to study the trees and to try to produce their own varieties, and soon the British government established a cinchona plantation at Ootacamund, in what today is Tamil Nadu, in southern India. But they in turn were out-competed by Dutch scientists starting in 1872, who produced a better variety from their plantations in Java and sold it in Amsterdam. "By 1897," Headrick writes, "the Netherlands provided two-thirds of the world's cinchona. The supply rose from 10 tons in 1884 to 516.6 tons in 1913, while the price dropped from twenty-four pounds per kilogram to between one and two in 1913. This was the source of the quinine used during the Scramble for Africa."[10] In this way, a biotechnology derived from a South American tree was produced in Indonesia and sold to British imperialists, who used it to build an empire in Africa.

Continued industrial improvement made steam shipping continually cheaper and more reliable. Better steam engines meant ships could travel farther on the same amount of coal; the spread of telegraph cables after the 1850s meant they could make decisions based on market information before departing for their destinations. Travel and trade were no longer dependent on the weather, nor were they unpredictable and variable to the same degree as before.[11] Bulk commodities could be shipped profitably, contributing to the rise of wool exports from Argentina and wheat from the American plains, which from the late 1860s overtook Russian exports via Odessa as the main source of European food grain.[12] Argentine wool fed continued textile industrialization (especially in France), and a flood of cheap American grain on the world market allowed for low wages.[13] It also undercut existing grain-export industries in Russia, Austria, and the Ottoman Empire, which also depleted the tax revenues of each government.[14] In Argentina, the creation of the wool export market led to an immense expansion of land under cultivation, first producing a boom in small independent farmers (one shepherd could profitably care for 2,000 sheep on 500 hectares of land, with little start-up capital), and then later led to a consolidation in the hands of powerful wealthy families once the supply of new land ran out.[15]

Just as steamships carried bulk goods to a newly integrated world market, so too did they carry people, in unprecedented numbers. The years from the 1840s until 1914 were the age of migration on the largest scale ever seen in human history. In the century from "1815 and 1914, at least 82 million people moved voluntarily from one country to another," especially across the Atlantic, and millions more migrated in forced-labor systems around the Pacific and Indian Oceans.[16] By far the most common destination was the United States, followed by Argentina. There were both push and pull factors involved: Waves of migrants arrived after disasters like the Irish potato famine in the 1840s, the wars of Italian and German unification in the 1860s and 1870s, and Russian pogroms in the first decade of the 1900s. But many people moved looking for higher wages. Better public health, better nutrition, and more food production in Europe led to a demographic boom: The population of Europe nearly tripled between 1700 and 1900, leading to a kind of demographic "rise of the West" that poured over into the Americas, Australia, and New Zealand.[17]

Migration from India began on a large scale in the 1820s, and reached a peak in the 1850s, but still continued on a large scale through 1910, mostly to Southeast Asia and eastern and southern Africa.[18] It was matched by substantial migration *within* India, as political violence, droughts, famines, and deindustrialization sent people looking for means of survival. Chinese migration began after the Opium War of 1842, and reached its peak in the 1860s–80s, often following gold rushes in California, Australia, and finally South Africa. The last substantial phase was 1905, when about 62,000 workers from northern China were shipped in unfree indenture to the gold mines in the Transvaal, the northern part of modern South Africa and Eswatini, undercutting local African wages.[19] In 1906, the Transvaal government required that all Indian and Chinese workers be registered and recorded, in one of many "pass laws" designed to produce racial segregation and control over migrant labor. The protest movement against the 1906 law was led by a young Indian lawyer named Mohandas Gandhi, who had spent a decade trying to organize the Indian migrant community in South Africa.[20]

The "pass laws" were one example of a wider trend. There were essentially two giant oceanic circuits of migration, one in the Atlantic and one in the Pacific and Indian Oceans, and they existed at very different levels of wages and labor freedom—a white, free, high-wage circuit and a brown, poor, largely unfree one.[21] Wherever they met or overlapped, exclusionary racial laws followed. The American Chinese Exclusion Act of 1882 is probably the most famous example, but there were many others: Chinese Restriction Acts in Australia in 1888 and the "White Australia policy" formalized in 1901, a poll tax in New Zealand in 1881, a head tax in Canada in 1885, and the Aliens Act in Britain in 1905, which was aimed at excluding Russian Jews fleeing pogroms. In this way, the concept of citizenship and labor rights was re-formed on a global level, creating what was then known as a "color line" that structured global politics and labor markets, both within empires and without.[22]

Steamships were vital for building a global market and for extending empire to places previously unreachable, but nothing exemplified 19th-century capitalism more than railroads. They were the most expensive and complicated economic projects of the age, absorbing enormous amounts of capital and labor, contributing to several global cycles of boom-and-bust in financial markets, and stitching agricultural interiors into the new global commodity markets. Railroads even refashioned people's experience of time, from rapid movement across long distances to understanding precise timetables to the creation of standardized time zones in 1883, provoked by the need to coordinate rail traffic.[23]

The first commercial steam-engine railroads were constructed in the mid-1820s: the Stockton & Darlington in England, which mainly carried coal, and the Baltimore & Ohio in the United States in 1827. But railroads remained relatively small, and concentrated in coal and iron haulage, and also, through the 1830s, were often pulled by draft animals. The real boom in railroads happened in the second half of the century. In 1850, there were only 2,201 miles of railroad track in the United States (and about 6,000 miles in England), but the number more than tripled over the next decade.[24] The 1850s saw the first railroads built in Norway, Brazil, Romania, Australia, Portugal, and the Ottoman Empire. The first American transcontinental railroad opened in 1869. In just four years, between 1869 and 1873, over 24,000 new miles were built in the United States, and in 1877, the American network was more than 79,000 miles, owned by about 50 corporations for a value of over $5 billion, at a time when the US government's outstanding debt was $2.1 billion.[25] The Pennsylvania Railroad Company was the largest of them, and indeed the largest corporation in the world by revenue.[26]

Railroads were gargantuan undertakings. The Pennsylvania Company employed about 200,000 people, and around the world, railroad construction sites were at the center of the employment of cheap migrant labor. They also functioned a bit like banks, providing mortgages along their lines, as well as elevator receipts for deposited grain, which circulated like local currency, and eventually they extended credit from the Chicago Board of Trade to various "line companies," thereby forming a credit chain from farmers to urban retailers.[27]

The coal needs of the railroads created company towns in southern Appalachia and Colorado, where hundreds of thousands of workers mined hundreds of millions of tons of coal per year: 243 million tons by 1900, which overtook Britain to make the United

States the world's leading coal producer.[28] Thanks to the railroads themselves, places like the coal towns of Colorado's Front Range were only five days from anywhere in the United States, and at most a month from anywhere else in the world.[29] Fossil energy allowed for the collapse of space and time.

The railroads also connected agricultural producers to markets. Four lines in Argentina connected the inland wool districts to the port.[30] In his classic book *Nature's Metropolis*, the environmental historian William Cronon shows how the railroad network that centered on Chicago created a vast agricultural hinterland throughout the core of the United States, converting immense amounts of land into lumber, grain, and above all, meat production.[31] These resources would be shipped by train from dozens of transit points to the core in Chicago, where they would be refined and processed, then shipped out to supply the rapidly growing and urbanizing East Coast cities. The Union Stock Yards in Chicago was a united project of the nine largest railroad companies and the Chicago Pork Packers Association, and once it was fully operational in the 1870s, it could process 21,000 cattle, 75,000 hogs, 22,000 sheep, and 200 horses all at the same time, turning them into half a million dollars in transactions every day.[32] Cincinnati was the second meatpacking city, able to slaughter 21,000 cattle and 75,000 pigs simultaneously, killing and processing over 17 million animals by 1905.[33] These vast plains of death and decay formed the setting of Upton Sinclair's classic 1906 novel, *The Jungle*, which led to sanitation reforms rather than socialism.

The American continent was not the only one tied by railroads to the global market. The British Parliament guaranteed 4.5 to 5 percent profits to Indian railroads after the 1850s, with any deficit to be paid by the Indian treasury. As a result, by the mid-1870s, India had over 5,000 miles of track, with an investment capital of some £95 million, and nearly all of its industrial equipment imported from Britain.[34] By 1900, there were over 23,000 track miles, and upwards of 338,000 people worked in the railroad sector, increasingly government owned after the 1880s.[35] It was by far the most expensive investment program in the history of the British Empire, intended to be useful for military purposes and famine relief. For those reasons, the impact of railroads on colonial India continues to be at the heart of debate over the consequences of the empire.[36] There were terrible famines in India in 1876–78, 1896–97, and 1899–1900, which together killed between 13 and 16 million people.[37] Some argue that the British officials thought famines were a problem of distribution, not production, so they thought building railroads relieved them of any further responsibilities and markets would solve the rest. Others argue that access to cheap imported food (especially Burmese rice) meant that Indians switched to cash-crop production (especially raw cotton, and especially when the disruption of the American Civil War in cotton markets caused a price spike), which left them vulnerable to price swings and crop failures. Still others argue that railroads and global markets meant India continued to export wheat, or to move it to areas following price incentives instead of humanitarian relief, so (as with Ireland in the 1840s) a commitment to laissez-faire ideology produced mortality disasters. And still others argue that railroads produced price convergence, market integration, and lower freight costs, which together had the effect of raising real incomes and providing social-capital investment that India otherwise would not have been able to provide for itself.[38] That counterfactual seems impossible to resolve. For our purposes, the point is that the railroads were tools of empire, and they brought capitalism, not humanitarianism or stability, everywhere they went.

All around the world, governments built railroads to stimulate cash-crop commodity production, from cocoa in West Africa to coffee in East Africa and Brazil, cotton in India, and wool, nitrates, and copper in South America.[39] Colonial and independent governments alike were funded by foreign capital, almost all of it British.

Britain owned the companies and manufactured the locomotives and freight cars, and often also owned the commodities that were shipped, and the shipping lines they were loaded onto. In this way, railroads connected the worlds of financial capitalism and actual territorial imperialism as well as informal empire, labor struggle, and a global division of labor.

Beyond transportation, other technologies aided in the expansion of empires. Standard military guns were effectively unchanged from roughly 1700 until the 1840s: slow, dangerous, and accurate only at about 50 yards, which is a distance that many people can throw a ball. In 1842, the Prussian Army adopted a new gun that was far more efficient and accurate, and then, in the 1850s, first Americans and then the British developed a system of interchangeable parts and industrial manufacturing for weapons. In 1884, an inventor named Hiram Maxim, who had also developed automatic sprinklers and coffee substitutes, created the first machine gun.[40] These guns in turn needed a steel industry, a precision machine-tool industry, and a chemical industry to make smokeless powder. As Headrick puts it, "Industrialized nations had the wherewithal to make such weapons. Only the larger European countries and the United States had the steel mills, chemical plants, and arms factories they needed to arm themselves. The Latin American republics imported what they could afford. The rest of the world fell far behind."[41]

Telegraphs were another essential technology for governing empires. In the early modern period, it might take 18 months or longer for a message to travel round trip from Amsterdam to Batavia, making any claim to imperial control difficult to substantiate. The first submarine telegraph cable was laid across the Hooghly River in Calcutta, but it took two more years to discover that gutta-percha sap from Malaysia could work as an insulator to keep it from immediately decaying.[42] By 1852, a cable crossed the English Channel, and another went to Ireland. In 1859, a cable crossed the

Red Sea: It weighed one ton per mile, and was soon eaten by teredo worms. The first cable line to India cost £800,000 and never successfully transmitted a single message, but by the 1870s, an imperial system was up and running that could convey information from India to London in about five hours.[43] On land, telegraphs followed railroads: Washington, DC, was connected to Baltimore in 1844, and the American coasts were connected in 1861. In the 1870s, most telegraph companies in the British Empire were consolidated into a giant monopoly called Eastern and Associated Telegraph Company, which owned almost three-quarters of the 190,000 miles of submarine cables in the world in 1900. The network hinged on remote places like the islands of Ascension, Saint Helena, Guam, and Midway, thereby bringing capitalism to some of the most isolated parts of the world.[44]

The story of the West African palm oil industry provides another clear picture of the various mechanisms of capitalist imperialism. The British abolition of the slave trade in 1807 undercut the fiscal basis of several West African polities and left them without an export commodity to trade for European imports, especially the guns that they had been buying in large numbers. (During the last decade of the slave trade, Europeans probably sold 300,000 to 400,000 guns per year to West Africa, half of them from Britain.)[45] Faced with a need for exports, and with an excess of slaves who could not be sold, West Africans turned to palm oil, which was in high demand as an industrial lubricant.[46] In some cases, as in Dahomey, states were unable to maintain centralized control as new people entered the market, opening routes for social mobility, while in others, like in Asante, government distribution of monopolies facilitated a successful commercial transition by the 1870s.[47] So in some cases the development of palm oil exports happened thanks to government coordination, and sometimes at private initiative. From the 1815–20 period to 1845–50, Britain's imports of palm oil increased by a factor of 10, to over 22,000 tons valued at some £725,000 per year.[48] The palm oil trade followed the same locations and power structures as the slave trade had, and involved many of the same people, skills, and knowledge. But the new scale of the trade increased land under cultivation and provided regular buyers, which meant more Africans switched to palm oil gathering and processing, and that meant more competition, more bankruptcies, more turmoil.[49]

In 1851, the British bombarded Lagos and pushed out the local ruler, the Oba Kosoko, whom they viewed as a pillar of the slave trade. A permanent formal colonial presence in Lagos after 1861 brought more British investment. Local traders began pledging property as security for loans, creating a mortgage market and a commercial credit system.[50] By the 1870s, there were 20 European firms operating 60 trading posts with over 200 merchants in the Niger Delta, and four companies operating steamship lines connecting them.[51] These ships would occasionally be attacked by locals, and the Royal Navy would respond by destroying towns, like Onitsha, Idah, and Aboh. The regional political fragmentation meant a series of increasingly escalating local campaigns of retaliation that ended in the occupation of much of Nigeria and the establishment of the Oil Rivers Protectorate in 1884. It continued to expand and be amalgamated with other protectorates through 1914, when it was the core of the entire colonial possession of British Nigeria. The annexation satisfied merchant demands for law and order, as well as a government to recognize and enforce land transfers and property rights, which became additionally important once railway construction began.[52] In this way, an African response to the end of slavery depended on British industrial demand, and British merchants who profited from satisfying that demand produced a set of incentives that led to violence and colonial occupation. Without steamships and quinine, the British presence would have been impossible.

The Opium Wars in China provide another illustrative example of how European imperialism worked, but in the context of a centralized state. The practice of mixing opium with tobacco to smoke it originated in Java in the 17th century, and it moved from there to the (temporary) Dutch colony of Taiwan, and on to the coastal cities of China by the 1720s.[53] As the 18th century wore on, three trends converged: First, the age-old drain of silver from Europe to China continued; second, the Qing rulers allowed for trade and commercial contact on a larger scale, but confined it to customs stations where foreigners had to register and pay taxes, with Canton (now Guangzhou) the most significant. And third, in 1757, the East India Company took territorial control over Bengal and began collecting taxes on land and agriculture, expanding the British Empire in India. The rise of the opium trade from India to China combined all three of these longer changes.

The East India Company did not itself traffic in opium. Instead it had a monopoly on production in Bengal and would sell its opium to private traders at auctions in Calcutta, and they would ship it to Canton, thus bearing the risk.[54] They would be paid in silver or bills of exchange, which in turn would be used to repay the company or buy goods from Europe. But although the company had a monopoly on Bengal production, it could not control a rival trade from western India, and after a series of failed attempts to block this rival out, in the 1820s it decided to compete on price by ramping up production and flooding the market.[55] The timing was not fortuitous. Global silver flows slumped as the wars of liberation in Latin America disrupted the supply. The collapse of a unified Spanish imperial silver standard meant its replacement by a wide variety of new types of coins, from new mints and new Latin American governments, which varied widely in quality and fineness.[56] Supply disruption and unpredictable quality produced internal monetary disorder in China, including the hoarding of quality silver, and that compounded social problems because peasants had to pay taxes in fixed amounts of silver, which was increasingly difficult to acquire. Much of the local-level commerce was still conducted in copper coins, and those soon depreciated in value relative to silver, meaning that by the 1830s, the real tax burden had increased by something like 40 percent.[57] The government blamed foreign trade; peasants blamed corrupt government officials (who would sometimes manipulate the exchange rate and pocket the difference), and the pressures of a century of population growth meant declining available land and a surplus of educated young men who could not find prestigious jobs in government administration. The result was a weak government with continual problems in legitimacy and enforcement.

In 1837–38, a reformer named Deng Tingzhen cracked down on the opium trade and almost wiped it out. Another scholar-official, named Lin Zexu, wrote a famous open letter to Queen Victoria, hoping to persuade her that the opium trade was morally wrong. Charles Elliot, the British superintendent of trade in China, tried to defuse the growing conflict by cooperating, and ordered British traders to hand over their opium supplies, claiming they would be reimbursed by the British government. The government, however, had no intention of paying out some £2 million to opium traders (who were a relatively weak, dispersed, and disliked constituency), especially since it was in the midst of paying a £20 million indemnity to former slave owners for the loss of their human property at abolition.[58] It was cheaper to send gunboats, which rapidly succeeded at destroying, bombarding, and blockading Chinese ports and ships. As a result, the Treaty of Nanking in 1842 was the first of what are known as "unequal treaties," several of which followed throughout the 19th century. China opened five ports to British merchants and gave over Hong Kong to the British Empire, as well as paying an indemnity of £21 million, and granted British merchants exemptions from local laws.[59] The treaty did not legalize the opium trade: That followed the second Opium War, in 1858. And it did not deliver long-term opium profits to the East India Company, because once the trade was legalized, local merchants squeezed out the European middlemen and utterly dominated the trade by the 1870s. It did, however, produce long-run social dislocation in China, and served as a precedent for how to use violence to force legal and commercial privileges out of the Chinese government.

The violent opening of the Chinese treaty ports should not be taken as a claim that there was no such thing as indigenous Chinese capitalism, or that the Chinese economy consisted of a vibrant, foreign-oriented coast and a stagnant, timeless agrarian hinterland. Chinese merchants had of course been engaged in substantial trade and commerce, both internally and with Korea and Southeast Asia. Before the 19th century, there were many *capitalists* in China, though I am skeptical of a socially-general *capitalism*. By the 19th century, there were signs of substantial capitalist sectors. The Sichuan salt industry is a classic example: It lasted for more than a century, involving probably a million people, a third of whom (plus 30,000 buffalo) were involved in direct salt production, boiling brine by burning underground natural gas.[60] The salt, as much as 390 million pounds per year, was sold across a wide expanse of central China, an arc from Yunnan to Guizhou to Hubei.[61] Also across the 19th century, merchant bankers called *piaohao* in Shanxi province engaged in an immense network of remittances, moving money for government and business alike. Especially when the movement of physical silver was difficult and dangerous (as during the long chaos of the Taiping Rebellion, 1850–64), about 30 different *piaohao* banks operated branches in 40 different cities in China, moving hundreds of thousands of payments from place to place.[62] This certainly constituted a kind of financial capitalism, to add to the salt industry's industrial capitalism. But until 1904, China had no limited-liability law and no means to reduce the risk of business debt in bankruptcy court, so Chinese firms remained relatively undercapitalized, and the combination of a large state and limited wage labor markets meant that Chinese capitalism never became socially general in the way it did elsewhere.[63] It was also pushed off course by the intrusion of foreign imperial projects.

Unlike in West Africa, in China there was a unified central government to grant concessions to Europeans, and to enforce property rights, thus obviating the need to set up a permanent occupying colonial government. But both stories began with merchants meeting local resistance and calling upon the greater industrialized violence of the empire, which then forced larger-scale transformations and subjugation than the merchants had initially imagined. We speak of "British" or "European" imperialism, but imperial violence was very often a matter of private, local initiative, almost entrepreneurial in its character, and state involvement came as a kind of bailout when private actors got into trouble, socializing the costs and privatizing the gains.[64] In both cases, the imperial intervention would have been impossible without the new technologies of steamships, guns, and ultimately, finance.

The capitalist expansion of empire in the late 19th century was primarily a European phenomenon, but with two corollaries: the United States and Japan. The United States had continued territorial imperial expansion from its inception, reaching the Pacific coast through an expansionary war with Mexico in 1848. It continued this process of colonial settlement and the different governance of territories and populations until well into the 20th century.[65] In the 1890s, it began a phase of Pacific imperial expansion. The government of Hawaii was overthrown in 1893 by a committee of American businessmen, and in 1898, following war with Spain, the United States seized the Philippines and Puerto Rico. By then it was also actively involved in the financial imperialism that will be discussed in the next section, mainly in Latin America. The Philippines especially became a laboratory for the American version of capitalist imperialism. The Americans brought their gold-standard system, which eased the flow of trade and movement of capital, but which brought budgetary austerity for the colonial government. As the historian Lisandro Claudio argues, the austerity policies that have become common in the 20th century actually originated in a colonial context: Low inflation, strong currency, and budget restraint were all tools for disciplining colonized people who were thought to be unable to control their own economic lives.[66]

Japan was a surprising exception to the club of imperialists. Until the 1850s, it remained isolated from the rest of the world, with a restriction on overseas trade except through the station at Nagasaki that the Dutch had captured from the Portuguese in 1641. Then an American naval fleet, using threats of force and intimidation, coerced the long-reigning Tokugawa shogunate to open to American trade, partly as a station for coal replenishment for ships bound for China. These treaties were widely perceived by the Japanese elite as a humiliation, and provoked a political crisis that led to the collapse of the Tokugawa ruling family and the creation of a self-consciously modernizing new oligarchical government in 1868 under the authority of the restored emperor.[67]

This new Meiji elite embarked on a large-scale project of political, military, educational, economic, and cultural reform. They modeled themselves on Germany—newly unified, militarily successful, rapidly industrializing. They employed thousands of foreign experts as advisers to modernize their universities, military, and industries. The first railroad opened in 1872, between Tokyo and Yokohama, and the traditional textile industry mechanized rapidly through the 1870s and 1880s. The government heavily subsidized giant centralized companies that coordinated economic activity across sectors: a distinctive form of industrial organization known as *zaibatsu*, which went on to be a feature of Japanese capitalism through the 20th century. But it seemed above all that the central proof of great-power success in the last half of the 19th century was the successful acquisition of an empire, so the new elite immediately began a project of creating one in the Pacific.[68]

Today we think of Hokkaido as the northernmost island of Japan, but that was the result of a settler colonial project that began in 1869, one year after the creation of the Meiji government. With American agricultural advisers, the Japanese Development Commission displaced the Indigenous Ainu people, relocated thousands of Japanese farmers to Hokkaido, and founded the capital city of Sapporo in the 1870s—about the same time that Minneapolis was converted from fort to town. Okinawa was next, annexed in 1879, followed by a war with much-beleaguered China in 1894–95. That war was a test of Japan's newly industrialized and re-formed military, and it succeeded, allowing the Japanese to annex Taiwan. An unequal treaty of 1876 opened Korean ports to Japanese trade, and in 1878, Japanese investors founded a branch of the Dai-Ichi Bank with the ability to issue banknotes, slowly making it into the de facto central bank of Korea.[69] A continual flow of settlers, merchants, landlords, bankers, and sometimes-violent political meddling pulled Korea into the Japanese imperial sphere well before its formal acquisition in 1910.[70] In 1905, Japan went to war with Russia and scored a shocking victory, provoking an attempted revolution in Russia and resulting in Japanese control of Sakhalin Island, and the Chinese city then called Port Arthur, now called Dalian.

The story of Japanese imperialism is striking in the ways that it exactly mirrored the patterns of European imperialism.[71] It depended on industrial production of warfare (ships, guns, trains) and on new forms of finance like central banks and sovereign debt. The Tokyo–Yokohama railroad was financed by loans borrowed in London, on a yen-to-gold exchange rate established in 1871 to allow for trade and capital flows with Britain.[72] A second loan in 1873 converted old samurai pensions into government bonds, thereby tying the old elite to the new. When it defeated China in 1895, Japan extracted an indemnity of 230 million silver *taels* (equivalent to about 25 percent of Japan's GDP that year) and used it as the basis of central-bank reserves to adopt the gold standard, just as Germany used its indemnity from the Franco-Prussian War of 1871 to adopt gold.[73] The remainder went to cover the costs of the war and to fund the construction of the Yawata steelworks. The indemnity itself was borrowed on the London market, so the entire process of the Sino-Japanese war was funded by European capital.

■ ■ ■

In Africa, the main form of capitalist imperialism was occupation and the establishment of formal colonial governments. In China, it was unequal treaties and special port zones. In the Ottoman Empire, it was concessions and capitulations, when core state functions or property were sold to or seized by European investors. In Latin America and other independent countries, it was debt-for-equity swaps and receiverships, when tax collection, government assets, or export revenues were granted to foreign investors, usually bondholders, after a government debt crisis. And all over the world, foreign (mostly British) direct investment in railroads, ports, and other infrastructure meant that much of the new apparatus of the global market economy was owned by Europeans. Each of these processes is a different version of financial imperialism, each with different implications.

Britain invested abroad an average of 5 percent of gross national product during 1873–1913, rising to 10 percent at the end: a truly immense scale, even by today's standards.[74] In peak years, £4.5 for every human in England, Scotland, and Wales went abroad, at a time when average annual income was about £40 per year.[75] France was second, at about half as much, also increasing at the end. It is useful to split the capital flows into those going to independent countries and those going to the colonies or other imperial territories, and later to compare each to rates of profit and returns for domestic investment. Table 2 below shows the main sources and destinations of investment in the late 19th century. The overall picture is clear: Britain was the main supplier of the world's finance, but the empire was not the major recipient. The United States was by far the largest destination of British capital and the main imperial recipient was Canada.[76] Capital sequentially incorporated new parts of the world into the global market, starting with the United States in the 1870s and earlier, then Australia and Argentina in the 1880s, then Canada and Brazil around 1900, with a much smaller series of bursts of investment in the colonies.[77] But the consequences of capital investment in small, poor imperial possessions had disproportionate long-run consequences for the people and economies on the receiving end.

It is also useful to distinguish between private investment, in companies and enterprises, and public investment in government debt. Throughout the late 19th century, about two-thirds of British

Table 2. **Proportion of English, French, and German Foreign Investment by Destination, 1870–1914**[78]

	England	France	Germany
Russia	3.4%	25.1%	7.7%
Ottoman Empire	1.0%	7.3%	7.7%
Total Europe	9.7%	61.1%	53.3%
United States	20.5%	4.4%	15.7%
Canada	10.1%		
Australia	8.3%		—
Latin America (total)	17.7%	13.3%	16.2%
Africa (total)	9.1%	7.3%	8.5%
Asia (total)	11.5%	4.9%	4.3%
Colonies	16.9%	8.9%	2.6%

overseas investment was private, and more than half of that money went into transport and infrastructure, especially railroads.[79] Government finance was more common in the empire than elsewhere, absorbing over half of all investment, partly because colonial debt was guaranteed by Parliament, so it was a safe asset. Transport, agriculture, and extractive industries (like mining gold in Mysore or coal in the Bengal uplands) were overrepresented in imperial investment relative to elsewhere.[80]

There was no clear relationship between empire and profitability. Over 1860–1914, profit rates in Britain averaged about 1.6 percent, though they declined toward the end to about 1.3 percent. Imperial profits also averaged about 1.6 percent, though their decline was less pronounced, down to about 1.5 percent per year.[81] Returns for the agricultural and extractive sectors were higher in the empire than at home, though higher still in independent foreign countries. Railroads were far more lucrative in foreign countries than in either Britain or the empire. Indeed, British capitalists invested in railroads in 70 countries and colonies, and in Latin America, 75 percent of railroad miles were owned by foreign firms, 70 percent of them by British investors.[82] Commerce and industry was more profitable in Britain than abroad.[83]

But beyond profit, overseas finance had other consequences. Many governments borrowed, especially to fight wars, and later found that they could not repay their debts, because of either defeat or disadvantageous movements in the prices for their main export commodities. Between 1875 and 1899, at least 22 different countries defaulted on their external debt at least 28 times.[84] About half of them experienced what economic historians euphemistically call "supersanctions," meaning either military intervention or some form of foreign financial control.[85] Outright military intervention was relatively rare, though always a credible threat, as with British occupation in Egypt after 1882, or the British, German, and Italian naval blockade of Venezuela in 1902, or the American invasion of Haiti in 1915. More often, a default would be followed by a renegotiation of the debt, and the new agreement would involve foreign ownership of public assets, or a swap of outstanding debt for majority shares in some domestic industry or infrastructure. To take one example, Peru defaulted in 1849.[86] The new renegotiated loan was backed by half of all proceeds from sales of guano, which was the most important fertilizer in the world before new chemical alternatives were developed. New loans were issued in 1854, 1862, and 1865, all secured by guano sales, but the last one also had a debt-for-equity provision. When Peru was unable to pay, the state monopoly on guano was handed over to Dreyfus Brothers & Co. of Paris, which also became the official financial agent for the Peruvian government abroad. In that capacity, Peru secured another loan in 1872, two-thirds of which went to repay past loans, and the rest was spent on railroads.

Similar foreign takeover of state assets or land-tax revenues occurred frequently, as a result of government debt crises. One early example was Spain, where the mercury mines at Almadén that had once enabled the silver extraction from Potosí were finally leased to the Rothschild banking family in exchange for loans to fight the First Carlist War in 1833–40. Table 3 below is a minimum list of debt-for-equity swaps and the assets turned over as collateral.

The alternative to taking over assets was receiverships, when debtors surrendered control of tax administration (often customs stations in ports) to foreign bondholders, who would set up a parallel bureaucracy to collect revenues, register and supervise economic activity, and sometimes even control budgetary spending. There were receiverships in Tunisia in 1870–81; Egypt with the British occupation in 1882–1913; parts of Ottoman Turkey also in 1882–1913; Serbia in 1895–1913; Greece in 1898–1913; Venezuela in 1902–3; Uruguay in 1903; Morocco in 1905–11; the Dominican Republic in 1905–13; Costa Rica and China both

Table 3. **Debt-for-Equity Swaps, 1835–1906**[87]

Place	Year	Assets
Spain	1835	Mercury
Ecuador	1855	Land
Paraguay	1855	Land
Colombia	1861	Land
Peru	1865	Guano
Costa Rica	1871	Railroads
Paraguay	1877	Railroads
Serbia	1881	Railroads, salt, tobacco
Costa Rica	1885	Railroads
Venezuela	1886	Railroads
Portugal	1891	Tobacco
Greece	1893	Salt, petroleum, cigarette paper
Dominican Republic	1893	Railroads
El Salvador	1899	Railroads
Bulgaria	1904	Tobacco
Brazil	1906	Coffee

in 1911; Nicaragua in 1912; and Liberia in 1912–13.[88] So each of these independent countries lost control of its revenue collection, government budgets, or exports. The Ottoman case is especially instructive: The empire first borrowed from foreigners in 1854, and two years later a consortium of London bankers established the International Ottoman Bank, which acquired the monopoly on the issue of paper money within the empire. With successive debt crises, the IOB obtained the right to have all state revenue paid in and disbursed out through its coffers, essentially becoming the Ottoman central bank, but entirely under foreign ownership.[89] By

1881, the Ottoman fiscal system was almost entirely under foreign financial control. Japan followed the same procedure in Korea.

The United States was particularly enamored with receiverships, often claiming that its experts would bring better management, efficiency, and state capacity. One study of eight American receiverships in Latin America, which involved the ownership or operation of customhouses, taxation, government debt ceilings, and budgetary expenditures, found that American intervention failed *in every case* to improve revenue or bureaucratic efficiency and capacity.[90] Instead, investments led to receiverships, which led to empire. As the economic historian Noel Maurer puts it, "Once American officials were on the ground managing core state functions, it became impossible to withdraw when the countries fell into political instability. In Haiti and the Dominican Republic, the United States installed American occupation governments. In Nicaragua, the United States never officially displaced the local government, but in practice this was a distinction without a difference."[91] The results also had an impact on financial profits: Over 1870–1914, the real return on sovereign bonds averaged 6.19 percent, but the highest returns were for serial defaulters, which had a premium of 4.2 percent over safe, secure British debt in that same period.[92] In sum, foreign debt was profitable for investors, and the mechanics of imperial intervention or "supersanctions" were effective at continuing to extract returns for investors, undercutting state capacity and governmental legitimacy in the debtor countries, which were often locked into serial defaults and onerous debt they could never repay, subject to foreign fiscal control they could never escape.

■ ■ ■

Despite the huge volumes of foreign investment, in practice, actual money seldom left London. Instead, companies and governments maintained accounts with London banks and sold their bonds and stocks on the London market, often with the help of London underwriters, who are financial intermediaries that assess risk and sell assets. Payments and debts would be settled by clearing accounts at different London banks. The whole system hinged on London and operated through the free flow of capital in the gold-standard system.

We've seen how early central banks were created as part of the Financial Revolution, and how a series of errors and short-term decisions at the Royal Mint in London led to the accidental adoption of the gold standard in Britain. For more than a century, the rest of the world continued on a variety of bimetallic systems, since Spanish silver remained abundant, globally recognized, and still the accepted currency in China.[93] But countries that wished to trade with Britain increasingly needed either gold or currencies backed by gold in their central banks.[94] In, say, 1730, global trade with Britain was substantial, but much of it was within the British Empire, and not nearly on the staggering scale that it would be a century later. By 1830, however, the Industrial Revolution meant Britain was exporting a gargantuan volume of cotton textiles, guns, and other manufactured goods to the entire world, which meant a stronger incentive for countries to move entirely to a gold standard. As some countries joined, network effects grew stronger: the more countries within the gold network, the higher the costs of staying out. There were also gold strikes in California in 1849 and Australia in 1851 (and then in South Africa in 1886 and Alaska in 1896), which vastly increased the world supplies of gold relative to silver. In the case of California, the establishment of US rule and the ensuing mining settlement accentuated an ongoing demographic catastrophe for the Indigenous people. Disease, forced labor, and captivity by colonists and missionaries had already reduced the California Indigenous population by at least half; between 1846 and 1870, the Native American population of the state plunged from 150,000 to 30,000 thanks to dislocation, forced removal to reservations, unfree labor, and outright massacre, in a process that many historians now call a genocide.[95] South Africa, Australia, and Alaska were also places where gold mining and mass settler colonial violence went hand in hand.

The tipping point for the establishment of the gold standard as the international monetary system was the early 1870s. In 1873, the victorious unified Germany, having defeated France in the Franco-Prussian war two years earlier, used the indemnity it extracted as the basis for its gold reserves. The United States also demonetized silver in 1873, in what was then known as the "Crime of 1873" because it seemed later to signal the start of a long, grinding price deflation that was blamed on insufficient supplies of specie.[96] Denmark, Sweden, Norway, and the Netherlands also went on gold in the 1870s, and countries continued to adopt it until 1914. Austria-Hungary used a loan in 1892 to get on gold and the colonial government of India demonetized silver and moved to gold in 1893. Japan denominated the yen in gold immediately after the monetary instability of the end of the Tokugawa regime and the start of the Meiji, then conducted a decade of deliberate deflation to drive down domestic prices and wages (which helped make exports competitive) before adopting the gold standard entirely with the Chinese indemnity.[97]

In order to go on the gold standard, countries had to do three things: They had to specify how much gold backed each unit of currency (one US dollar was 1.50463 grams of gold, for instance), they had to allow for the free import and export of gold, and they had to declare that their central bank (or its equivalent) would exchange currency for gold at that stated, fixed rate. These may not sound like important rules, but they had world-altering consequences.

Since currencies represented a set quantity of gold, and since a gram of gold is a gram of gold everywhere, the result was fixed exchange rates between currencies. Thus, if one dollar was about 1.5 grams, and one British pound was about 7.3 grams, then the dollar-pound exchange rate would be $7.3 \div 1.5 = 4.8$ dollars per pound. And indeed it was, for the entirety of the late 19th century. Fixed exchange rates are great for business, because they are predictable and allow for businesses to easily and accurately conduct international trade. Capital could flow freely across international borders, including in the form of physical gold: exactly the process of international finance described above. Central banks had to keep gold in their vaults in order to exchange it for currency. The Bank of England needed 7.3 grams per pound, never the total amount of pounds in circulation, but some large proportion. In a moment of panic or crisis, banks, investors, and businesspeople would rush to central banks to exchange their currency for gold, including foreign investors or investors who otherwise wanted to send their money abroad, to get higher rates of return or to escape the panic. Gold would drain out of central-bank vaults, raising the possibility that they would eventually run out of gold and have to suspend conversion of currency to gold, effectively leaving the gold standard. Bankers and policymakers perceived that as an unthinkable disaster—they were willing to temporarily suspend conversion in a crisis moment, but always on the very public understanding that they would never, ever leave gold permanently. Faced with a drain of gold, what could central banks do? They could raise interest rates. If interest rates are, say, 2 percent, perhaps investors are scared and willing to take their money out and either hoard it or send it elsewhere. But what about at 5 percent? Or 8 percent? There is some tipping point where the interest rate is high enough that people will be willing to put their money in the bank, even at some risk. The saying in the late 19th century was that at 7 percent, the Bank of England could draw in gold from the moon.[98]

The problem is that raising interest rates in a crisis makes the crisis worse. Money that goes into the Bank of England's vaults does not get spent on goods and services. Businesses do not borrow to expand production if they have to borrow at 10 percent. Businesses that have to borrow constantly and are earning, say, a 5 percent profit may fail if they have to borrow at 10 percent. People don't buy houses, businesses close, people lose their jobs. When they lose their jobs, they don't spend, so other businesses don't make money, and *they* close, and more people lose their jobs. For these reasons, in today's world, when a crisis hits, central banks move to *lower* interest rates, not raise them.

Economic historians say that the gold-standard system meant that there was no policy autonomy: Central bankers could not respond to crises the way they would have liked, but instead were forced to respond the way the gold standard made them respond. Put another way, the gold-standard system facilitated a world of international trade and free capital flows, but enforced the costs of crises on domestic working populations by requiring central bankers to save themselves by raising interest rates and making crises worse for everyone else. And crises abounded: There was a major international financial crisis in 1825, 1837, 1848, 1857, 1866, 1873, 1879, 1884, 1893, 1897, 1907, and 1913, at the very least. The system "worked" because most of the people harmed were disenfranchised, and most central banks were privately owned corporations anyway, so when they moved to protect themselves, their profits, their shareholders, and the international monetary system, they did so by wreaking misery and ruin on millions of people without any possibility of democratic accountability.

■ ■ ■

We've already seen many examples of workers resisting the spread of industrial capitalism. The Luddites, the Swing rioters, and the machine-breakers were all engaged in a kind of collective labor action, but without much in the way of permanent institutional structures, political parties, or coherent working-class ideology.

In some ways, the spread and intensity of strikes and labor conflicts after the 1870s is a measure of the spread of industrialization from Britain to the European continent and the United States.

Where industry and factories and railroads went, labor conflict followed, usually beginning with relatively powerful artisanal skilled workers who were being displaced by the new technologies, then moving on to mass proletarian strikes organized by unions or political organizations. By the first decade of the 20th century, mass strikes and general strikes were appearing on national scales, incorporating hundreds of thousands of workers across many branches of economic activity, and threatening the political order itself. Anticapitalist working-class political parties also began to appear, especially as voting franchises slowly and reluctantly expanded to include poorer men (with a few exceptions, women's suffrage began only during and after the First World War). In 1880, these parties were negligible, including only the German Social Democratic Party, which was small and fractious. But by 1914, they were major political players in most industrialized countries, even the United States, where the socialist Eugene Debs got one million votes for president while in jail.[99]

But it was unions more than socialist parties that accounted for most of the labor conflict in the late 19th century. Unions mostly acquired legal standing between about 1865 and 1875, so even conservative governments were unable to simply abolish them, even though they had few qualms about using the military or police to help employers break strikes. In the summer of 1877, railroad workers in Martinsburg, West Virginia, went on strike to oppose a second round of wage cuts imposed by the Baltimore & Ohio railroad company. A violent attempt by the local militia to suppress it made it a famous cause, and the strike spread along the railway lines so that within six days, workers were on strike in West Virginia, Maryland, Pennsylvania, New York, New Jersey, Ohio, Indiana, Kentucky, Missouri, and Iowa, comprising maybe 80,000 railroad workers and half a million others.[100] Over the course of the next 45 days, federal troops moved from city to city, violently dispersing crowds and breaking the strikes.

That was nowhere near the end. Hundreds of thousands of coal miners across the United States went on strike in 1894. There was a bitter strike among silver miners in Leadville, Colorado, in 1896–97, a strike for the eight-hour day and against wage cuts among smelters in the Front Range in 1899, and another large-scale miners' strike in 1903–4 across the entire state of Colorado.[101] Prolonged strikes in the Colorado coalfields in 1913–14 culminated in the Ludlow Massacre of April 20, 1914, when soldiers from the Colorado National Guard murdered 21 people, including women and children.[102] American labor conflict continued well into the 20th century: The Battle of Blair Mountain in West Virginia in 1921 was the largest armed conflict on US territory since the Civil War, pitting coal miners who were attempting to unionize against strikebreakers, police, and the National Guard.

In France there were mass-strike waves in 1890, 1899, 1900, 1904, and 1906, each involving hundreds of thousands of workers, who, increasingly, were unskilled proletarian factory workers, whereas earlier in the century strikers had mainly been skilled artisanal workers trying to protect their privileged positions.[103] One study found a total of 2,924 strikes in France between 1871 and 1890.[104] Labor conflict in France had a particularly political tinge, because of the memory of the Paris Commune of 1871. Following the defeat of the French army in the Franco-Prussian War, the workers and citizens of Paris had declared a popular revolutionary government, which ruled the city for two months. The French army, despite its recent defeat, fought its way into Paris, suppressed the Commune, and killed something like 10,000 to 15,000 people in the process. The leaders of the Commune were executed, others were deported to the colonies. The story of the Commune became and has remained a famous example in radical left political history.

Labor uprisings were violently repressed around the world, from Colorado to South Africa to India. In 1869, striking iron puddlers in Belgium were shot by the civil militia; road workers were shot in Draveil-Vigneux in France in 1908; in 1906, the Chilean army murdered at least 58 striking railway workers in the coastal town of Antofagasta.[105] In 1897 a sheriff's posse murdered 19 immigrant anthracite workers at the Lattimer Mine in Pennsylvania. In Siberia in 1912, Imperial Russian troops shot into a crowd of striking gold workers, killing hundreds.

But strikes continued on a larger and larger scale as the 19th century came to a close. In London, strikes by the Union of Women Match Makers, bus conductors, and gas company workers in 1888 were followed by a strike of 100,000 dockworkers the next year.[106] In 1905–6, there were 3,300 industrial conflicts in Germany, involving 270,000 workers, at the cost of some 13.2 million marks in expenditure from the union strike funds.[107] In 1907 alone, there were at least 231 strikes in the city of Buenos Aires.[108] The most proportionally immense strike of the age was the Swedish General Strike of 1909, which involved 300,000 workers in a small country.[109] The strike was a failure, and the Swedish Trade Union Confederation lost half its members, while employers fired 20,000 workers in retaliation. A case could be made instead for the most successful work stoppage in history being the general strike of enslaved Americans, which, as W. E. B. Du Bois argued, was the death blow to the Confederacy and the southern slave economy.[110]

In nearly all cases, these workers were not trying to stage a revolution, or upend the social order, or destroy capitalism and usher in a new age of collective ownership over the means of production. They wanted higher wages, shorter hours, and safer working conditions. In many cases, they were striking in response to some sudden outrage, often including cuts to their wages or arbitrary firings. Having had their wages cut by profitable corporations, they would stop work in protest, and promptly be murdered either by hired killers or by the soldiers of their own governments. There was not much subtlety to the relation between governments and capitalists in the late 19th century. Nor was the violence entirely on the side of the government and employers (though it disproportionately was). From 1878 through the 1920s, anarchists especially waged an international campaign of terrorist violence. Following failed popular uprisings, terrorists made numerous attacks on kings, tsars, and emperors.[111] Many attacks were announced as retribution for previous acts of state or capitalist violence: King Umberto I of Italy was killed by an anarchist in retribution for the hundreds of people shot by government troops in the bread riots of 1898. The American President William McKinley was shot by an anarchist in retaliation for the Lattimer Massacre. Other anarchists tried and failed to blow up John D. Rockefeller because of the Ludlow Massacre, and another tried and failed to shoot Leopold of Belgium for his atrocities in the Congo. In 1881, Tsar Alexander II was killed by a socialist populist group; in 1894, the French President Sadi Carnot was stabbed to death by an anarchist; in 1897, the Spanish Prime Minister Antonio Cánovas del Castillo was shot at a thermal bath resort. There were many others. Taking advantage of the new invention of dynamite, anarchists carried out dozens of bombings, including the bombing of Wall Street in September of 1920. None of these provoked the revolutions they intended, nor even a lasting victory in the long class conflict. They are now mostly forgotten, but for the decades of high capitalist imperialism at the end of the 19th century, elites feared anarchist violence more than socialist revolution, and certainly more than they fear terrorism today.

■ ■ ■

Since about 2010, a field of history has arisen that calls itself "the new history of capitalism." It is overwhelmingly focused on the United States in the 19th century, especially on Southern cotton slavery, and it argues that the slave plantation was the emblematic form of capitalist organization.[112] This field has been explicitly unwilling to define what it means by "capitalism," but it is very clear that it considers the central driving element to have been Southern slavery, and although different scholars differ, they mainly claim that slavery not only *was* capitalism but in various ways represented the *essence* of capitalism.[113]

By contrast, this book has shown that capitalism and capitalists can be found much earlier, and doing a wide variety of things. The first wholly capitalist society was the Dutch Republic in the 17th century, followed by Britain not much later, and capitalism was spread around the world through the force of industrialization and empire. Slavery played an important role in that process, but the originating force was mostly not 19th-century American slavery. Cotton was not widely grown in the American South until the 1810s, by which point the Industrial Revolution was nearly completed. New historians of capitalism claim that the Industrial Revolution could not have been sustained without access to American cotton, which may be true, and that the scale of American cotton production could not have increased without slavery, which is more questionable. Cotton production vastly increased after the end of slavery despite no obvious technological revolution, which suggests it could have increased if slavery had ended earlier, and that in turn suggests that, if anything, slavery held back cotton production.[114] And while it is true that cotton represented the bulk of American exports, exports were a small part of the overall American economy, and, as we saw in the last chapter, the annual hay crop was probably of similar value, not to mention wheat. Cotton was about 5 to 7 percent of US GDP throughout the entire antebellum period.[115] The most recent estimate has calculated that enslaved people contributed about 12.6 percent of American gross national product in 1860—roughly proportionate to their share of the population.[116]

The antebellum Southern economy was a poor, undercapitalized, extractive colonial system, more like Brazil than Boston or Britain. Since slaves were a mobile form of property, slave owners had little reason to invest in land or infrastructure.[117] The sharply stratified and unequal society meant elites had little reason to invest in things like education or other public goods. Slavery and cotton were profitable enough not to provoke diversification (to the extent that when gold was discovered in the South Carolina Piedmont region, local plantation owners didn't bother to mine it), but since slaves were a fixed cost, planters kept them working all year on a variety of crops, which is why the South actually specialized more in cotton cropping *after* the Civil War, opting to import food from the North and West.[118] Instead of the slave South being the core of the American economy, to my view the bigger story was the continual expulsion and extermination of Native people in the continental interior, and the large-scale immigration from Europe. We can debate the counterfactual of whether the Industrial Revolution and modern capitalism could have emerged without Southern slavery, but it seems incontrovertible that it could not have happened if Native Americans had retained their own system of property rights over the entire territory of North and South America.[119]

The focus on the United States is also misplaced. American economic growth only really took off in the 1870s. The economic historian Robert Gordon has exhaustively traced the impact and diffusion of a range of technological and industrial transformations, and finds that the sustained rise in standards of living began in that decade.[120] The American economy overtook the British one in aggregate output, and in terms of energy production, only by about the 1890s. Global American dominance followed the catastrophe of the First World War, the demise of the British-dominated financial system during the Great Depression, and the emergence of American manufacturing power in the Second World War. The decline of Britain and the destruction of Germany and Japan were at least as responsible for 20th-century capitalism being a specifically American capitalism as was any intrinsic element of American dynamism.

Instead of arguing that the slave plantation was the definitive form of American capitalism (after all, it existed previously, in the case of Caribbean sugar, and later, in the case of Brazilian coffee or West African palm oil), it is more accurate to consider the vertically integrated, capital-intensive corporation. We have already encountered corporations, but after the 1870s, they emerged in the United States on a scale and complexity that had never existed before. Instead of hiring labor on an unpredictable daily pattern, they developed human resources bureaucracies and internal promotion mechanisms.[121] They separated ownership from management, creating a new managerial class that had training, education, and a commitment to scientific efficiency. They developed manufacturing with interchangeable parts on a previously impossible scale (especially Ford Motors after 1903), and they marshaled more capital than anything ever had before.[122] These new forms of organization made people like John D. Rockefeller, Andrew Carnegie, Henry Frick, Thomas and Andrew Mellon, and J. P. Morgan preposterously rich, and they guarded their power and wealth with systems of organized violence. When a multinational corporation controlled by distant billionaires dispatched local police to murder striking workers in West Virginia or Colorado in the 1880s or 1890s, that was more emblematic of the coming world of 20th- and 21st-century capitalism than the antebellum slave plantation had been.

■ ■ ■

Why did all of this happen, this rapid and bloody expansion of capitalist imperialism? The socialist answer in the late 19th century was clear: Empire was a means to keep capitalism alive, providing a profitable outlet for surplus capital, a source of raw materials, and a captive market for manufactures. The liberal critic J. A. Hobson published his book *Imperialism* in 1902, arguing that empire was the result of capitalist oligarchy, a symptom of inequality in Britain and other rich countries. In 1913, the Polish Marxist Rosa Luxemburg published her *Accumulation of Capital*, which argued that imperialism was a kind of safety valve for capitalism, which otherwise would run into crises of overproduction and overaccumulation. And finally, in 1916, Vladimir Lenin drew heavily on Hobson in his *Imperialism: The Highest Stage of Capitalism*, to claim that financial capitalism specifically drew on the profits of colonial exploitation, having reached the end stage of concentration and monopoly in capitalist competition. A deep socialist tradition maintained that workers had no homeland, and that national pride and imperial rivalries were mechanisms of elite rule, ways to divide the workers and to obscure the true antagonism of class society.

As we have seen, many of these claims about profitability and the direction and destination of overseas investment are not accurate. There were still plenty of profits to be made in Britain, the largest destination for investment was the United States, and imperial investment was not especially large or especially profitable. However, it was very concentrated in ownership. Wealth was immensely concentrated in the late 19th century, to a degree only matched by the 2010s and 2020s.[123] In that sense, the numbers presented above about the average amount of investment per capita are misleading, because most people still died with no wealth whatsoever.[124] Instead, the average obscures the fact that most investment came from a relatively small group of grotesquely wealthy people. The British elite in particular had a distinctive investment portfolio. They "held less than 30 percent of domestic, but almost 40 percent of foreign and Empire shares" in companies and were much more likely to invest in imperial government debt than domestic debt.[125]

As the economic historians Lance Davis and Robert Huttenback put it, "If the Empire investors were not the same people who paid the taxes, imperialism, at least in part, can be viewed as a process of income transfer from British taxpayers to imperial investors."[126] Indeed, there is no question that from 1860 to 1914, residents of Britain paid considerably more in taxes than anyone else in the world, and essentially all tax systems everywhere were regressive.[127] Davis and Huttenback calculate that the taxpaying middle classes were net losers of empire by more than £2.5 million at the minimum, though if the calculation is weighted for opportunity costs and the distribution of benefits and many other assumptions, the figure could be many multiples higher.[128] To that loss could be added a loss of life: One historian estimates that between 1750 and 1913, something like 280,000 to 300,000 European and American soldiers died in overseas colonial wars.[129] European, American, and Japanese imperial soldiers killed many times more people on the receiving end of their ferocious new industrial technologies, including explicit and deliberate policies of exterminatory genocide by British settlers in Tasmania, by the German army in what is now Namibia, and by Leopold in the Congo.[130] Whether the millions of deaths of the First World War should be counted among the casualties of capitalist imperial competition remains debated, but the continuities with colonial wars are stronger than the differences.

The bureaucracy of the British Empire itself constituted a surprisingly small set of people: The Colonial Office in London had a staff of only 23 people in 1849, and still only 125 in 1907. The total imperial employment was about 2,400 people in 1892, plus another 3,000 in India, but that includes even indigenous officials and retired people still on the payroll.[131] There were probably 75,000 troops in India and another 45,000 elsewhere in the empire, but many of them were drawn from imperial subject populations rather than British settlers. The empire was not a full-employment program: It was an investment protection mechanism, and a way of socializing losses while privatizing gains. As the economic historian Patrick O'Brien puts it, the elite constituted

> social and occupational groups who benefited most directly and tangibly from military and other governmental expenditures allocated to support imperial rule, to foster imperial trade and to miti-

gate the risks of private investment in the dominions and colonies. Britain's "gentlemanly capitalists," resident in large part in the home counties (financiers, bankers, merchants, shippers and other intermediaries involved in servicing commerce between the metropolis and the empire) derived the largest gains (net of taxes) from military and other forms of imperial subsidy. Meanwhile the majority of English people cheerfully and even proudly shouldered a tax bill for an empire from which they derived very little in the form of tangible pecuniary gains for decades before or decades after the Great War.[132]

Nevertheless, despite paying for the empire in blood and taxes, despite mostly not migrating to the empire, despite mostly not working in industries that exported to the empire or depended on inputs from colonial exports, by the 1880s or 1890s, average Europeans and Americans felt very strongly in favor of empire. This puzzle is at the heart of most current historical research on imperialism, which tends to focus on the cultural preconditions, legitimation, representation, and popular understanding of empire in their daily lives. But in that sense, although the socialists of the time were wrong about the profits and investment patterns, they seem to have been exactly right about the politics. Empire was an expression of capitalist oligarchy, and it was indeed a way of dividing the global working class, to ensure the preservation of elite rule and elite profits. The members of that elite proceeded to steer their empires into a global cataclysm that in some cases destroyed the empires, their rulers, and in many cases, themselves. It almost destroyed capitalism as well.

Vladimir Lenin in 1917: Capitalism's Near-Death Experience

Effective history deprives the self of the reassuring stability of life and nature, and it will not permit itself to be transported toward a millennial ending. It will uproot its traditional foundations and relentlessly disrupt its pretended continuity. This is because knowledge is not made for understanding; it is made for cutting.

—Michel Foucault[1]

Close to midnight on April 16, 1917 (by our calendar), an energetic little red-haired man arrived by train at the Finland Station, on the north side of the Neva River in Saint Petersburg. It was Vladimir Ilych Ulyanov, better known by his revolutionary code name "Lenin." He had traveled from his exile in Zurich through Germany, which was then three years into bitter warfare with the

Russian Empire, north through Sweden, then down through Finland to Saint Petersburg. He was there to try to take charge of the ongoing revolution against the tsarist government that had broken out among the furious female textile workers of Saint Petersburg that February. (The anniversary of their uprising lives on as International Women's Day.) He spent the late spring and summer tirelessly agitating for further revolution, an end to the war, and the establishment of the world's first workers' state. The Provisional Government that took charge after the tsar abdicated continued the war and was unable to solve the ongoing subsistence crises in the cities, resulting in the continual deterioration of its legitimacy. In October, Lenin's Bolshevik Communist Party staged a coup and seized power in Saint Petersburg.[2] For the next five years, they fought a bitter war for survival, culminating with their victory and the establishment of the Soviet Union.

The capitalism of Lenin's time would have been unrecognizable to Newton 200 years earlier, let alone Luther 200 years before that. The gulf between 1717 and 1917 was immeasurably wider than the one between 1517 and 1717. Lenin and his comrades spent most of their lives in exile, in prison, or in various states of hiding and underground activity, but still their living standards would have been incomprehensible to someone like Isaac Newton. They also existed in a world of print culture, constantly writing articles attacking one another in the small radical émigré press. Little wonder: By 1900, there were over 31,000 newspapers in the world, including 600 in India and 195 in Africa, some reaching hundreds of thousands of readers.[3] They traveled to the Americas on rare occasions, and across Europe frequently and rapidly by railroad, often to go to party conferences at hotels lit by electric lights and warmed by radiators.[4] They devoted their lives to trying to organize the millions of new industrial workers in the new manufacturing and technology sectors all over the world.

Above all, the capitalism Lenin knew was profoundly unequal, both between societies and within them. The Russia he came to rule was desperately poor, and serfdom was still a living memory. Most people still lived and worked in small, rural communities, and things like railroads, electricity, and manufacturing were still limited to richer urban centers, where there was considerable economic dynamism.[5] Most rural Russians were integrated into labor and agricultural markets, but remained illiterate (over half of men could read by the 1890s, but very few women), with ferocious rates of infant mortality and malnutrition.[6] Average incomes in western Europe were about $3,700 (in standardized 1990 US dollars) in 1913, while in Russia they were about $1,500, comparable to Latin America at the time.[7] The Russian aristocracy that Lenin and his comrades overthrew were often well educated, French speaking, and with extravagant consumer tastes that they satisfied with their control of some 20 percent of national income.[8] Russia was not abnormally unequal: In Britain, France, Germany, Japan, and the United States the richest 1 percent of people in 1914 received at least 20 percent of national income. There is no better description of the life of elites in the world before 1914 than the famous one given by John Maynard Keynes in his *Economic Consequences of the Peace*:

The inhabitant of London could order by telephone, sipping his morning tea in bed, the various products of the whole earth, in such quantity as he might see fit, and reasonably expect their early delivery upon his doorstep; he could at the same moment and by the same means adventure his wealth in the natural resources and new enterprises of any quarter of the world, and share, without exertion or even trouble, in their prospective fruits and advantages; or he could decide to couple the security of his fortunes with the good faith of the townspeople of any substantial municipality in any continent that fancy or information might recommend. . . . He regarded this state of affairs as normal, certain, and permanent, except in the direction of further improvement, and any deviation from it as aberrant, scandalous, and avoidable. The projects and politics of militarism and imperialism, of racial and cultural rivalries, of monopolies, restrictions, and exclusion, which were to play the serpent to this paradise, were little more than the amusements of his daily newspaper, and appeared to exercise almost no influence at all on the ordinary course of social and economic life, the internationalization of which was nearly complete in practice.[9]

Not many people had telephones, or wealth to adventure, but even an exile like Lenin could enjoy coffee at the Café Landolt in Geneva, simple dinners with beer at London restaurants, and Italian vacations.[10] By 1912, about 60 percent of the population of Moscow (or about 800,000 people, mostly living in very dense apartment housing) had either indoor plumbing or flush toilets, or both.[11] To be sure, very few people could afford to live alone, some slept in their workplaces, and others traded off shifts in their bare-plank beds.[12] Most people in the world were still very poor and most still worked in agriculture, but the set of people living and working for wages in cities was massively greater than it had been even at the beginning of the 19th century, with vastly higher standards of living, and even the poorest people's lives would be touched in some way by new industrial technologies, whether electricity, railroads, telegraphs, or cheaper commodities conveyed by steam. Or through industrialized violence, which after 1914 took place on a scale never before imagined. The First World War killed between 15 and 22 million people, and it was the last war in human history in which the majority of people killed were probably soldiers instead of civilians. Most of them were killed through an intense version of the industrialized violence previously employed in the colonies: machine guns and artillery, barbed wire, and after 1915, chemical weapons like chlorine gas, which was manufactured by giant industrial corporations.[13] The landscape was pulverized, entire towns lost generations of young men, and economic warfare (especially the blockade of Germany) produced hunger and deprivation. Members of the capitalist class appeared helpless to stop the destruction they had unleashed, and it did not take long to wonder why they should have the right to rule.

Between 1917 and 1933, capitalism faced its greatest crisis and came the closest it ever has to being destroyed. The Soviet Revolution of 1917 was the first time a self-consciously anticapitalist political force had ever taken power anywhere, and through 1921, it appeared very likely that some form of communism or socialism would spread throughout Europe, and perhaps the world.[14] There were brief communist revolutions and even governments in Finland, Bavaria, and Hungary. Another revolution failed in Berlin in 1919 and was brutally repressed by protofascist paramilitaries with the support of the new centrist Social Democratic government.[15] Violent open conflict between communists and fascists continued until Adolf Hitler took power in 1933 and set about murdering communists, socialists, and trade unionists, or sending them to concentration camps. From 1917 to 1922, the Soviets fought a bitter civil war, both against many factions of the old regime and against British, Czech, French, Japanese, and American intervention that tried to strangle the communist experiment before it could spread. In 1919–21, the Soviets tried to intervene in Poland to support another communist revolution, but were defeated. Across Europe, riots, protests, strikes, and rebellions against the old capitalist order were violently suppressed throughout 1919–23, and eventually the so-called Red Wave was turned back.[16] Even in the archcapitalist United States, a first "Red Scare" against anarchists, communists, and socialists, especially foreign ones who opposed the war, culminated in the Palmer Raids of 1919–20, in which Attorney General Mitchell Palmer arrested 6,000 people and deported about 550, essentially wiping out the leadership of the American political left.[17]

But the violent repression of the anticapitalist movements did not end the crisis. The interwar years were one long, grinding series of economic disasters. Britain had a "lost decade" without wage growth or overall economic growth, and was paralyzed by a national general strike in 1926. Germany had hyperinflation in 1923, leaving lasting political, social, and economic scars. Global agricultural depression began as early as 1925, and in 1929, the stock market crash in New York precipitated a banking crisis through 1930–33, and the panic was transmitted around the world through the strictures of the newly re-created gold-standard system.[18] Capitalism appeared to be unable to avert the First World War, unable to recover after it, and unable to solve its own economic problems.

The first months of 1933 were the historic low point of global capitalism. The Depression was at its deepest trough, and about one-quarter of Americans and Germans were unemployed. The Soviet economy, however, was booming under the first Five-Year Plan, which the Soviets completed in only four years. Planning instead of markets appeared to be the way of the future. In Germany, after years of political instability, austerity, and grinding deflation enacted by the Brüning government, Adolf Hitler was appointed chancellor and soon began rapidly consolidating the Nazi dictatorship. Observers around the world agreed that capitalism was a relic of the 19th century and had proved to be inadequate to the challenges of the modern age. Even people sympathetic to capitalism concluded it was doomed and the future belonged to the communist and fascist challengers.[19] If capitalism was ever going to collapse and be replaced by a newer rival, it would have happened between 1917 and 1933. But the machine survived.

■ ■ ■

In 1989, a US State Department functionary named Francis Fukuyama published a famous article asking whether history was coming
to an end. He meant History in the big sense of a civilizational conflict between different totalizing visions of organizing human society, and he thought that the alternative rivals to capitalism were
exhausted, leaving liberal capitalist democracy as the only, and final,
form of human social life.[20] In part, Fukuyama's idea was popular-
ized through a concerted effort of billionaire-funded think tanks,
and also in part, many people have had a good laugh since 1989 at
the naivete of believing that History would have an end. But in
some ways, Fukuyama was right, and even radical-left critics like
Fredric Jameson have asked a different version of the same question,
and one that opened this book: Why is it easier to imagine the end
of the world than to imagine the end of capitalism?[21]

Today capitalism is more dominant than it has ever been. There
are more markets in more things than ever before, and more of
human life is oriented toward market activity than ever.[22] Capitalism has no serious rival, and the major political rivals to American
capitalist hegemony offer only alternative versions of capitalism.
In that sense, History *did* end in 1989–91, but it was only one of
many ends of History, because of course different people have different histories. In a different way, History also ended in 1917–33,
since that was the last moment when it was credible and possible
that capitalism as a whole would collapse and be replaced by something else. The 1989 end was the end of the coexistence of systemic
rivals. The remaining end is a planetary one. It is too late to prevent the catastrophic consequences of climate change, which has
been driven by the burning of fossil fuels for industrial purposes.
The exact structures of capitalism, with its private-profit motivation, short-term temporalities, and absence of mechanisms for collective action, are precisely the elements that have led to climatic

disaster and that prevent any meaningful action to mitigate it.[23] We can focus on survival, on local amelioration, and on creating new structures of meaning and historical time to replace permanent economic growth as the justificatory end point of human activity. But it is too late to stop the catastrophe.

The world has ended before. The history of capitalism told in this book has involved the end of the world for many groups of people, and that history is at least as instructive as the history of the successful mechanisms of capital accumulation, industrialization, technology, and rising living standards. Living standards have risen immensely since the time of Luther, but not for the Taino and the Arawak, for the people of the Banda Islands and Tasmania, or for those of the North American plains and the Aztec cities. The workers and, for that matter, the slaves who lived through the fossil-fueled creation of modern economic growth did not experience it as a great human achievement. The past is littered with dead worlds, ways of life and meaning once held by thousands of people and now so irrevocably lost as to be unintelligible to us. Capitalism has not been the only mechanism for ending the world, but it is the only one to make it profitable.

If asked, many people would say that the reason to learn history is to learn lessons from the past, perhaps to avoid repeating past mistakes. Almost no historian believes that to be the case. Instead, historians emphasize context, and difference. But that does not mean there is no reason to study history, or that history has no contemporary relevance. Instead, history is a radical, emancipatory, imaginative act. When we learn history, we are learning that nothing about the world around us is natural, permanent, or inevitable. Instead, it was all created by people, which means it can be changed by people. The world does not have to be this way. If the world used to be different, it can be different again. The specific challenge posed by capitalism is exactly the way that it has organized social life around individual struggles for survival instead of intentional, democratic collective action. The first step to any kind of change is understanding how that happened, that it could have happened differently, and thus to recognize that capitalism has a history, which means it also has an end.

Instead of easily applied lessons, history offers us other things. Community, solidarity, and meaning begin with the recognition of a shared condition and shared struggle, and history helps us realize that we share conditions and struggles not just across space but also across time. The central argument of this book is that there was nothing inevitable about the capitalism that we have, and that means that when we recognize it and attempt to resist or change the gravity of capitalist inevitability, when we struggle for a more equal world and a better future, we do so in community and solidarity with those who came before us. When we recognize our community with the past, and the fact that history is not a separate thing that has already happened, but rather that we are *in* it, and *of* it, we can see that we are not so isolated and atomized as we have been led to believe. The knowledge that the world has ended before is also the knowledge that something comes after the end, something which is as impossible to imagine as it is impossible to imagine the kinds of people who will inhabit that future, and how they will look back on us as historical actors. This book argues that capital is in some ways immortal, and the changes it has wrought on the world have happened on a time scale different from that of human lives. That recognition, in turn, allows us to see that the struggle of people against capital is also immortal. There is no escape from the march through time, and we don't know where we're going. But we are not alone.

ACKNOWLEDGMENTS

In a sonnet from 1931, Edna St. Vincent Millay wrote that "time does not bring relief." As usual, she was right. History writing can do many things, but it does not rectify past injustices; it only creates small replicas of them to be handed down to others. This book is a record of many injustices, and written at a time of great injustice and cruelty. I hope the majority of its readers live in a time of greater relief. There is a specific and finite number of books that any of us gets to read, and an even smaller number that any of us gets to write, and a limited number of times that these words will be read by anyone. I'm glad to get to use them to express my gratitude to others.

I thought out this book, did most of the reading for it, and wrote the first chapters while part of the Capitalism's Hardwiring research seminar hosted by the Warren Center at Harvard University in 2022–23. I owe a great debt to Christine Desan and Kenneth Mack for providing an excellent place to work and for such stimulating discussion. Thanks are also due to my fellow Chuck Warrenites: Ann Daly, Devin Fergus, Pierre-Christian Fink, Nicolas Jabko, Sohaib Khan, Andrew Konove, R. H. Lossin, Simon

Middleton, Ellen Nye, and Christopher Todd. I am additionally grateful to the library staff at both Harvard and UC Berkeley.

Simon Middleton, Bruce Hall, Matt Shutzer, Nicolas Radburn, Eric Schluessel, Sam Wetherell, and Jan de Vries all read portions of the manuscript and provided valuable corrections. Thanks are due to James Vernon and to the graduate students in my fall 2023 Capitalism seminar at UC Berkeley for reading a draft of the entire manuscript: Diego Ayala, Emma Bates, Nate Dolton-Thompson, Bennett Fees, Matt Hamilton, Thomas Kingston, Diene Grapengiesser, Vahid Mazdeh, Vincent Pacheco, Flavio Santini, and Jacob Smiley.

I need to thank Lauren Benton and Mark Peterson for a conversation that helped clarify the periodization. Joanna Korey taught me many things, and helped save chapter 3. Erika Hornmark was an ideal research assistant: She both helped me get the notes and bibliography right and saved me from many infelicitous locutions. Charlotte Robertson has been a source of great encouragement and camaraderie. It was my great fortune to come to the attention of Matt Weiland, who saw what this book could be and helped make it possible. I'm grateful to Tim Stallman for the maps, to Sarah Johnson and Rebecca Springer for their thoughtful and incisive copyediting, and to the production team at W. W. Norton, especially Yumiko Gonzalez Rios.

Keith Young read and provided valuable reactions to a very early draft. Danny Kelly helped me clarify my thinking on the introduction. As with everything I write, Julia Shatz has been present, supportive, and brilliant every step of the way, always pushing me to be better, by example more than anything else. Sam Wetherell continues to set the aspirational edge for how to be a person who is also an academic. Shawn Walsh is a patient and thoughtful craftsman, as well as a very good neighbor. And of course I am most grateful to Absinthe the Cat and my wife Beki, for taking the long road back to California, right back where we started from.

NOTES

Introduction

1. Jameson, *Political Unconscious*, 102.
2. For example, McCloskey, *Bourgeois Virtues*.
3. Lazear, "Economic Imperialism."
4. Most famous, but by no means the only example, is Becker and Lewis, "On the Interaction." Lutter, "Valuing Children's Health," argues that there is probably too much effort put into not poisoning children with lead. Carlin and Sandy, "Estimating the Implicit Value," 196, helpfully calculates that the life of a young child is worth about $500,000 to its mother. See also Roth et al., "Kidney Exchange."
5. Jameson, "Future City," 76.
6. The increase in living standards depends on where we are looking, when we are starting, and how we are measuring. Average incomes in England, for instance, have increased 24-fold from the end of the Black Death until today.
7. Christophers, *Price Is Wrong*.
8. The following draws heavily on my *Impunity and Capitalism*, 6–8.
9. Gelderblom, *Cities of Commerce*.
10. For a classic version of this argument, see Heilbroner, *Nature and Logic of Capitalism*.
11. For a polemical development of this argument, see Mau, *Mute Compulsion*.
12. Alfani, "Inequality in History."
13. A similar argument can be found in Chibber, *Class Matrix*.
14. North and Thomas, *Rise of the Western World*.
15. Findlay and O'Rourke, *Power and Plenty*.
16. Allen, *British Industrial Revolution in Global Perspective*.
17. Smith, *Wealth of Nations*, 17.

18. For useful overviews of this field, see Lipartito, "Reassembling the Economic"; Hilt, "Economic History, Historical Analysis."
19. Kershaw, "Hamlet Without the Prince of Denmark"; Schakenbach Regele, "Brief History of the History."
20. Kocka, *Capitalism*; Sonenscher, *Capitalism*.
21. Amin, *Eurocentrism*.
22. Moore, "Metabolic Rift or Metabolic Shift?"
23. Fressoz, *More and More and More*.

Prologue: Martin Luther in 1517: The World Before Capitalism

1. Brady, *German Histories in the Age of Reformations*.
2. Two examples who disagree with each other are Tawney, *Religion and the Rise of Capitalism* and Weber, *Protestant Ethic*.
3. On household economies, see Wrightson, *Earthly Necessities*, part 1.
4. Humphries and Weisdorf, "Unreal Wages?"
5. On living standards, see the exhaustive account of Braudel, *Civilization and Capitalism*.
6. de Vries, *Economy of Europe*, 32.
7. Muldrew, *Economy of Obligation*.
8. Findlay and O'Rourke, *Power and Plenty*, 127–40.
9. Hill, *Century of Revolution*, 32.
10. Sylvester et al., *Medieval Dress and Textiles*, 210.
11. Curtin, *Economic Change in Precolonial Africa*, 153–97; Manning, *Slavery and African Life*.
12. Hirth, *Aztec Economic World*, 24–48.
13. On the variety and history of slavery, see Patterson, *Slavery and Social Death*.
14. Carmichael et al., "European Marriage Pattern."
15. de Vries, "Population." The massive Benedictow, *Black Death*, 380–86, puts European mortality as high as 60 percent.
16. On premodern inequality, see Alfani, *As Gods Among Men*.
17. Milanovic, *Haves and Have-Nots*, 100.
18. Bray, *Rice Economies*.
19. Kishimoto, "Property Rights and Factor Markets."
20. Brook, *Price of Collapse*, 57–58.
21. United Nations, *World Urbanization Prospects*.
22. Engels, *Peasant War in Germany*; Petterson, "Bloch's Münzer and the Horizons of History."

Chapter 1: Money, 1415–1650s

1. Cipolla, *Guns, Sails and Empires*.
2. Green, "Africa and Capitalism," 303, and many other examples follow.
3. Arrighi, *Long Twentieth Century*.
4. Newitt, *History of Portuguese Overseas Expansion*, 25.

5. For superb work on African economic activity, see Green, *Fistful of Shells*, part 1.

6. Newitt, *History of Portuguese Overseas Expansion*, 40.

7. Newitt, *History of Portuguese Overseas Expansion*, 46.

8. Anderson, *History of Portugal*, 55.

9. Radburn, *Traders in Men*, 9.

10. Curtin, "Africa and the Wider Monetary World," 235.

11. Vilar, *History of Gold and Money*, 63.

12. Vilar, *History of Gold and Money*, 66.

13. Livi-Bacci, "Depopulation of Hispanic America," gives a helpful overview of the many different population estimates and many different causes of catastrophe.

14. Lane, *Potosí*, 20–21, 31–32.

15. Bakewell, *Silver Mining and Society*.

16. Bakewell, *Silver Mining and Society*, 57, 78.

17. Bakewell, *Silver Mining and Society*, 115.

18. Vilar, *History of Gold and Money*, 134.

19. Stein and Stein, *Silver, Trade, and War*, 30.

20. Arroyo Abad and Palma, "Fruits of El Dorado," 98.

21. Lane, *Potosí*, 34.

22. Lane, *Potosí*, 47–48.

23. Lane, *Potosí*, 71.

24. Lane, *Potosí*, 72.

25. Lane, *Potosí*, 83–84.

26. Hamilton, *American Treasure*, 20.

27. Stein and Stein, *Silver, Trade, and War*, 12.

28. von Glahn, *Fountain of Fortune*, 117–18.

29. Flynn and Giráldez, "Cycles of Silver," 393.

30. Arroyo Abad et al., "Between Conquest and Independence"; Arroyo Abad and van Zanden, "Growth Under Extractive Institutions?"

31. Kindleberger, "Economic and Financial Crises," 75.

32. Flynn, "Early Capitalism," 43; Flynn, "New Perspective," 397.

33. Parker, *Military Revolution*, 59.

34. Stein and Stein, *Silver, Trade, and War*, 45.

35. Flynn, "New Perspective," 397.

36. Drelichman and Voth, *Lending to the Borrower from Hell*, 89–94.

37. Stein and Stein, *Silver, Trade, and War*, 45, 62.

38. Munro, "Monetary Origins," 25.

39. Flynn, "New Perspective," 397.

40. Stein and Stein, *Silver, Trade, and War*, 52.

41. Barrett, "World Bullion Flows," 250.

42. Appleby, *Relentless Revolution*, 42.

43. Flynn, "New Perspective," 399.

44. Brook, *Price of Collapse*, 70.

45. von Glahn, *Fountain of Fortune*, 135.

46. von Glahn, *Fountain of Fortune*, 135.

47. Irigoin, "New World," 272.

48. Irigoin, "New World," 272–73.

49. Gaastra, "Exports of Precious Metals," 451, table 1.

50. von Glahn, *Fountain of Fortune*, 140–41.

51. Brook, *Price of Collapse*, 104–5.

52. von Glahn, *Fountain of Fortune*, 177–78, 192–93.

53. Chen et al., "Sung and Ming Paper Monies."

54. Brook, *Price of Collapse*, chap. 5.

55. von Glahn, *Fountain of Fortune*, 207, 213–14.

56. von Glahn, "Myth and Reality," 450–51. See also Kishimoto-Nakayama, "Kangxi Depression."

57. Munro, "Monetary Origins," 2–3, table 1.1.

58. Barrett, "World Bullion Flows," 242–43, table 7.3.

59. Munro, "Monetary Origins," 6.

60. Munro, "Monetary Origins," 7.

61. von Glahn, *Fountain of Fortune*, 237.

62. For the political history of money in England over the long run, see Desan, *Making Money*.

63. Kindleberger, "Currency Debasement," 51.

64. Bills of exchange could be used in more complicated ways than this. See Trivellato, *Promise and Peril of Credit*.

65. Sahillioğlu, "International Monetary and Metal Movements," 279.

66. Guyer, *Marginal Gains*, chap. 2.

67. Curtin, "Africa and the Wider Monetary World," 257.

68. Radburn, *Traders in Men*, 71–74.

69. Millon, "When Money Grew on Trees"; Sampeck, "Constitutional Approach to Cacao Money."

70. Sahillioğlu, "International Monetary and Metal Movements," 284–85.

71. Pamuk, *Monetary History of the Ottoman Empire*, 141.

72. Kindleberger, "Currency Debasement," 52.

73. Kindleberger, "Currency Debasement," 53.

74. Stein and Stein, *Silver, Trade, and War*, 19.

75. Stein and Stein, *Silver, Trade, and War*, 54–56.

76. Flynn and Giráldez, "Global Economic Unity," 405.

Chapter 2: Finance, 1650–1720

1. Neal, *Rise of Financial Capitalism*, 44.

2. Brewer, *Sinews of Power*, 88.

3. North and Weingast, "Constitutions and Commitment."

4. This is the general argument of Brewer, *Sinews of Power*.

5. Shovlin, *Trading with the Enemy*.

6. Bindseil, *Central Banking Before 1800.*

7. de Roover, *Rise and Decline.*

8. Bindseil, *Central Banking,* 71, 172.

9. For an extensive discussion of *giro* banking, see Mueller, *Venetian Money Market.*

10. Häberlein, *Fuggers of Augsburg,* 16.

11. Häberlein, *Fuggers of Augsburg,* 35.

12. Häberlein, *Fuggers of Augsburg,* 41. Here I think "mark" is referring not to a currency but to a weight: the Cologne mark, which was about 234 grams.

13. Häberlein, *Fuggers of Augsburg,* 53.

14. Häberlein, *Fuggers of Augsburg,* 77.

15. Graulau, "Finance, Industry and Globalization."

16. Häberlein, *Fuggers of Ausburg,* 92.

17. Tracy, *Financial Revolution,* 26–27.

18. Tracy, *Financial Revolution,* 90.

19. Tracy, *Financial Revolution,* 97, 107.

20. Israel, *Dutch Republic,* chap. 5.

21. Prak and van Zanden, *Pioneers of Capitalism.*

22. Prak and van Zanden, *Pioneers of Capitalism,* chap. 3. Robert Allen finds that wages and living standards in Amsterdam and London diverged from the rest of Europe and the rest of the world as early as 1500–1550 in a "little divergence" of northwestern Europe. Allen, "Great Divergence."

23. van Bavel and van Zanden, "Jump-Start of the Holland Economy"; Sewell, "Emergence of Capitalism," agrees, as does Prak and van Zanden, *Pioneers of Capitalism.*

24. de Vries, *Dutch Rural Economy.*

25. de Vries, *Dutch Rural Economy,* 136–74, and for some surprising consequences of the Dutch dairy industry, van Bavel and Gelderblom, "Economic Origins of Cleanliness."

26. Prak and van Zanden, *Pioneers of Capitalism,* 84.

27. Alfani, *As Gods Among Men,* 102.

28. de Vries and van der Woude, *First Modern Economy,* 57–72.

29. de Vries, *Barges and Capitalism.*

30. Gelderblom, *Cities of Commerce.*

31. de Vries and van der Woude, *First Modern Economy,* 279–334; on books, Prak and van Zanden, *Pioneers of Capitalism,* 23–24.

32. Prak and van Zanden, *Pioneers of Capitalism,* 104.

33. Berg and Hudson, *Slavery, Capitalism and the Industrial Revolution,* 64.

34. de Vries and van der Woude, *First Modern Economy,* 561–96.

35. de Vries and van der Woude, *First Modern Economy,* 384.

36. t'Hart, *Making of a Bourgeois State.*

37. Gelderblom, *Cities of Commerce.*

38. Tracy, *Financial Revolution,* 216.

39. Gelderblom and Jonker, "Completing a Financial Revolution," 649–50.

40. Tracy, *Financial Revolution*, 197.

41. Alfani, *As Gods Among Men*, 138–39.

42. Gelderblom and Jonker, "Completing a Financial Revolution," 654. The profit figure is from Neal, *Rise of Financial Capitalism*, 17.

43. de Vries, "Connecting Europe and Asia," 68–74.

44. Quinn and Roberds, *How a Ledger Became a Central Bank*, 44.

45. Gelderblom and Jonker, "Completing a Financial Revolution."

46. Alfani, *As Gods Among Men*, 140–41.

47. Gelderblom and Jonker, "Completing a Financial Revolution," 645.

48. Gelderblom and Jonker, "Completing a Financial Revolution," 648.

49. Quinn and Roberds, *How a Ledger Became a Central Bank*, 141.

50. Quinn and Roberds, *How a Ledger Became a Central Bank*, 6–7.

51. Petram, *World's First Stock Exchange*, 51–68.

52. Goldgar, *Tulipmania*.

53. Alfani, *As Gods Among Men*, 96.

54. de Vries and van der Woude, *First Modern Economy*, 392.

55. de Vries, "Limits of Globalization," 728.

56. Klooster, *Dutch Moment*, 35.

57. Klooster, *Dutch Moment*, 60.

58. Klooster, *Dutch Moment*, 24–25.

59. Klooster, *Dutch Moment*, 70, 159–60.

60. Klooster, *Dutch Moment*, 72, 146.

61. For a wide variety of interpretations, see the essays in Israel, *Anglo-Dutch Moment*.

62. Parker, *Military Revolution*.

63. Brewer, *Sinews of Power*, 8.

64. Brewer, *Sinews of Power*, 34.

65. Brewer, *Sinews of Power*, 35.

66. Brewer, *Sinews of Power*, 36.

67. Shaw-Taylor, "Rise of Agrarian Capitalism."

68. Allen, *Enclosure and the Yeoman*.

69. From entirely different political perspectives, see Crafts and Harley, "Precocious British Industrialisation"; Meiksins Wood, *Origin of Capitalism*.

70. The classic example is Hill, *Century of Revolution*; but also more recently, Healy, *Blazing World*.

71. Hill, *World Turned Upside Down*.

72. Brewer, *Sinews of Power*, chap. 4.

73. Carruthers, *City of Capital*, 63.

74. Temin and Voth, *Prometheus Shackled*, 76–84.

75. For example, many works by Russell, like his *Causes of the English Civil War*; also Braddick, *God's Fury, England's Fire*.

76. For examples of other emphases, see Morrill, *Revolt of the Provinces*; Harris,

London Crowds; for doubts about Stuart tyranny harming trade, Zahedieh, "Regulation, Rent-Seeking, and the Glorious Revolution."

77. For a strong argument that the Glorious Revolution of 1688 was indeed very revolutionary, see Pincus, *1688*.

78. Kynaston, *Till Time's Last Sand*, 11–33.

79. Carruthers, *City of Capital*, 149–50. It's a bit more complicated: There was an old and a new company, but the old was the biggest investor in the new, and they overlapped in personnel, so I am simplifying.

80. Carruthers, *City of Capital*, 80.

81. Velde, "Lottery Loans in the Eighteenth Century," 3.

82. Stigler, *Casanova's Lottery*.

83. Carruthers, *City of Capital*, 76.

84. Temin and Voth, *Prometheus Shackled*, 27.

85. Carruthers, *City of Capital*, 76.

86. A classic discussion of the linked London-Amsterdam capital markets is in Neal, *Rise of Financial Capitalism*.

87. Neal, *Rise of Financial Capitalism*, 169.

88. Murphy, *Origins of English Financial Markets*, 25.

89. Neal, *Rise of Financial Capitalism*, 46.

90. Neal, *Rise of Financial Capitalism*, 18.

91. Neal, *Rise of Financial Capitalism*, esp. chap. 3.

92. Temin and Voth, *Prometheus Shackled*, 98.

93. The best biography of Law remains Murphy, *John Law*.

94. It's still on display in the Louvre, and it's about the size of an egg.

95. The story of the diamond deal is told in Neal, *"I Am Not Master of Events,"* chap. 3.

96. Murphy, *John Law*, chap. 14, gives an excellent overview.

97. Shovlin, *Trading with the Enemy*.

98. Kaiser, "Money, Despotism, and Public Opinion."

99. Neal, *Rise of Financial Capitalism*, 84.

100. Harris, "Bubble Act."

101. Deringer, *Calculated Values*.

102. Hoppit, "Myths of the South Sea Bubble."

103. Neal, *Rise of Financial Capitalism*, 117.

104. Neal, *Concise History*, 85.

105. Temin and Voth, *Prometheus Shackled*, 179–80.

106. Kaiser, "Money, Despotism, and Public Opinion"; Spang, "Ghost of Law."

107. Keynes, "Economic Possibilities for Our Grandchildren," 324.

108. Keynes, "Economic Possibilities for Our Grandchildren."

109. Outhwaite, "Royal Borrowing in the Reign of Elizabeth I."

110. Smith, "Global Interests of London's Commercial Community," 1122–23.

111. Israel, *Dutch Primacy*, 162.

112. Klooster, *Dutch Moment*, 47.

113. Pressman, "Oscar Hartzell," 55–63.

114. For a theoretical Marxist version of this argument, see Nichols, "Disaggregating Primitive Accumulation."

115. Brecht, *Threepenny Opera*, act 3, sc. 3.

116. This is an enormous subject of debate. For excellent recent entries, see Kwass, *Privilege and the Politics*; Sonenscher, *Before the Deluge*.

Intermission: Isaac Newton in 1717: Capitalism Under Construction

1. Gleick, *Isaac Newton*, 101.

2. Gleick, *Isaac Newton*, 106; and see also Newman, *Newton the Alchemist*, 415–34.

3. On Newton's religious beliefs, see Iliffe, *Priest of Nature*.

4. Gleick, *Isaac Newton*, 108.

5. Gleick, *Isaac Newton*, 145.

6. Gleick, *Isaac Newton*, 190.

7. Wennerlind, *Casualties of Credit*, 123–61.

8. Craig, *Newton at the Mint*, 20.

9. Craig, *Newton at the Mint*, 43.

10. Mayhew, *Sterling*, 103.

11. Craig, *Newton at the Mint*, 106.

12. Craig, *Newton at the Mint*, 84–85.

13. Westfall, *Never at Rest*, 620.

14. On the emergence of the new civic episteme, see Deringer, *Calculated Values*.

15. Westfall, *Never at Rest*, 861.

16. Westfall, *Never at Rest*, 862.

17. Gleick, *Isaac Newton*, 191.

18. Westfall, *Never at Rest*, 579–80.

19. Allen et al., "Colonial Origins of the Divergence," 872.

20. Gleick, *Isaac Newton*, 33.

21. Peterson, "Capitalism," 71–79.

Chapter 3: Land and Labor, 1640s–1800s

1. Tomlins, *Freedom Bound*, 349.

2. Tomlins, *Freedom Bound*, 422. For more on this see Patterson, *Slavery and Social Death*.

3. Camp, *Closer to Freedom*; Fuentes, *Dispossessed Lives*; Finley, *Intimate Economy*.

4. de Vries, *Industrious Revolution*.

5. Williams, *Capitalism and Slavery*, 98. The crux of the argument is chap. 5, and note that Williams is more careful and detailed than later accounts of his argument often recognize.

6. Mörner, "Spanish Historians on Spanish Migration," 252.

7. Eltis, *Rise of African Slavery*, 5.

8. Haselby, "Muslims of Early America."

9.   Manning, *Slavery and African Life*, 30.
10.   Klein, "Atlantic Slave Trade," 208.
11.   Schwartz, "Commonwealth," 159.
12.   Schwartz, "Commonwealth," 161, 163.
13.   Schwartz, "Commonwealth," 164. And also Curtin, *Rise and Fall*, 43.
14.   Klein, "Atlantic Slave Trade," 208.
15.   Schwartz, "Commonwealth," 166, 175.
16.   Schwartz, "Commonwealth," 174.
17.   Schwartz, "Commonwealth," 166.
18.   McCusker and Menard, "Sugar Industry," 295; Klooster, *Dutch Moment*, 173.
19.   Menard, *Sweet Negotiations*, 20–24.
20.   Menard, *Sweet Negotiations*, 34–38.
21.   Klein, "Atlantic Slave Trade," 209.
22.   McCusker and Menard, "Sugar Industry," 297.
23.   Curtin, *Rise and Fall*, 82–83; Menard, *Sweet Negotiations*, 65.
24.   For the economic explanation for the switch from servitude to slavery, see Galenson, "Rise and Fall of Indentured Servitude."
25.   Menard, *Sweet Negotiations*, 106.
26.   Menard, *Sweet Negotiations*, 108.
27.   Menard, *Sweet Negotiations*, 111.
28.   Menard, *Sweet Negotiations*, 18.
29.   Curtin, *Rise and Fall*, 82.
30.   Morgan, *Slavery, Atlantic Trade and the British Economy*, 21.
31.   Klein, "Atlantic Slave Trade," 209; Menard, *Sweet Negotiations*, 48.
32.   Menard, *Sweet Negotiations*, 79.
33.   Morgan, *Slavery and Servitude*, 36, 57.
34.   Morgan, *Slavery and Servitude*, 40.
35.   Radburn, *Traders in Men*, 7.
36.   McCusker and Menard, "Sugar Industry," 305.
37.   Menard, *Sweet Negotiations*, 17.
38.   Menard, *Sweet Negotiations*, 56.
39.   The classic statement is Lewis, "Economic Development."
40.   Aston and Philpin, *Brenner Debate*; Meiksins Wood, *Origin of Capitalism*.
41.   de Vries, "Netherlands and the Polder Model."
42.   Cantor, *Changing English Countryside*, 29, 36.
43.   Allen, *Enclosure and the Yeoman*, 45–47.
44.   Allen, *Enclosure and the Yeoman*, 14.
45.   Allen, *Enclosure and the Yeoman*, 66–67.
46.   Allen, *Enclosure and the Yeoman*, 94.
47.   Allen, *Enclosure and the Yeoman*, 92.
48.   Humphries, "Enclosures, Common Rights, and Women."
49.   Allen, *Enclosure and the Yeoman*, 218.
50.   Allen, *Enclosure and the Yeoman*, 235.

51. Thompson, *Whigs and Hunters*.

52. Hay, "Property, Authority and the Criminal Law," 18.

53. Linebaugh, *London Hanged*, 18.

54. Eltis, *Rise of African Slavery*, 75.

55. Cantor, *English Countryside*, 36.

56. Cantor, *English Countryside*, 60.

57. Allen, "Price of Freehold Land," 43, table 2.

58. Allen, *Enclosure and the Yeoman*, 285.

59. Pistor, *Code of Capital*.

60. Blaufarb, *Great Demarcation*.

61. Acemoglu et al., "Consequences of Radical Reform."

62. Horning, *Ireland in the Virginian Sea*, 275 and 314–16.

63. Horning, *Ireland in the Virginian Sea*, 1. This book contains much more on the linkages between colonialism in Virginia and Ireland.

64. Morgan, *Slavery and Servitude*, 44.

65. Morgan, *Slavery and Servitude*, 9.

66. Morgan, *Slavery and Servitude*, 13–15.

67. Eltis, *Rise of African Slavery*, 44.

68. Eltis, *Rise of African Slavery*, 8.

69. Morgan, *Slavery and Servitude*, 20.

70. Tomlins, *Freedom Bound*, 64–65; Grubb, "Does Bound Labour Have to Be Coerced?"

71. Steinfeld, *Invention of Free Labor*, 56.

72. Morgan, *Slavery and Servitude*, 45–47.

73. Steinfeld, *Invention of Free Labor*, 19–20, 40.

74. Steinfeld, *Invention of Free Labor*, 27.

75. Grubb, "End of European Immigrant Servitude."

76. Morgan, *Slavery and Servitude*, 11; Tomlins, "Early British America," 134.

77. Priest, *Credit Nation*, esp. 25–27.

78. Weaver, *Great Land Rush*, 100.

79. Priest, *Credit Nation*, 23.

80. McCusker and Menard, *Economy of British America*, 245, 254.

81. Greer, *Property and Dispossession*, 360–67.

82. Greer, *Property and Dispossession*, 372–75.

83. Greer, *Property and Dispossession*, 376–79.

84. Greer, *Property and Dispossession*, 383.

85. On the company's history, see Stern, *Company-State*.

86. The classic work on the subject is an intellectual history: Guha, *Rule of Property for Bengal*. See also Stokes, *English Utilitarians and India*.

87. On the material economics instead of the intellectual history, see Roy, "Where Is Bengal?" and Roy, "Permanent Settlement." For a case showing how the creation of property in Bengal and fossil-fuel extraction interacted, see Shutzer, "Subterranean Properties."

88. For a similar story in Punjab, see Bhattacharya, *Great Agrarian Conquest*.

89. Steinfeld, *Invention of Free Labor*, 79. For the classic statement, see Macpherson, *Political Theory of Possessive Individualism*.

90. Eltis, *Rise of African Slavery*, 22.

91. For much more on the pervasive new ideology of "improvement," see Slack, *Invention of Improvement*.

92. Weaver, *Great Land Rush*, 81.

93. Eltis, *Rise of African Slavery*, 61.

94. Morgan, *Slavery and Servitude*, 35.

95. Kruer, *Time of Anarchy*, 118–19.

96. Morgan, *American Slavery, American Freedom*, 270.

97. For example, Fields, "Slavery, Race, and Ideology," 101–16.

98. McCusker and Menard, *Economy of British America*, 39.

99. Morgan, *Slavery, Atlantic Trade and the British Economy*, 18.

100. Berg and Hudson, *Slavery, Capitalism and the Industrial Revolution*, 57.

101. de Vries, "Connecting Europe and Asia," 92, table 2.14.

102. Morgan, *Slavery, Atlantic Trade and the British Economy*, 12.

103. Menard, *Sweet Negotiations*, 51.

104. Morgan, *Slavery and the British Empire*, 35.

105. Morgan, *Slavery and Servitude*, 30.

106. Klein, "Atlantic Slave Trade," 215.

107. Morgan, *Slavery and Servitude*, 66.

108. Radburn, *Traders in Men*, 28–31.

109. Radburn, *Traders in Men*, 40.

110. Manning, *Slavery and African Life*, 51–53, 128.

111. Kea, *Settlements, Trade, and Polities*.

112. Fynn, *Asante and Its Neighbours*.

113. Radburn, *Traders in Men*, 43–46.

114. Nwokeji, *Slave Trade and Culture*, 22–81.

115. Radburn, *Traders in Men*, 57.

116. Curtin, *Rise and Fall*, 126–27.

117. Curtin, *Rise and Fall*, 131.

118. Manning, *Slavery and African Life*, 34; and Curtin, *Rise and Fall*, 126.

119. Curtin, *Rise and Fall*, 120.

120. Manning, *Slavery and African Life*, 64, 91.

121. On the magnitude of slave revolts, see Taylor, *If We Must Die*.

122. Eltis, *Rise of African Slavery*, 192.

123. Manning, *Slavery and African Life*, 91.

124. Eltis, *Rise of African Slavery*, 180; Curtin, *Rise and Fall*, 124.

125. Radburn, *Traders in Men*, 76–77.

126. I am grateful to Bruce Hall for pointing this out.

127. Manning, *Slavery and African Life*, 94.

128. On this process, see Smallwood, *Saltwater Slavery*, esp. chap. 2; and Mustakeem, *Slavery at Sea*.

129. Manning, *Slavery and African Life*, 64.

130. Radburn, *Traders in Men*, 206.

131. Berg and Hudson, *Slavery, Capitalism and the Industrial Revolution*, 95, table 4.1.

132. Berg and Hudson, *Slavery, Capitalism and the Industrial Revolution*, 140.

133. Curtin, *Rise and Fall*, 117.

134. Radburn, *Traders in Men*, 211.

135. Morgan, *Slavery and the British Empire*, 68.

136. Morgan, *Slavery, Atlantic Trade and the British Economy*, 23.

137. These numbers, and figure 6, are from the Trans-Atlantic Slave Trade Database at slavevoyages.org.

138. Eltis et al., "Slave Prices," 677–78.

139. Manning, *Slavery and African Life*, 23.

140. Manning, *Slavery and African Life*, 95; Curtin, *Rise and Fall*, 133.

141. Curtin, *Rise and Fall*, 133.

142. Morgan, *Slavery and the British Empire*, 74.

143. Morgan, *Slavery and Servitude*, 69.

144. Manning, *Slavery and African Life*, 37.

145. McCusker and Menard, *Economy of British America*, 176, 183. On rice, see Carney, *Black Rice*.

146. McCusker and Menard, *Economy of British America*, 98.

147. On Atlantic cod, see Grafe, *Distant Tyranny*; also McCusker and Menard, *Economy of British America*, 99.

148. Morgan, *Slavery, Atlantic Trade and the British Economy*, 59.

149. Morgan, *Slavery and Servitude*, 74.

150. Morgan, *Slavery, Atlantic Trade and the British Economy*, 59.

151. Morgan, *Slavery, Atlantic Trade and the British Economy*, 63.

152. Morgan, *Slavery, Atlantic Trade and the British Economy*, 22.

153. Curtin, *Rise and Fall*, 142.

154. Muldrew, *Food, Energy and the Creation of Industriousness*, 26.

155. Muldrew, *Food, Energy and the Creation of Industriousness*, 227.

156. The classic account is Thompson, "Time, Work-Discipline, and Industrial Capitalism," but he is not very specific about the time, place, or prevalence of these habits.

157. Humphries and Weisdorf, "Unreal Wages?" provides several estimates from different scholars. One puts the medieval working year at 168 days, while the 19th-century industrial one was as many as 330 days. A five-day workweek with two weeks of vacation is 250 days.

158. de Vries, *Industrious Revolution*, 88–91.

159. Voth, *Time and Work in England*, 244–49.

160. de Vries, *Industrious Revolution*, 43–57.

161. de Vries, *Industrious Revolution*, esp. 113–21.

162. Eltis et al., "Slave Prices," 678.

163. For a critique of overlooking women and gender history in the history of capitalism, see Stanley, "Histories of Capitalism and Sex Difference."

164. Humphries, "Enclosures, Common Rights, and Women."

165. Linebaugh, *London Hanged*, 407.

166. Steinfeld, *Invention of Free Labor*, 115.

167. Tomlins, *Freedom Bound*, 355–58.

168. Although many readers turn to Karl Marx for theory and critique, chapter 8 ("The Working Day") and chapter 13 ("Machinery and Large-Scale Industry") in his *Capital* contain some magnificent historical evidence and analysis of these processes.

169. Muldrew, *Food, Energy and the Creation of Industriousness*, 242.

170. Millward, "Emergence of Wage Labor," 28.

171. Millward, "Emergence of Wage Labor," 22.

172. On patterns and limits of proto-industry and other industrious family activities, see de Vries, *Industrious Revolution*, 97–107.

173. Muldrew, *Food, Energy and the Creation of Industriousness*, 26.

174. Morgan, *Slavery, Atlantic Trade and the British Economy*, 44; Anstey, "Volume and Profitability of the British Slave Trade," 3–31. There is an enormous debate about these numbers, covering dozens of publications over decades.

175. Menard, *Sweet Negotiations*, 86. These numbers are actually from Craton, *Sinews of Empire*, 138–39.

176. Berg and Hudson, *Slavery, Capitalism and the Industrial Revolution*, 43.

177. Eltis, *Rise of African Slavery*, 269.

178. Morgan, *Slavery, Atlantic Trade and the British Economy*, 45.

179. Berg and Hudson, *Slavery, Capitalism and the Industrial Revolution*, 42 (their italics).

180. Eltis, *Rise of African Slavery*, 267.

181. The classic statement of this view is Genovese, *World the Slaveholders Made*.

182. Rosenthal, *Accounting for Slavery*; Murphy, *Banking on Slavery*; Johnson, *Soul by Soul*.

183. Berg and Hudson, *Slavery, Capitalism and the Industrial Revolution*, 90–91.

184. Berg and Hudson, *Slavery, Capitalism and the Industrial Revolution*, 165.

185. The most comprehensive effort to compile the contributions of Africans, both enslaved and free, to British economic growth is Inikori, *Africans and the Industrial Revolution in England*.

186. The story of Haitian independence and the indemnity is of vital importance. Among many others, see the classic James, *Black Jacobins*; Dubois, *Avengers of the New World*; and for later consequences, Hallward, *Damming the Flood*.

187. Martinez, *Slave Trade and the Origins*.

188. On repaying the slave-owners, see Draper, *Price of Emancipation*; Hall et al., *Legacies of British Slave-Ownership*; on abolition as a pretext for empire, Scanlan, *Slave Empire*. University College London maintains a database where you

can look up your least-favorite British person to see if they or their family owned slaves: https://www.ucl.ac.uk/lbs/.
189. Manning, *Slavery and African Life*, 137–40.
190. Steinfeld, *Invention of Free Labor*, 147.

Chapter 4: Industry, 1710–1830

1. Hobsbawm, *Industry and Empire*, 1.
2. Smith, *Wealth of Nations*, 21–26.
3. Moore, "Environmental Crises and the Metabolic Rift."
4. Wrigley, *Energy*.
5. Feinstein, "Pessimism Perpetuated."
6. For the many dimensions of the Acceleration, see Bonneuil and Fressoz, *Shock of the Anthropocene*.
7. For a survey of world history that contextualizes capitalism in a wider set of human relations to the environment, see Amrith, *Burning Earth*.
8. The best discussion of the technical elements of all these inventions remains Mokyr, *Lever of Riches*, chap. 5.
9. Timmins, *Last Shift*, 19.
10. Riello, *Cotton*, 204.
11. Olmstead and Rhode, "Biological Innovation."
12. Riello, *Cotton*, 207.
13. Riello, *Cotton*, 212.
14. Fernihough and O'Rourke, "Coal and the European Industrial Revolution," 1137.
15. Richards, *Unending Frontier*, 238.
16. Allen, *British Industrial Revolution in Global Perspective*, 164–68.
17. Berg and Hudson, *Slavery, Capitalism and the Industrial Revolution*, 132.
18. Malm, *Fossil Capital*, 54.
19. Malm, *Fossil Capital*, 55–56.
20. Radburn, *Traders in Men*, 213–15.
21. Bulstrode, "Black Metallurgists."
22. Bulstrode, "Black Metallurgists," 19.
23. Evans, "Industrial Revolution in Iron," 25.
24. Pluymers, *No Wood, No Kingdom*, 2–3.
25. Fressoz, *More and More and More*.
26. Pluymers, *No Wood, No Kingdom*, 12.
27. Pluymers, *No Wood, No Kingdom*, 221–24.
28. Richards, *Unending Frontier*, 224–25.
29. Richards, *Unending Frontier*, 221.
30. Richards, *Unending Frontier*, 221–22.
31. Wrigley, *Energy*, 16.
32. Richards, *Unending Frontier*, 235.
33. Kander et al., *Power to the People*, 56–59.

34. Wrigley, *Energy*, 39.
35. Kander et al., *Power to the People*, 114.
36. Malm, *Fossil Capital*, 13.
37. Kander et al., *Power to the People*, 71.
38. Kander et al., *Power to the People*, 75.
39. Wrigley, *Energy*, 94, table 4.2.
40. Richards, *Unending Frontier*, 239.
41. Fressoz, *More and More and More*.
42. Pollard, "Factory Discipline," 258n5.
43. Pollard, "Factory Discipline," 256.
44. Pollard, "Factory Discipline," 265–66.
45. Pollard, "Factory Discipline," 268–69.
46. Pollard, "Factory Discipline," 260–61.
47. Humphries, *Childhood and Child Labour*, 176–77.
48. Pollard, "Factory Discipline," 259–60.
49. Humphries, *Childhood and Child Labour*, 45.
50. Humphries, *Childhood and Child Labour*, 184.
51. Hobsbawm, "Machine Breakers," 59–62.
52. Horn, "Machine-breaking," 148.
53. Hobsbawm, "Machine Breakers," 62.
54. Horn, "Machine-breaking," 148.
55. Hobsbawm, "Machine Breakers," 58.
56. Horn, "Machine-breaking," 150.
57. Horn, "Machine-breaking," 150.
58. Hobsbawm and Rudé, *Captain Swing*.
59. Horn, "Machine-breaking," 155.
60. Thompson, *Making of the English Working Class*, 807–32.
61. Pollard, "Factory Discipline," 270.
62. Malm, *Fossil Capital*, 69.
63. Malm, *Fossil Capital*, 70.
64. The fate of the handloom weavers is told in E. P. Thompson's classic *Making of the English Working Class*, 269–314.
65. Timmins, *Last Shift*, 28, table 1.4.
66. Parthasarathi, *Why Europe Grew Rich*, 101–8.
67. Cuenca Esteban, "British Balance of Payments," table 1.
68. Clingingsmith and Williamson, "Deindustrialization," 220.
69. Parthasarathi, *Why Europe Grew Rich*, 126–27.
70. Parthasarathi, *Why Europe Grew Rich*, 24, 138.
71. Chang, *Kicking Away the Ladder* and *Bad Samaritans*.
72. DuPlessis, "Cottons Consumption," 227.
73. DuPlessis, "Cottons Consumption," 228.
74. Findlay and O'Rourke, *Power and Plenty*, 314, table 6.2.
75. Balderston, "The Economics of Abundance," 573.

76. Clingingsmith and Williamson, "Deindustrialization," 217.
77. Clingingsmith and Williamson, "Deindustrialization," 217; see also Roy, *Economic History of Early Modern India*.
78. Clingingsmith and Williamson, "Deindustrialization," 218; in more detail, Roy, *Crafts and Capitalism*.
79. Kander et al., *Power to the People*, 143.
80. On air pollution see Mosley, *Chimney of the World*; Uekoetter, *Age of Smoke*; Thorsheim, *Inventing Pollution*.
81. Kumekawa, "Measuring the Cost of Pollution," 339–40.
82. Cushman, *Guano and the Opening of the Pacific World*.
83. Otter, *Diet for a Large Planet*.
84. Richards, *Unending Frontier*, 6.
85. Whitney, *From Coastal Wilderness*, 150.
86. Rosenthal, *Accounting for Slavery*; and also Olmstead and Rhode, "Biological Innovation," 1124–25.
87. Dean, "Deforestation in Southeastern Brazil," 61–63.
88. Mokyr, "Irish History with the Potato," 8–11.
89. Ó Gráda, *Ireland Before and After the Famine*, 138–44.
90. Read, *Great Famine in Ireland*.
91. Jackson et al., "Historical Overfishing," 629.
92. Whitney, *From Coastal Wilderness*, 306.
93. Richards, *Unending Frontier*, 510–11.
94. Whitney, *From Coastal Wilderness*, 300–301.
95. Whitney, *From Coastal Wilderness*, 144. See also Isenberg, *Destruction of the Buffalo*, esp. chap. 4.
96. Richards, *Unending Frontier*, 606.
97. Richards, *Unending Frontier*, 606.
98. Richards, *Unending Frontier*, 611.
99. Richards, *Unending Frontier*, 613, table 16.1; Demuth, *Floating Coast*, 15, 68.
100. Demuth's *Floating Coast*, chap. 2, is astonishingly good on this.
101. Kander et al., *Power to the People*, 191.
102. Greene, *Horses at Work*, 8, 51–60, 180–82.
103. Greene, *Horses at Work*, 41, 166.
104. Greene, *Horses at Work*, 63–65.
105. Greene, *Horses at Work*, 71–79.
106. Greene, *Horses at Work*, 170.
107. Cronon, *Nature's Metropolis*.
108. McShane and Tarr, *Horse in the City*, 135.
109. Ron, "When Hay Was King," 186.
110. Ron, "When Hay Was King," 208.
111. The best version of this argument focuses on a slightly later period: Edgerton, *Shock of the Old*.
112. Daggett, *Birth of Energy*, 3–4; and in the US case, Ron, "When Hay Was King."

113. Jackson, "Revolution and Extinction."
114. Kander et al., *Power to the People*, 132.
115. Baines, *History of the Cotton Manufacture*, 244.
116. Riello, *Cotton*, 214.
117. Kander et al., *Power to the People*, 125.
118. Kander et al., *Power to the People*, 131.
119. Balderston, "Economics of Abundance," 583.

Chapter 5: Empire, 1840s–1914

1. This is an important part of the story of the modern economy, but it is not our focus here, because it mainly involves the geographical extension of processes we have already discussed. But see the classics: Milward and Saul, *Development of the Economies*; Trebilcock, *Industrialization of the Continental Powers*.
2. Chandler, *Visible Hand*.
3. Headrick, *Power over Peoples*, 177.
4. Pakenham, *Scramble for Africa*. This book is outdated, and not widely esteemed by scholars in its field, but I know of no other broad survey of the subject.
5. A dramatic journalistic account can be found in Hochschild, *King Leopold's Ghost*, but see also Vanthemsche, *Belgium and the Congo*.
6. Headrick, *Power over Peoples*, 181.
7. Headrick, *Power over Peoples*.
8. Headrick, *Tools of Empire*, 170.
9. Headrick, *Power over Peoples*, 196.
10. Headrick, *Power over Peoples*, 234.
11. Allen, *Institutional Revolution*, chap. 2.
12. Nelson, *Oceans of Grain*, chaps. 7–9.
13. O'Rourke, "European Grain Invasion."
14. Nelson, *Oceans of Grain*, chaps. 9–10.
15. Sabato, *Agrarian Capitalism*, argument at 48 and quote at 193.
16. Osterhammel, *Transformation of the World*, 154.
17. Osterhammel, *Transformation of the World*, 118.
18. Osterhammel, *Transformation of the World*, 159.
19. Osterhammel, *Transformation of the World*, 162.
20. A recent study on this phase of Gandhi's life is Desai and Vahed, *South African Gandhi*.
21. Lewis, *Evolution of the International Economic Order*.
22. Lake and Reynolds, *Drawing the Global Colour Line*; Behm, *Imperial History and the Global Politics of Exclusion*.
23. For an exquisite study of the cultural impact of railroads see Schivelbusch, *Railway Journey*.
24. Foner, *Great Labor Uprising*, 13.

25. Foner, *Great Labor Uprising*, 13–14.

26. Foner, *Great Labor Uprising*, 14.

27. Nelson, *Oceans of Grain*, 153.

28. Shifflett, *Coal Towns*, 27.

29. Andrews, *Killing for Coal*, 112.

30. Sabato, *Agrarian Capitalism*, 222.

31. Cronon, *Nature's Metropolis*.

32. Cronon, *Nature's Metropolis*, 210–11.

33. Osterhammel, *Transformation of the World*, 230.

34. Headrick, *Tools of Empire*, 184–86.

35. Roy, *Economic History of India*, 264.

36. A useful overview of the following arguments can be found in Sweeney, "Indian Railways and Famine." Just to be clear, there were no good consequences of empire.

37. Roy, *Economic History of India*, 294.

38. Donaldson, "Railroads of the Raj."

39. Frankema et al., "Economic Rationale," 239. Also Jedwab and Moradi, "Permanent Effects."

40. Headrick, *Power over Peoples*, 258–65.

41. Headrick, *Power over Peoples*, 265.

42. Headrick, *Tools of Empire*, 158.

43. Headrick, *Tools of Empire*, 160.

44. Headrick, *Tools of Empire*, 161–63.

45. Headrick, *Power over Peoples*, 266–67.

46. Frankema et al., "Economic Rationale."

47. Austin, *Labour, Land and Capital in Ghana*, 47.

48. Lovejoy and Richardson, "Initial 'Crisis of Adaptation,'" 47.

49. Lynn, "West African Palm Oil Trade," 60, 64, 69.

50. Mann, "Owners, Slaves and the Struggle," 145–48.

51. Headrick, *Power over Peoples*, 211–12.

52. Frankema et al., "Economic Rationale," 255; Lynn, "West African Palm Oil Trade," 72.

53. Platt, *Imperial Twilight*, 224.

54. Platt, *Imperial Twilight*, 195–96.

55. Platt, *Imperial Twilight*, 197.

56. Irigoin, "End of a Silver Era." Irigoin puts more weight on the inadequate new standard, but does show silver inflows to China slumping after the late 1820s.

57. Platt, *Imperial Twilight*, 305; Rowe, *China's Last Empire*, 157.

58. Platt, *Imperial Twilight*, 388.

59. Platt, *Imperial Twilight*, 426.

60. Zelin, *Merchants of Zigong*, esp. 120 and 278.

61. Zelin, *Merchants of Zigong*, 6, 24.

62. Wang, *Chinese Hinterland Capitalism*, 6–7, 12.

63. Zelin, *Merchants of Zigong*, xviii.
64. Benton, *They Called It Peace*, esp. chap. 3.
65. The literature on American imperialism is huge. A readable recent overview is Immerwahr, *How to Hide an Empire*.
66. Claudio, *Profligate Colonial*.
67. For a helpful overview, Jansen, *Making of Modern Japan*.
68. See the essays in Myers and Peattie, *Japanese Colonial Empire*.
69. Metzler, *Lever of Empire*, 52–53.
70. Duus, *Abacus and the Sword*; Uchida, *Brokers of Empire*.
71. And American Pacific imperialism: Iriye, *Pacific Estrangement*.
72. Metzler, *Lever of Empire*, 22–23.
73. Metzler, *Lever of Empire*, 3, 31, 51.
74. Fishlow, "Lessons from the Past," 384.
75. Davis and Huttenback, *Mammon and the Pursuit of Empire*, 38.
76. Davis and Huttenback, *Mammon and the Pursuit of Empire*, 43.
77. Fishlow, "Lessons from the Past," 395.
78. Daudin et al., "Europe and Globalization," 26, table 1.4.
79. Davis and Huttenback, *Mammon and the Pursuit of Empire*, 55.
80. Davis and Huttenback, *Mammon and the Pursuit of Empire*, 72. On Bengali coal see Shutzer, "Subterranean Properties."
81. Davis and Huttenback, *Mammon and the Pursuit of Empire*, 88.
82. Queralt, *Pawned States*.
83. Davis and Huttenback, *Mammon and the Pursuit of Empire*, 102–5.
84. Reinhart and Rogoff, *This Time Is Different*, 90, table 6.
85. Mitchener and Weidenmier, "Supersanctions and Sovereign Debt Repayment."
86. The following draws on Queralt, *Pawned States*, 44.
87. Queralt, *Pawned States*, 95.
88. Queralt, *Pawned States*, 96.
89. Queralt, *Pawned States*, 135–38.
90. Maurer and Arroyo Abad, "Can Europe Run Greece?"
91. Maurer, *Empire Trap*, 184.
92. Meyer et al., "Sovereign Bonds Since Waterloo."
93. On bimetallic systems, see Redish, *Bimetallism*.
94. The following draws heavily on Eichengreen, *Globalizing Capital*, chap. 2; Eichengreen and Flandreau, *Gold Standard in Theory and History*; Bordo, "The Gold Standard."
95. For instance, Madley, *American Genocide*.
96. Until the 1930s, people referred to the price deflation of 1873–96 as "the Great Depression." Scholars today no longer think of it that way, because overall economic growth continued, trade grew rapidly, and even real wages, in the aggregate, also grew. What declined was agricultural prices, immiserating farmers, and leading to political demands to remonetize silver, as with

the Populists in the United States. For the revisionist view of the deflation, see Bordo et al., "Good Versus Bad Deflation."

97.   Metzler, *Lever of Empire*, 26–30.
98.   Dornbusch and Frenkel, "Gold Standard and the Bank of England," 254.
99.   For a brief overview, see Hobsbawm, *Age of Empire*, 116–18.
100. Foner, *Great Labor Uprising*, 189.
101. Andrews, *Killing for Coal*, 179, 240.
102. Andrews, *Killing for Coal*, 272–73.
103. Shorter and Tilly, *Strikes in France*, 107, 112.
104. Perrot, *Workers on Strike*, 13.
105. Delalande, *Struggle and Mutual Aid*, 153, 258; Bayly, *Birth of the Modern World*, 193.
106. Delalande, *Struggle and Mutual Aid*, 218–19.
107. Delalande, *Struggle and Mutual Aid*, 258.
108. Bayly, *Birth of the Modern World*, 193.
109. Delalande, *Struggle and Mutual Aid*, 259.
110. Du Bois, *Black Reconstruction*, chaps. 4 and 5. Saville, *Work of Reconstruction*, and Hahn, *Nation Under Our Feet*, both provide detailed recent substantiations of this argument.
111. Jensen, "Daggers, Rifles and Dynamite."
112. The clearest statements of the field and its aims can be found in the introduction to Beckert and Rockman's *Slavery's Capitalism*; and Rockman, "What Makes the History of Capitalism Newsworthy?" The core books in the field are Beckert, *Empire of Cotton*; Johnson, *River of Dark Dreams*; Baptist, *Half Has Never Been Told*.
113. Extensive critiques of the methods and empirical claims of the field can be found in Hilt, "Economic History, Historical Analysis"; Olmstead and Rhode, "Cotton, Slavery, and the New History"; Burnard and Riello, "Slavery and the New History of Capitalism."
114. Wright, "Slavery and the Rise."
115. Wright, "Slavery and Anglo-American Capitalism," 374–75.
116. Rhode, "What Fraction of Antebellum."
117. Wright, *Old South, New South*, 18–19.
118. Wright, *Old South, New South*, 28, 34.
119. Research on this subject is only belatedly happening. See Carlos et al., "Indigenous Nations."
120. Gordon, *Rise and Fall of American Growth*.
121. The classic works are Chandler, *Visible Hand*; Berle and Means, *Modern Corporation and Private Property*.
122. For an excellent overview, see Levy, *Ages of American Capitalism*, chaps. 8 and 11.
123. This is part of the famous argument of Piketty, *Capital in the Twenty-First Century*, especially chap. 2.
124. Cummins, "Where Is the Middle Class?"

125. Davis and Huttenback, *Mammon and the Pursuit of Empire*, 200, 212.

126. Davis and Huttenback, *Mammon and the Pursuit of Empire*, 195.

127. O'Brien, "Costs and Benefits," 187.

128. Davis and Huttenback, *Mammon and the Pursuit of Empire*, 252.

129. Etemad, *Possessing the World*, cited in Osterhammel, *Transformation of the World*, 125–26.

130. On Namibia, see Hull, *Absolute Destruction*.

131. Davis and Huttenback, *Mammon and the Pursuit of Empire*, 13–14.

132. O'Brien, "Costs and Benefits," 194–95.

Epilogue: Vladimir Lenin in 1917: Capitalism's Near-Death Experience

1. Foucault, "Nietzsche, Genealogy, History," 154.

2. For a dramatic account of the events of the revolution, see Miéville, *October*.

3. Bayly, *Birth of the Modern World*, 19–20.

4. For a story about Lenin and hotel radiators see Valentinov, *Encounters with Lenin*, 37–38.

5. The case for dynamism is made in Mironov, "Wages and Prices in Imperial Russia," and Mironov and A'Hearn, "Russian Living Standards Under the Tsars."

6. Dennison and Nafziger, "Living Standards in Nineteenth-Century Russia," 416–17.

7. Allen, *Farm to Factory*, 5, table 1.1.

8. Novokmet et al., "From Soviets to Oligarchs."

9. Keynes, *Economic Consequences of the Peace*, 11.

10. Gorky, *Days with Lenin*. Circa 1903, the Café Landolt was the headquarters of several political movements, including Zionism and various anticolonial projects. Hillis, *Utopia's Discontents*, chap. 1.

11. Bradley, *Muzhik and Muscovite*, 197–98.

12. Bradley, *Muzhik and Muscovite*, 201–2.

13. Haber, *Poisonous Cloud*.

14. For overviews of the revolution, see Fitzpatrick, *Russian Revolution*, and Smith, *Russia in Revolution*.

15. Jones, *Founding Weimar*.

16. For a masterful account, see Maier, *Recasting Bourgeois Europe*.

17. For an overview of open social conflict, see Gage, *Wall Street Exploded*. See also Schmidt, *Red Scare*; and Montgomery, *Fall of the House of Labor*.

18. The essential history remains Eichengreen, *Golden Fetters*.

19. Schumpeter, *Capitalism, Socialism and Democracy*.

20. Fukuyama, "The End of History?"; the full book version is Fukuyama, *End of History and the Last Man*.

21. This story is detailed in George, "How to Win the War of Ideas."

22. This is the argument of Milanovic, *Capitalism, Alone*.

23. For a detailed recent account of the problem, see Malm and Carton, *Overshoot*.

Acemoglu, Daron, Davide Cantoni, Simon Johnson, and James Robinson. "The Consequences of Radical Reform: The French Revolution." *American Economic Review* 101, no. 7 (2011): 3286–307.

Alfani, Guido. *As Gods Among Men: A History of the Rich in the West*. Princeton University Press, 2023.

Alfani, Guido. "Inequality in History: A Long-Run View." *Journal of Economic Surveys* 39, no. 2 (2025): 546–66.

Allen, Douglas. *The Institutional Revolution: Measurement and the Economic Emergence of the Modern World*. University of Chicago Press, 2012.

Allen, Robert. *The British Industrial Revolution in Global Perspective*. Cambridge University Press, 2009.

Allen, Robert. *Enclosure and the Yeoman*. Oxford University Press, 1992.

Allen, Robert. *Farm to Factory: A Reinterpretation of the Soviet Industrial Revolution*. Princeton University Press, 2003.

Allen, Robert. "The Great Divergence in European Wages and Prices from the Middle Ages to the First World War." *Explorations in Economic History* 38, no. 4 (2001): 411–47.

Allen, Robert. "The Price of Freehold Land and the Interest Rate in the Seventeenth and Eighteenth Centuries." *Economic History Review* 41, no. 1 (1988): 33–50.

Allen, Robert, Tommy Murphy, and Eric Schneider. "The Colonial Origins of the Divergence in the Americas: A Labor Market Approach." *Journal of Economic History* 72, no. 4 (2012): 863–94.

Amin, Samir. *Eurocentrism*. Monthly Review Press, 1989.

Amrith, Sunil. *The Burning Earth: A History*. W. W. Norton, 2024.

Anderson, James Maxwell. *The History of Portugal*. Greenwood Press, 2000.

Andrews, Thomas. *Killing for Coal: America's Deadliest Labor War*. Harvard University Press, 2008.

Anstey, Roger. "The Volume and Profitability of the British Slave Trade, 1761–1807." In *Race and Slavery in the Western Hemisphere*, edited by Stanley Engerman and Eugene Genovese. Princeton University Press, 1975.

Appleby, Joyce. *The Relentless Revolution: A History of Capitalism*. W. W. Norton, 2010.

Arrighi, Giovanni. *The Long Twentieth Century: Money, Power and the Origins of Our Times*. Verso, 2010.

Arroyo Abad, Leticia, Elwyn Davies, and Jan Luiten van Zanden. "Between Conquest and Independence: Real Wages and Demographic Change in Spanish America, 1530–1820." *Explorations in Economic History* 49, no. 2 (2012): 149–66.

Arroyo Abad, Leticia, and Nuno Palma. "The Fruits of El Dorado: The Global Impact of American Precious Metals." In *The Fruits of the Early Globalization: An Iberian Perspective*, edited by Rafael Dobado-González and Alfredo García-Hiernaux. Palgrave Macmillan, 2021.

Arroyo Abad, Leticia, and Jan Luiten van Zanden. "Growth Under Extractive Institutions? Latin American Per Capita GDP in Colonial Times." *Journal of Economic History* 76, no. 4 (2016): 1182–215.

Aston, T. H., and C. H. E. Philpin, eds. *The Brenner Debate: Agrarian Class Structure and Economic Development in Pre-Industrial Europe*. Cambridge University Press, 1987.

Austin, Gareth. *Labour, Land and Capital in Ghana: From Slavery to Free Labour in Asante, 1807–1956*. University of Rochester Press, 2005.

Baines, Edward. *History of the Cotton Manufacture in Great Britain*. H. Fisher, R. Fisher, and P. Jackson, 1835.

Bakewell, P. J. *Silver Mining and Society in Colonial Mexico: Zacatecas, 1546–1700*. Cambridge University Press, 1971.

Balderston, Theo. "The Economics of Abundance: Coal and Cotton in Lancashire and the World." *Economic History Review* 63, no. 3 (2010): 569–90.

Baptist, Edward. *The Half Has Never Been Told: Slavery and the Making of American Capitalism*. Basic Books, 2014.

Barrett, Ward. "World Bullion Flows, 1450–1800." In *The Rise of Merchant Empires: Long-Distance Trade in the Early Modern World, 1350–1750*, edited by James Tracy. Cambridge University Press, 1990.

Bayly, C. A. *The Birth of the Modern World, 1780–1914: Global Connections and Comparisons*. Blackwell, 2004.

Becker, Gary, and H. Gregg Lewis. "On the Interaction Between the Quantity and Quality of Children." *Journal of Political Economy* 81, no. 2, part 2 (1973): S279–S288.

Beckert, Sven. *Empire of Cotton: A Global History*. Vintage, 2014.

Beckert, Sven, and Seth Rockman. Introduction to *Slavery's Capitalism: A New History of American Economic Development*, edited by Sven Beckert and Seth Rockman. University of Pennsylvania Press, 2016.

Behm, Amanda. *Imperial History and the Global Politics of Exclusion: Britain, 1880–1940*. Palgrave Macmillan, 2018.

Benedictow, Ole J. *The Black Death, 1346–1353: The Complete History*. Boydell Press, 2006.

Benton, Lauren. *They Called It Peace: Worlds of Imperial Violence*. Princeton University Press, 2024.

Berg, Maxine, and Pat Hudson. "Rehabilitating the Industrial Revolution." *Economic History Review* 45, no. 1 (1992): 24–50.

Berg, Maxine, and Pat Hudson. *Slavery, Capitalism and the Industrial Revolution*. Polity Press, 2023.

Berle, Adolf, and Gardiner Means. *The Modern Corporation and Private Property*. Transaction Publishers, 1968.

Bhattacharya, Neeladri. *The Great Agrarian Conquest: The Colonial Reshaping of a Rural World*. State University of New York Press, 2020.

Bindseil, Ulrich. *Central Banking Before 1800: A Rehabilitation*. Oxford University Press, 2019.

Blaufarb, Rafe. *The Great Demarcation: The French Revolution and the Invention of Modern Property*. Oxford University Press, 2016.

Bonneuil, Christophe, and Jean-Baptiste Fressoz. *The Shock of the Anthropocene: The Earth, History and Us*. Verso, 2017.

Bordo, Michael. "The Gold Standard: The Traditional Approach." In Bordo and Schwartz, *Retrospective on the Classical Gold Standard*.

Bordo, Michael, John Landon-Lane, and Angela Redish. "Good Versus Bad Deflation: Lessons from the Gold Standard Era." In *Monetary Policy in Low-Inflation Economies*, edited by David Altig and Ed Nosal. Cambridge University Press, 2009.

Bordo, Michael, and Anna Schwartz, eds. *A Retrospective on the Classical Gold Standard, 1821–1931*. University of Chicago Press, 1984.

Braddick, Michael. *God's Fury, England's Fire: A New History of the English Civil Wars*. Allen Lane, 2008.

Bradley, Joseph. *Muzhik and Muscovite: Urbanization in Late Imperial Russia*. University of California Press, 1985.

Brady, Thomas. *German Histories in the Age of Reformations, 1400–1650*. Cambridge University Press, 2009.

Braudel, Fernand. *Civilization and Capitalism, 15th–18th Century*. Vol. 1, *The Structures of Everyday Life: The Limits of the Possible*. Translated by Siân Reynolds. Harper & Row, 1981.

Bray, Francesca. *The Rice Economies: Technology and Development in Asian Societies*. University of California Press, 1986.

Brecht, Bertolt. *Threepenny Opera*. Grove Press, 1994. Originally published in 1928.

Brewer, John. *The Sinews of Power: War, Money and the English State, 1688–1783*. Harvard University Press, 1989.

Brook, Timothy. *The Price of Collapse: The Little Ice Age and the Fall of Ming China*. Princeton University Press, 2023.

Bulstrode, Jenny. "Black Metallurgists and the Making of the Industrial Revolution." *History and Technology: An International Journal* 39, no. 1 (2023): 1–41.

Burnard, Trevor, and Giorgio Riello. "Slavery and the New History of Capitalism." *Journal of Global History* 15, no. 2 (2020): 225–44.

Camp, Stephanie M. H. *Closer to Freedom: Enslaved Women and Everyday Resistance in the Plantation South.* University of North Carolina Press, 2004.

Cantor, Leonard. *The Changing English Countryside, 1400–1700.* Routledge, 1987.

Carlin, Paul, and Robert Sandy. "Estimating the Implicit Value of a Young Child's Life." *Southern Economic Journal* 58, no. 1 (1991): 186–202.

Carlos, Ann, Donna Feir, and Angela Redish. "Indigenous Nations and the Development of the U.S. Economy: Land, Resources, and Dispossession." *Journal of Economic History* 82, no. 2 (2022): 516–55.

Carmichael, Sarah, Alexandra de Pleijt, Jan Luiten van Zanden, and Tine de Moor. "The European Marriage Pattern and Its Measurement." *Journal of Economic History* 76, no. 1 (2016): 196–204.

Carney, Judith. *Black Rice: The African Origins of Rice Cultivation in the Americas.* Harvard University Press, 2002.

Carruthers, Bruce. *City of Capital: Politics and Markets in the English Financial Revolution.* Princeton University Press, 1996.

Chandler, Alfred. *The Visible Hand: The Managerial Revolution in American Business.* Harvard University Press, 1977.

Chang, Ha-Joon. *Bad Samaritans: The Myth of Free Trade and the Secret History of Capitalism.* Bloomsbury Press, 2008.

Chang, Ha-Joon. *Kicking Away the Ladder: Development Strategy in Historical Perspective.* Anthem Press, 2002.

Chen, Chau-Nan, Pin-Tsun Chang, and Shikuan Chen. "The Sung and Ming Paper Monies: Currency Competition and Currency Bubbles." *Journal of Macroeconomics* 17, no. 2 (1995): 273–88.

Chibber, Vivek. *The Class Matrix: Social Theory After the Cultural Turn.* Harvard University Press, 2022.

Chibber, Vivek. *Postcolonial Theory and the Specter of Capital.* Verso, 2013.

Christophers, Brett. *The Price Is Wrong: Why Capitalism Won't Save the Planet.* Verso, 2023.

Cipolla, Carlo. *Guns, Sails and Empires: Technological Innovation and the Early Phases of European Expansion, 1400–1700.* Pantheon Books, 1965.

Clapham, J. H. "The Transference of the Worsted Industry from Norfolk to the West Riding." *Economic Journal* 20 (1910): 195–210.

Claudio, Lisandro. *The Profligate Colonial: How the U.S. Exported Austerity to the Philippines.* Cornell University Press, 2025.

Clingingsmith, David, and Jeffrey Williamson. "Deindustrialization in 18th and 19th Century India: Mughal Decline, Climate Shocks, and British Industrial Ascent." *Explorations in Economic History* 45 (2008): 209–34.

Crafts, N. F. R. "British Economic Growth, 1700–1831: A Review of the Evidence." *Economic History Review* 36, no. 2 (1983): 177–99.

Crafts, N. F. R., and C. Knick Harley. "Precocious British Industrialisation: A General-Equilibrium Perspective." In *Exceptionalism and Industrialisation: Britain and Its European Rivals, 1688–1815*, edited by Leandro Prados de la Escosura. Cambridge University Press, 2004.

Craig, John. *Newton at the Mint*. Cambridge University Press, 1946.

Craton, Michael. *Sinews of Empire: A Short History of British Slavery*. Anchor Press, 1974.

Cronon, William. *Nature's Metropolis: Chicago and the Great West*. W. W. Norton, 1991.

Cuenca Esteban, Javier. "The British Balance of Payments, 1772–1820: India Transfers and War Finance." *Economic History Review* 54, no. 1 (2001): 58–86.

Cummins, Neil. "Where Is the Middle Class? Evidence from 60 Million English Death and Probate Records, 1892–1992." *Journal of Economic History* 81, no. 2 (2021): 359–404.

Curtin, Philip. "Africa and the Wider Monetary World, 1250–1850." In Richards, *Precious Metals*.

Curtin, Philip. *Economic Change in Precolonial Africa: Senegambia in the Era of the Slave Trade*. University of Wisconsin Press, 1975.

Curtin, Philip. *The Rise and Fall of the Plantation Complex: Essays in Atlantic History*. Cambridge University Press, 1998.

Cushman, Gregory. *Guano and the Opening of the Pacific World: A Global Ecological History*. Cambridge University Press, 2013.

Daalu, Kwame Yeboa. *Trade and Politics on the Gold Coast, 1600–1720: A Study of the African Reaction to European Trade*. Clarendon Press, 1970.

Daggett, Cara New. *The Birth of Energy: Fossil Fuels, Thermodynamics, and the Politics of Work*. Duke University Press, 2019.

Daudin, Guillaume, Matthias Morys, and Kevin H. O'Rourke. "Europe and Globalization, 1870–1914." OFCE Working Paper No. 2008–17 (2008).

Davis, Lance, and Robert Huttenback. *Mammon and the Pursuit of Empire: The Political Economy of British Imperialism, 1860–1912*. Cambridge University Press, 1986.

de Roover, Raymond. *The Rise and Decline of the Medici Bank, 1397–1494*. Harvard University Press, 1963.

de Vries, Jan. *Barges and Capitalism: Passenger Transportation in the Dutch Economy, 1632–1839*. HES Publishers, 1981.

de Vries, Jan. "Connecting Europe and Asia: A Quantitative Analysis of the Cape-Route Trade, 1497–1795." In Flynn et al., *Global Connections and Monetary History*.

de Vries, Jan. *The Dutch Rural Economy in the Golden Age, 1500–1700*. Yale University Press, 1974.

de Vries, Jan. *The Economy of Europe in an Age of Crisis, 1600–1750*. Cambridge University Press, 1976.

de Vries, Jan. *The Industrious Revolution: Consumer Behavior and the Household Economy, 1650 to the Present*. Cambridge University Press, 2008.

de Vries, Jan. "The Limits of Globalization in the Early Modern World." *Economic History Review* 63, no. 3 (2010): 710–33.

de Vries, Jan. "The Netherlands and the Polder Model: Questioning the Polder Model Concept." *BMGN Low Countries Historical Review* 129, no. 1 (2014): 99–111.

de Vries, Jan. "Population." In *Handbook of European History, 1400–1600*. Vol. 1, *Structures and Assertions*, edited by Thomas Brady, Heiko Oberman, and James Tracy. Brill, 1994.

de Vries, Jan, and Ad van der Woude. *The First Modern Economy: Success, Failure, and Perseverance of the Dutch Economy, 1500–1815*. Cambridge University Press, 1997.

Dean, Warren. "Deforestation in Southeastern Brazil." In *Global Deforestation in the Nineteenth-Century World Economy*, edited by Richard Tucker and J. F. Richards. Duke Press Policy Studies, 1983.

Delalande, Nicolas. *Struggle and Mutual Aid: The Age of Worker Solidarity*. Other Press, 2023.

Demuth, Bathsheba. *Floating Coast: An Environmental History of the Bering Strait*. W. W. Norton, 2019.

Dennison, Tracy, and Steven Nafziger. "Living Standards in Nineteenth-Century Russia." *Journal of Interdisciplinary History* 42, no. 3 (2013): 397–441.

Deringer, William. *Calculated Values: Finance, Politics, and the Quantitative Age*. Harvard University Press, 2018.

Desai, Ashwin, and Goolem Vahed. *The South African Gandhi: Stretcher-Bearer of Empire*. Stanford University Press, 2016.

Desan, Christine. *Making Money: Coin, Currency, and the Coming of Capitalism*. Oxford University Press, 2015.

Donaldson, Dave. "Railroads of the Raj: Estimating the Impact of Transportation Infrastructure." *American Economic Review* 108, nos. 4–5 (2018): 899–934.

Dornbusch, Rudiger, and Jacob A. Frankel. "The Gold Standard and the Bank of England in the Crisis of 1847." In Bordo and Schwartz, *Retrospective on the Classical Gold Standard*.

Draper, Nicholas. *The Price of Emancipation: Slave-Ownership, Compensation and British Society at the End of Slavery*. Cambridge University Press, 2013.

Drelichman, Mauricio, and Hans-Joachim Voth. *Lending to the Borrower from Hell: Debt, Taxes, and Default in the Age of Philip II*. Princeton University Press, 2014.

Du Bois, W. E. B. *Black Reconstruction in America, 1860–1880*. Scribner, 1995. Originally published in 1935.

Dubois, Laurent. *Avengers of the New World: The Story of the Haitian Revolution*. Harvard University Press, 2004.

DuPlessis, Robert. "Cottons Consumption in the Seventeenth- and Eighteenth-Century North Atlantic." In *The Spinning World: A Global History of Cotton Textiles, 1200–1850*, edited by Giorgio Riello and Prasannan Parthasarathi. Oxford University Press, 2009.

Duus, Peter. *The Abacus and the Sword: The Japanese Penetration of Korea, 1895–1910*. University of California Press, 1998.

Edgerton, David. *The Shock of the Old: Technology and Global History Since 1900.* Oxford University Press, 2011.

Eichengreen, Barry. *Globalizing Capital: A History of the International Monetary System.* 3rd ed. Princeton University Press, 2019.

Eichengreen, Barry. *Golden Fetters: The Gold Standard and the Great Depression, 1919–1939.* Oxford University Press, 1996.

Eichengreen, Barry, and Marc Flandreau, eds. *The Gold Standard in Theory and History.* Routledge, 1997.

Eltis, David. *The Rise of African Slavery in the Americas.* Cambridge University Press, 1999.

Eltis, David. "The Volume and Structure of the Transatlantic Slave Trade: A Reassessment." *William and Mary Quarterly* 58, no. 1 (2011): 17–46.

Eltis, David, Frank Lewis, and David Richardson. "Slave Prices, the African Slave Trade, and Productivity in the Caribbean, 1674–1807." *Economic History Review* 58, no. 4 (2005): 673–700.

Engels, Friedrich. *The Peasant War in Germany.* International Publishers, 1996. Originally published in 1850.

Etemad, Bouda. *Possessing the World: Taking the Measurements of Colonisation from the Eighteenth to the Twentieth Century.* Berghahn Books, 2007.

Evans, Chris. "The Industrial Revolution in Iron in the British Isles." In *The Industrial Revolution in Iron: The Impact of British Coal Technology in Nineteenth-Century Europe*, edited by Chris Evans and Göran Rydén. Ashgate Publishing, 2005.

Feinstein, Charles H. "Pessimism Perpetuated: Real Wages and the Standard of Living in Britain During and After the Industrial Revolution." *Journal of Economic History* 58, no. 3 (1998): 625–58.

Fernihough, Alan, and Kevin O'Rourke. "Coal and the European Industrial Revolution." *Economic Journal* 131 (April 2020): 1135–49.

Fields, Barbara. "Slavery, Race, and Ideology in the United States of America." *New Left Review* 181 (May/June 1990): 95–118.

Findlay, Ronald, and Kevin H. O'Rourke. *Power and Plenty: Trade, War, and the World Economy in the Second Millennium.* Princeton University Press, 2007.

Finley, Alexandra. *An Intimate Economy: Enslaved Women, Work, and America's Domestic Slave Trade.* University of North Carolina Press, 2020.

Fishlow, Albert. "Lessons from the Past: Capital Markets During the 19th Century and the Interwar Period." *International Organization* 39, no. 3 (1985): 383–439.

Fitzpatrick, Sheila. *The Russian Revolution.* 4th ed. Oxford University Press, 2017.

Flynn, Dennis O. "Early Capitalism Despite New World Bullion." *Revista de Historia Economica* 2, no. 2 (1984): 29–58.

Flynn, Dennis O. "A New Perspective on the Spanish Price Revolution: The Monetary Approach to the Balance of Payments." *Explorations in Economic History* 15, no. 4 (1978): 388–406.

Flynn, Dennis O., and Arturo Giráldez. "Cycles of Silver: Global Economic Unity Through the Mid-Eighteenth Century." *Journal of World History* 13, no. 2 (2002): 391–427.

Flynn, Dennis O., Arturo Giráldez, and Richard von Glahn, eds. *Global Connections and Monetary History, 1470–1800*. Ashgate Publishing, 2003.

Foner, Philip. *The Great Labor Uprising of 1877*. Monad Press, 1977.

Foucault, Michel. "Nietzsche, Genealogy, History." In *Language, Counter-Memory, Practice: Selected Essays and Interviews*, edited by D. F. Bouchard. Cornell University Press, 1977.

Frankema, Ewout, Jeffrey Williamson, and Pieter Woltjer. "An Economic Rationale for the West African Scramble? The Commercial Transition and the Commodity Price Boom of 1835–1885." *Journal of Economic History* 78, no. 1 (2018): 231–67.

Fressoz, Jean-Baptiste. *More and More and More: An All-Consuming History of Energy*. Penguin, 2025.

Fuentes, Marisa J. *Dispossessed Lives: Enslaved Women, Violence, and the Archive*. University of Pennsylvania Press, 2016.

Fukuyama, Francis. "The End of History?" *National Interest* 16 (1989): 3–18.

Fukuyama, Francis. *The End of History and the Last Man*. Free Press, 1992.

Furet, François. *Interpreting the French Revolution*. Cambridge University Press, 1981.

Fynn, John Kofi. *Asante and Its Neighbours, 1700–1807*. Longman, 1971.

Gaastra, F. S. "The Exports of Precious Metals from Europe to Asia by the Dutch East India Company, 1602–1795." In Richards, *Precious Metals*.

Gage, Beverly. *The Day Wall Street Exploded: A Story of America in Its First Age of Terror*. Oxford University Press, 2009.

Galenson, David. "The Rise and Fall of Indentured Servitude in the Americas: An Economic Analysis." *Journal of Economic History* 44, no. 1 (1984): 1–26.

Gelderblom, Oscar. *Cities of Commerce: The Institutional Foundations of International Trade in the Low Countries, 1250–1650*. Princeton University Press, 2013.

Gelderblom, Oscar, and Joost Jonker. "Completing a Financial Revolution: The Finance of the Dutch East India Trade and the Rise of the Amsterdam Capital Market, 1595–1612." *Journal of Economic History* 64, no. 3 (2004): 641–72.

Genovese, Eugene. *The World the Slaveholders Made: Two Essays in Interpretation*. Pantheon Books, 1969.

George, Susan. "How to Win the War of Ideas: Lessons from the Gramscian Right." *Dissent* (Summer 1997): 47–53.

Gleick, James. *Isaac Newton*. Vintage, 2004.

Goldgar, Anne. *Tulipmania: Money, Honor, and Knowledge in the Dutch Golden Age*. University of Chicago Press, 2007.

Gordon, Robert. *The Rise and Fall of American Growth: The U.S. Standard of Living Since the Civil War*. Princeton University Press, 2016.

Gorky, Maxim. *Days with Lenin*. International Publishers, 1932.

Grafe, Regina. *Distant Tyranny: Markets, Power, and Backwardness in Spain, 1650–1800*. Princeton University Press, 2012.

Graulau, Jeannette. "Finance, Industry and Globalization in the Early Modern

Period: The Example of the Metallic Business of the House of Fugger." *Rivista di Studi Politici Internazionali* 75, no. 4 (2008): 554–98.

Green, Toby. "Africa and Capitalism: Repairing a History of Omission." *Capitalism* 3, no. 2 (2022): 301–32.

Green, Toby. *A Fistful of Shells: West Africa from the Rise of the Slave Trade to the Age of Revolution.* University of Chicago Press, 2019.

Greene, Anne Norton. *Horses at Work: Harnessing Power in Industrial America.* Harvard University Press, 2008.

Greer, Allan. *Property and Dispossession: Natives, Empires and Land in Early Modern North America.* Cambridge University Press, 2018.

Grubb, Farley. "Does Bound Labour Have to Be Coerced Labour? The Case of Colonial Immigrant Servitude Versus Craft Apprenticeship and Life-Cycle Servitude-in-Husbandry." *Itinerario* 21, no. 1 (1997): 28–51.

Grubb, Farley. "The End of European Immigrant Servitude in the United States: An Economic Analysis of Market Collapse, 1772–1835." *Journal of Economic History* 54, no. 4 (1994): 794–824.

Guha, Ranajit. *A Rule of Property for Bengal: An Essay on the Idea of Permanent Settlement.* Duke University Press, 1996. Originally published in 1963.

Guyer, Jane. *Marginal Gains: Monetary Transactions in Atlantic Africa.* University of Chicago Press, 2004.

Haber, L. F. *The Poisonous Cloud: Chemical Warfare in the First World War.* Oxford University Press, 1986.

Häberlein, Mark. *The Fuggers of Augsburg: Pursuing Wealth and Honor in Renaissance Germany.* University of Virginia Press, 2012.

Hahn, Steven. *A Nation Under Our Feet: Black Political Struggles in the Rural South from Slavery to the Great Migration.* Harvard University Press, 2005.

Hall, Catherine, Nicholas Draper, Keith McClelland, Katie Donington, and Rachel Lang. *Legacies of British Slave-Ownership: Colonial Slavery and the Formation of Victorian Britain.* Cambridge University Press, 2014.

Hallward, Peter. *Damming the Flood: Haiti and the Politics of Containment.* Verso, 2010.

Hamilton, Earl. *American Treasure and the Price Revolution in Spain, 1501–1650.* Harvard University Press, 1934.

Harley, C. Knick. "Output Growth and the Industrial Revolution: A Restatement of the Crafts-Harley View." *Economic History Review* 45, no. 4 (1992): 703–30.

Harris, Ron. "The Bubble Act: Its Passage and Its Effects on Business Organization." *Journal of Economic History* 54, no. 3 (1994): 610–27.

Harris, Tim. *London Crowds in the Reign of Charles II: Propaganda and Politics from the Restoration until the Exclusion Crisis.* Cambridge University Press, 1987.

Haselby, Sam. "Muslims of Early America." *Aeon,* May 20, 2019.

Hatton, Timothy, and Jeffrey Williamson. *Global Migration and the World Economy: Two Centuries of Policy and Performance.* MIT Press, 2005.

Hay, Douglas. "Property, Authority and the Criminal Law." In *Albion's Fatal Tree:*

Crime and Society in Eighteenth-Century England, edited by Douglas Hay. Allen Lane, 1975.

Headrick, Daniel. *Power over Peoples: Technology, Environments, and Western Imperialism, 1400 to the Present.* Princeton University Press, 2010.

Headrick, Daniel. *The Tools of Empire: Technology and European Imperialism in the Nineteenth Century.* Oxford University Press, 1981.

Healy, Jonathan. *The Blazing World: A New History of Revolutionary England, 1603–1689.* Knopf, 2023.

Heilbroner, Robert L. *The Nature and Logic of Capitalism.* W. W. Norton, 1985.

Hill, Christopher. *The Century of Revolution, 1603–1714.* W. W. Norton, 1961.

Hill, Christopher. *The World Turned Upside Down: Radical Ideas During the English Revolution.* Viking, 1972.

Hillis, Faith. *Utopia's Discontents: Russian Émigrés and the Quest for Freedom, 1830s–1930s.* Oxford University Press, 2021.

Hilt, Eric. "Economic History, Historical Analysis, and the 'New History of Capitalism.'" *Journal of Economic History* 77, no. 2 (2017): 511–36.

Hirth, Kenneth. *The Aztec Economic World: Merchants and Markets in Ancient Mesoamerica.* Cambridge University Press, 2016.

Hobsbawm, Eric. *The Age of Empire, 1875–1914.* Vintage Books, 1987.

Hobsbawm, Eric. *Industry and Empire: An Economic History of Britain Since 1750.* Weidenfeld & Nicolson, 1968.

Hobsbawm, Eric. "The Machine Breakers." *Past & Present* no. 1 (February 1952): 57–70.

Hobsbawm, Eric, and George Rudé. *Captain Swing.* Lawrence & Wishart, 1969.

Hochschild, Adam. *King Leopold's Ghost: A Story of Greed, Terror and Heroism in Colonial Africa.* Mariner Books, 1998.

Hoppit, Julian. "The Myths of the South Sea Bubble." *Transactions of the Royal Historical Society* 12 (December 2002): 141–65.

Horn, Jeff. "Machine-breaking in England and France During the Age of Revolution." *Labour/Le Travailleur* 55 (2005): 143–66.

Horning, Audrey. *Ireland in the Virginian Sea: Colonialism in the British Atlantic.* University of North Carolina Press, 2013.

Hull, Isabel. *Absolute Destruction: Military Culture and the Practices of War in Imperial Germany.* Cornell University Press, 2005.

Humphries, Jane. *Childhood and Child Labour in the British Industrial Revolution.* Cambridge University Press, 2010.

Humphries, Jane. "Enclosures, Common Rights, and Women: The Proletarianization of Families in the Late Eighteenth and Early Nineteenth Centuries." *Journal of Economic History* 50, no. 1 (1990): 17–42.

Humphries, Jane, and Jacob Weisdorf. "Unreal Wages? Real Income and Economic Growth in England, 1260–1850." *Economic Journal* 129, no. 623 (2019): 2867–87.

Iliffe, Rob. *Priest of Nature: The Religious Worlds of Isaac Newton.* Oxford University Press, 2017.

Immerwahr, Daniel. *How to Hide an Empire: A History of the Greater United States.* Macmillan, 2019.

Inikori, Joseph. *Africans and the Industrial Revolution in England: A Study in International Trade and Economic Development.* Cambridge University Press, 2002.

Irigoin, Alejandra. "The End of a Silver Era: The Consequences of the Breakdown of the Spanish Peso Standard in China and the United States, 1780s–1850s." *Journal of World History* 20, no. 2 (2009): 207–40.

Irigoin, Alejandra. "The New World and the Global Silver Economy, 1500–1800." In *Global Economic History*, edited by Giorgio Riello and Tirthankar Roy. Bloomsbury, 2019.

Iriye, Akira. *Pacific Estrangement: Japanese and American Expansion, 1897–1911.* Harvard University Press, 1972.

Isenberg, Andrew C. *The Destruction of the Buffalo: An Environmental History, 1750–1920.* Cambridge University Press, 2000.

Israel, Jonathan. *The Anglo-Dutch Moment: Essays on the Glorious Revolution and Its World Impact.* Cambridge University Press, 1991.

Israel, Jonathan. *Dutch Primacy in World Trade, 1585–1740.* Clarendon Press, 1989.

Israel, Jonathan. *The Dutch Republic: Its Rise, Greatness, and Fall, 1477–1806.* Clarendon Press, 1995.

Jackson, J. B. C., Michael X. Kirby, Wolfgang H. Berger, et al. "Historical Overfishing and the Recent Collapse of Coastal Ecosystems." *Science* 293, no. 5530 (July 27, 2001): 629–37.

Jackson, Trevor. *Impunity and Capitalism: The Afterlives of European Financial Crises, 1690–1830.* Cambridge University Press, 2022.

Jackson, Trevor. "Revolution and Extinction: The Chrono-economics of Capitalism." *Critical Historical Studies* 9, no. 2 (2022): 283–306.

James, C. L. R. *The Black Jacobins: Toussaint L'Ouverture and the San Domingo Revolution.* 2nd ed. Vintage, 1963.

Jameson, Fredric. "Future City." *New Left Review* no. 21 (May/June 2003): 65–81.

Jameson, Fredric. *The Political Unconscious: Narrative as a Socially Symbolic Act.* Cornell University Press, 1981.

Jansen, Marius. *The Making of Modern Japan.* Harvard University Press, 2002.

Jedwab, Remi, and Alexander Moradi. "The Permanent Effects of Transportation Revolutions in Poor Countries: Evidence from Africa." *Review of Economics and Statistics* 98, no. 2 (2016): 268–84.

Jensen, Richard Bach. "Daggers, Rifles and Dynamite: Anarchist Terrorism in Nineteenth Century Europe." *Terrorism and Political Violence* 16, no. 1 (2004): 116–53.

Johnson, Walter. *River of Dark Dreams: Slavery and Empire in the Cotton Kingdom.* Harvard University Press, 2013.

Johnson, Walter. *Soul by Soul: Life Inside the Antebellum Slave Market.* Harvard University Press, 1999.

Jones, Mark. *Founding Weimar: Violence and the German Revolution of 1918–1919.* Cambridge University Press, 2016.

Kaiser, Thomas. "Money, Despotism, and Public Opinion in Early Eighteenth-Century France: John Law and the Debate on Royal Credit." *Journal of Modern History* 63, no. 1 (1991): 1–28.

Kander, Astrid, Paolo Malanima, and Paul Warde. *Power to the People: Energy in Europe over the Last Five Centuries*. Princeton University Press, 2013.

Kea, Ray. *Settlements, Trade, and Polities in the Seventeenth-Century Gold Coast*. Johns Hopkins University Press, 1982.

Kershaw, Paul V. "Hamlet Without the Prince of Denmark: Bringing Capitalism Back into the 'New' History of Capitalism." *Journal of Historical Sociology* 33, no. 1 (2020): 61–73.

Keynes, John Maynard. *The Economic Consequences of the Peace*. Harcourt, Brace and Howe, 1920.

Keynes, John Maynard. "Economic Possibilities for Our Grandchildren." In *Essays in Persuasion*. Palgrave Macmillan, 2010. Originally published in 1931.

Kindleberger, Charles. "Currency Debasement in the Early Seventeenth Century and the Establishment of Deposit Banks in Central Europe." In *Essays in History*.

Kindleberger, Charles. "Economic and Financial Crises and Transformation in Sixteenth-Century Europe." In *Essays in History*.

Kindleberger, Charles. *Essays in History: Financial, Economic, Personal*. University of Michigan Press, 1999.

Kishimoto, Mio. "Property Rights and Factor Markets." In *The Cambridge Economic History of China*. Vol. 1, *To 1800*, edited by Debin Ma and Richard von Glahn. Cambridge University Press, 2022.

Kishimoto-Nakayama, Mio. "The Kangxi Depression and Early Qing Local Markets." *Modern China* 10, no. 2 (1984): 227–56.

Klein, Herbert. "The Atlantic Slave Trade to 1650." In Schwartz, *Tropical Babylons*.

Klooster, Wim. *The Dutch Moment: War, Trade, and Settlement in the Seventeenth-Century Atlantic World*. Cornell University Press, 2019.

Kocka, Jürgen. *Capitalism: A Short History*. Princeton University Press, 2016.

Kruer, Matthew. *Time of Anarchy: Indigenous Power and the Crisis of Colonialism in Early America*. Harvard University Press, 2021.

Kumekawa, Ian. "Measuring the Cost of Pollution: Economic Life, Economic Theory, and the Origins of Environmental Economics." *Journal of Modern History* 96, no. 2 (2024): 332–61.

Kwass, Michael. *Privilege and the Politics of Taxation in Eighteenth-Century France: Liberté, Égalité, Fiscalité*. Cambridge University Press, 2000.

Kynaston, David. *Till Time's Last Sand: A History of the Bank of England, 1694–2013*. Bloomsbury, 2017.

Lake, Marilyn, and Henry Reynolds, eds. *Drawing the Global Colour Line: White Men's Countries and the International Challenge of Racial Equality*. Cambridge University Press, 2008.

Lane, Kris. *Potosí: The Silver City That Changed the World*. University of California Press, 2019.

Law, Robin, ed. *From Slave Trade to 'Legitimate' Commerce: The Commercial Transition in Nineteenth-Century West Africa*. Cambridge University Press, 1995.

Lazear, Edward. "Economic Imperialism." *Quarterly Journal of Economics* 115, no. 1 (2000): 99–146.

Levy, Jonathan. *Ages of American Capitalism: A History of the United States*. Random House, 2021.

Lewis, William Arthur. "Economic Development with Unlimited Supplies of Labour." *Manchester School* 22, no. 2 (1954): 139–91.

Lewis, William Arthur. *The Evolution of the International Economic Order*. Princeton University Press, 1978.

Linebaugh, Peter. *The London Hanged: Crime and Civil Society in the Eighteenth Century*. Cambridge University Press, 1992.

Lipartito, Kenneth. "Reassembling the Economic: New Departures in Historical Materialism." *American Historical Review* 121, no. 1 (2016): 101–39.

Livi-Bacci, Massimo. "The Depopulation of Hispanic America After the Conquest." *Population and Development Review* 32, no. 2 (2006): 199–232.

Lovejoy, Paul, and David Richardson. "The Initial 'Crisis of Adaptation': The Impact of British Abolition on the Atlantic Slave Trade in West Africa, 1808–1820." In Law, *From Slave Trade to 'Legitimate' Commerce*.

Lutter, Randall. "Valuing Children's Health: A Reassessment of the Benefits of Lower Lead Levels." AEI–Brookings Joint Center for Regulatory Studies, Working Paper No. 00–02, 2000.

Lynn, Martin. "The West African Palm Oil Trade in the Nineteenth Century and the 'Crisis of Adaptation.'" In Law, *From Slave Trade to 'Legitimate' Commerce*.

Macpherson, C. B. *The Political Theory of Possessive Individualism: Hobbes to Locke*. Clarendon Press, 1962.

Madley, Benjamin. *An American Genocide: The United States and the California Indian Catastrophe, 1846–1873*. Yale University Press, 2016.

Maier, Charles. *Recasting Bourgeois Europe: Stabilization in France, Germany, and Italy in the Decade After World War I*. Princeton University Press, 1975.

Malm, Andreas. *Fossil Capital: The Rise of Steam Power and the Roots of Global Warming*. Verso, 2016.

Malm, Andreas, and Wim Carton. *Overshoot: How the World Surrendered to Climate Breakdown*. Verso, 2024.

Mann, Kristin. "Owners, Slaves and the Struggle for Labour in the Commercial Transition at Lagos." In Law, *From Slave Trade to 'Legitimate' Commerce*.

Manning, Patrick. *Slavery and African Life: Occidental, Oriental, and African Slave Trades*. Cambridge University Press, 1990.

Martinez, Jenny S. *The Slave Trade and the Origins of International Human Rights Law*. Oxford University Press, 2014.

Marx, Karl. *Capital: A Critique of Political Economy*. Vol. 1. Edited and translated by Paul North and Paul Reitter. Princeton University Press, 2024. Originally published in 1867.

Mau, Søren. *Mute Compulsion: A Marxist Theory of the Economic Power of Capital.* Verso, 2023.

Maurer, Noel. *The Empire Trap: The Rise and Fall of U.S. Intervention to Protect American Property Overseas, 1893–2013.* Princeton University Press, 2013.

Maurer, Noel, and Leticia Arroyo Abad. "Can Europe Run Greece? Lessons from U.S. Fiscal Receiverships in Latin America, 1904–31." SSRN Working Paper, June 13, 2017.

Mayhew, Nicholas. *Sterling: The Rise and Fall of a Currency.* Allen Lane, 1999.

McCloskey, Deirdre Nansen. *The Bourgeois Virtues: Ethics for an Age of Commerce.* University of Chicago Press, 2006.

McCusker, John, and Russell Menard. *The Economy of British America, 1607–1789.* University of North Carolina Press, 1985.

McCusker, John, and Russell Menard. "The Sugar Industry in the Seventeenth Century: A New Perspective on the Barbadian 'Sugar Revolution.'" In Schwartz, *Tropical Babylons.*

McShane, Clay, and Joel Tarr. *The Horse in the City: Living Machines in the Nineteenth Century.* Johns Hopkins University Press, 2007.

Meiksins Wood, Ellen. *The Origin of Capitalism: A Longer View.* Verso, 2017. Originally published in 1999.

Menard, Russell. *Sweet Negotiations: Sugar, Slavery, and Plantation Agriculture in Early Barbados.* University of Virginia Press, 2006.

Metzler, Mark. *Lever of Empire: The International Gold Standard and the Crisis of Liberalism in Prewar Japan.* University of California Press, 2006.

Meyer, Josefin, Carmen Reinhart, and Cristoph Trebesch. "Sovereign Bonds Since Waterloo." NBER Working Paper 25542, 2019.

Miéville, China. *October: The Story of the Russian Revolution.* Verso, 2017.

Milanovic, Branko. *Capitalism, Alone: The Future of the System That Rules the World.* Harvard University Press, 2019.

Milanovic, Branko. *The Haves and Have-Nots: A Brief and Idiosyncratic History of Global Inequality.* Basic Books, 2010.

Millon, Rene Francis. "When Money Grew on Trees: A Study of Cacao in Ancient Mesoamerica." PhD diss., Columbia University, 1955. https://www.proquest.com/dissertations-theses/when-money-grew-on-trees-study-cacao-ancient/docview/301991670/se-2.

Millward, R. "The Emergence of Wage Labor in Early Modern England." *Explorations in Economic History* 18 (1981): 21–39.

Milward, Alan, and S. B. Saul. *The Development of the Economies of Continental Europe, 1850–1914.* George Allen & Unwin, 1977.

Mironov, Boris. "Wages and Prices in Imperial Russia, 1703–1913." *Russian Review* 69, no. 1 (2010): 47–72.

Mironov, Boris, and Brian A'Hearn. "Russian Living Standards Under the Tsars: Anthropometric Evidence from the Volga." *Journal of Economic History* 68, no. 3 (2008): 900–929.

Mitchener, Kris, and Marc Weidenmier. "Supersanctions and Sovereign Debt Repayment." *Journal of International Money and Finance* 29, no. 1 (2010): 19–36.

Mokyr, Joel. "Irish History with the Potato." *Irish Economic and Social History* 8, no. 1 (1981): 8–29.

Mokyr, Joel. *The Lever of Riches: Technological Creativity and Economic Progress.* Oxford University Press, 1990.

Montgomery, David. *The Fall of the House of Labor: The Workplace, the State, and American Labor Activism, 1865–1925.* Cambridge University Press, 1988.

Moore, Jason W. "Environmental Crises and the Metabolic Rift in World-Historical Perspective." *Organization and Environment* 13, no. 2 (2000): 123–57.

Moore, Jason W. "Metabolic Rift or Metabolic Shift? Dialectics, Nature, and the World-Historical Method." *Theory and Society* 46, no. 4 (2017): 285–318.

Morgan, Edmund. *American Slavery, American Freedom: The Ordeal of Colonial Virginia.* W. W. Norton, 1975.

Morgan, Kenneth. *Slavery and Servitude in Colonial North America: A Short History.* New York University Press, 2001.

Morgan, Kenneth. *Slavery and the British Empire: From Africa to America.* Oxford University Press, 2008.

Morgan, Kenneth. *Slavery, Atlantic Trade and the British Economy, 1660–1800.* Cambridge University Press, 2000.

Mörner, Magnus. "Spanish Historians on Spanish Migration to America During the Colonial Period." *Latin American Research Review* 30, no. 2 (1995): 251–85.

Morrill, J. S. *The Revolt of the Provinces: Conservatives and Radicals in the English Civil War, 1630–1650.* Longman, 1980.

Mosley, Stephen. *Chimney of the World: A History of Smoke Pollution in Victorian and Edwardian Manchester.* Routledge, 2008.

Mueller, Reinhold. *The Venetian Money Market: Banks, Panics, and the Public Debt, 1200–1500.* Johns Hopkins University Press, 1997.

Muldrew, Craig. *The Economy of Obligation: The Culture of Credit and Social Relations in Early Modern England.* 2nd ed. Palgrave, 1998.

Muldrew, Craig. *Food, Energy and the Creation of Industriousness: Work and Material Culture in Agrarian England, 1550–1780.* Cambridge University Press, 2011.

Munro, John H. "The Monetary Origins of the 'Price Revolution': South German Silver Mining, Merchant Banking, and Venetian Commerce, 1470–1540." In Flynn et al., *Global Connections and Monetary History.*

Murphy, Anne. *The Origins of English Financial Markets: Investment and Speculation Before the South Sea Bubble.* Cambridge University Press, 2009.

Murphy, Antoin. *John Law: Economic Theorist and Policymaker.* Oxford University Press, 1997.

Murphy, Sharon Ann. *Banking on Slavery: Financing Southern Expansion in the Antebellum United States.* University of Chicago Press, 2023.

Mustakeem, Sowande' M. *Slavery at Sea: Terror, Sex, and Sickness in the Middle Passage.* University of Illinois Press, 2016.

Myers, Ramon H., and Mark R. Peattie. *The Japanese Colonial Empire, 1895–1945*. Princeton University Press, 1984.

Neal, Larry. *A Concise History of International Finance: From Babylon to Bernanke*. Cambridge University Press, 2015.

Neal, Larry. *"I Am Not Master of Events": The Speculations of John Law and Lord Londonderry in the Mississippi and South Sea Bubbles*. Yale University Press, 2012.

Neal, Larry. *The Rise of Financial Capitalism: International Capital Markets in the Age of Reason*. Cambridge University Press, 1990.

Nelson, Scott Reynolds. *Oceans of Grain: How American Wheat Remade the World*. Basic Books, 2022.

Newitt, Malyn. *A History of Portuguese Overseas Expansion, 1400–1668*. Routledge, 2005.

Newman, William. *Newton the Alchemist: Science, Enigma, and the Quest for Nature's 'Secret Fire.'* Princeton University Press, 2019.

Nichols, Robert. "Disaggregating Primitive Accumulation." *Radical Philosophy* no. 194 (November/December 2015): 18–28.

North, Douglass, and Robert Thomas. *The Rise of the Western World: A New Economic History*. Cambridge University Press, 1973.

North, Douglass, and Barry Weingast. "Constitutions and Commitment: The Evolution of Institutions Governing Public Choice in Seventeenth-Century England." *Journal of Economic History* 49, no. 4 (1989): 803–32.

Novokmet, Filip, Thomas Piketty, and Gabriel Zucman. "From Soviets to Oligarchs: Inequality and Property in Russia, 1905–2016." *Journal of Economic Inequality* 16 (2018): 189–223.

Nwokeji, G. Ugo. *The Slave Trade and Culture in the Bight of Biafra: An African Society in the Atlantic World*. Cambridge University Press, 2010.

Ó Gráda, Cormac. *Ireland Before and After the Famine: Explorations in Economic History, 1800–1925*. Manchester University Press, 1988.

O'Rourke, Kevin H. "The European Grain Invasion, 1870–1913." *Journal of Economic History* 57, no. 4 (1997): 775–801.

Olmstead, Alan, and Paul Rhode. "Biological Innovation and Productivity Growth in the Antebellum Cotton Economy." *Journal of Economic History* 68, no. 4 (2008): 1123–71.

Olmstead, Alan, and Paul Rhode. "Cotton, Slavery, and the New History of Capitalism." *Explorations in Economic History* 67 (January 2018): 1–17.

Osterhammel, Jürgen. *The Transformation of the World: A Global History of the Nineteenth Century*. Princeton University Press, 2014.

Otter, Chris. *Diet for a Large Planet: Industrial Britain, Food Systems, and World Ecology*. University of Chicago Press, 2020.

Outhwaite, R. B. "Royal Borrowing in the Reign of Elizabeth I: The Aftermath of Antwerp." *English Historical Review* 86, no. 339 (1971): 251–63.

Pakenham, Thomas. *The Scramble for Africa: The White Man's Conquest of the Dark Continent from 1876 to 1912*. 13th ed. Abacus, 1992.

Pamuk, Şevket. *A Monetary History of the Ottoman Empire*. Cambridge University Press, 2000.

Parker, Geoffrey. *The Military Revolution: Military Innovation and the Rise of the West, 1500–1800*. Cambridge University Press, 1996.

Parthasarathi, Prasannan. *Why Europe Grew Rich and Asia Did Not: Global Economic Divergence, 1600–1850*. Cambridge University Press, 2011.

Patterson, Orlando. *Slavery and Social Death: A Comparative Study*. Harvard University Press, 1982.

Perrot, Michelle. *Workers on Strike: France, 1871–1890*. Yale University Press, 1987.

Peterson, Mark. "Capitalism." In *The Princeton Companion to Atlantic History*, edited by Joseph C. Miller. Princeton University Press, 2015.

Petram, Lodewijk. *The World's First Stock Exchange*. Columbia University Press, 2014.

Petterson, Christina. "Bloch's Münzer and the Horizons of History." *Critical Research on Religion* 10, no. 3 (2022): 339–44.

Piketty, Thomas. *Capital in the Twenty-First Century*. Harvard University Press, 2014.

Pincus, Steve. *1688: The First Modern Revolution*. Yale University Press, 2009.

Pistor, Katharina. *The Code of Capital: How the Law Creates Wealth and Inequality*. Princeton University Press, 2019.

Platt, Stephen. *Imperial Twilight: The Opium War and the End of China's Last Golden Age*. Knopf, 2018.

Pluymers, Keith. *No Wood, No Kingdom: Political Ecology in the English Atlantic*. University of Pennsylvania Press, 2021.

Pollard, Sidney. "Factory Discipline in the Industrial Revolution." *Economic History Review* 16, no. 2 (1963): 254–71.

Pomeranz, Kenneth. *The Great Divergence: China, Europe, and the Making of the Modern World Economy*. Princeton University Press, 2000.

Prak, Maarten, and Jan Luiten van Zanden. *Pioneers of Capitalism: The Netherlands, 1000–1800*. Princeton University Press, 2023.

Pressman, Steven. "Oscar Hartzell and the Estate of Sir Francis Drake." In *Handbook of Frauds, Scams, and Swindles: Failures of Ethics in Leadership*, edited by Serge Matulich and David M. Currie. Taylor and Francis, 2009.

Priest, Claire. *Credit Nation: Property Laws and Legal Institutions in Early America*. Princeton University Press, 2021.

Queralt, Didac. *Pawned States: State Building in the Era of International Finance*. Princeton University Press, 2022.

Quinn, Stephen, and William Roberds. *How a Ledger Became a Central Bank: A Monetary History of the Bank of Amsterdam*. Cambridge University Press, 2024.

Radburn, Nicholas. *Traders in Men: Merchants and the Transformation of the Transatlantic Slave Trade*. Yale University Press, 2023.

Ransom, Roger, and Richard Sutch. *One Kind of Freedom: The Economic Consequences of Emancipation*. Cambridge University Press, 1977.

Read, Charles. *The Great Famine in Ireland and Britain's Financial Crisis*. Boydell Press, 2022.

Redish, Angela. *Bimetallism: An Economic and Historical Analysis*. Cambridge University Press, 2000.

Reinhart, Carmen, and Kenneth Rogoff. *This Time Is Different: Eight Centuries of Financial Folly*. Princeton University Press, 2009.

Rhode, Paul. "What Fraction of Antebellum US National Product Did the Enslaved Produce?" *Explorations in Economic History* 91 (2024): 1–15.

Richards, John F., ed. *Precious Metals in the Later Medieval and Early Modern Worlds*. Carolina Academic Press, 1983.

Richards, John F. *The Unending Frontier: An Environmental History of the Early Modern World*. University of California Press, 2006.

Riello, Giorgio. *Cotton: The Fabric That Made the Modern World*. Cambridge University Press, 2013.

Rockman, Seth. "What Makes the History of Capitalism Newsworthy?" *Journal of the Early Republic* 34, no. 3 (2014): 439–66.

Ron, Ariel. "When Hay Was King: Energy History and Economic Nationalism in the Nineteenth-Century United States." *American Historical Review* 128, no. 1 (2023): 177–213.

Rosenthal, Caitlin. *Accounting for Slavery: Masters and Management*. Harvard University Press, 2018.

Roth, Alvin, Tayfun Sönmez, and M. Utku Ünver. "Kidney Exchange." *Quarterly Journal of Economics* 119, no. 2 (2004): 457–88.

Rowe, William. *China's Last Empire: The Great Qing*. Harvard University Press, 2009.

Roy, Tirthankar. *The Crafts and Capitalism: Handloom Weaving Industry in Colonial India*. Routledge, 2020.

Roy, Tirthankar. *An Economic History of Early Modern India*. Routledge, 2013.

Roy, Tirthankar. *The Economic History of India, 1857–1947*. Oxford University Press, 2000.

Roy, Tirthankar. "The Permanent Settlement and the Emergence of a British State in Late-Eighteenth Century India." LSE Economic History Working Papers, No. 335, June 2023.

Roy, Tirthankar. "Where Is Bengal? Situating an Indian Region in the Early Modern World Economy." *Past & Present* 213, no. 1 (2011): 115–46.

Russell, Conrad. *The Causes of the English Civil War*. Clarendon Press, 1990.

Sabato, Hilda. *Agrarian Capitalism and the World Market: Buenos Aires in the Pastoral Age, 1840–1890*. University of New Mexico Press, 1990.

Sahillioğlu, Halil. "The Role of International Monetary and Metal Movements in Ottoman Monetary History, 1300–1750." In Richards, *Precious Metals*.

Sampeck, Kathryn E. "A Constitutional Approach to Cacao Money." *Journal of Anthropological Archaeology* 61 (March 2021).

Saville, Julie. *The Work of Reconstruction: From Slave to Wage Laborer in South Carolina, 1860–1870*. Cambridge University Press, 1996.

Scanlan, Padraic X. *Slave Empire: How Slavery Built Modern Britain*. Little, Brown, 2022.

Schakenbach Regele, Lindsay. "A Brief History of the History of Capitalism, and a New American Variety." *Enterprise & Society* 25, no. 1 (2024): 2–26.

Schivelbusch, Wolfgang. *The Railway Journey: The Industrialization of Time and Space in the Nineteenth Century.* University of California Press, 2014.

Schmidt, Regin. *Red Scare: FBI and the Origins of Anticommunism in the United States, 1919–1943.* University of Copenhagen, 2000.

Schumpeter, Joseph. *Capitalism, Socialism and Democracy.* Harper & Brothers, 1942.

Schwartz, Stuart. "A Commonwealth Within Itself: The Early Brazilian Sugar Industry, 1550–1670." In *Tropical Babylons.*

Schwartz, Stuart, ed. *Tropical Babylons: Sugar and the Making of the Atlantic World, 1450–1680.* University of North Carolina Press, 2004.

Sewell, William. "On the Emergence of Capitalism: Marx, Brenner, and the Troublesome Case of the Dutch." *Critical Historical Studies* 11, no. 1 (2024): 1–46.

Shaw-Taylor, Leigh. "The Rise of Agrarian Capitalism and the Decline of Family Farming in England." *Economic History Review* 65, no. 1 (2012): 26–60.

Shifflett, Crandall. *Coal Towns: Life, Work, and Culture in Company Towns of Southern Appalachia, 1880–1960.* University of Tennessee Press, 1991.

Shorter, Edward, and Charles Tilly. *Strikes in France, 1830–1968.* Cambridge University Press, 1974.

Shovlin, John. *Trading with the Enemy: Britain, France, and the Eighteenth-Century Quest for a Peaceful World Order.* Yale University Press, 2021.

Shutzer, Matthew. "Subterranean Properties: India's Political Ecology of Coal, 1870–1975." *Comparative Studies in Society and History* 63, no. 2 (2021): 400–432.

Slack, Paul. *The Invention of Improvement: Information and Material Progress in Seventeenth-Century England.* Oxford University Press, 2015.

Smallwood, Stephanie. *Saltwater Slavery: A Middle Passage from Africa to American Diaspora.* Harvard University Press, 2007.

Smith, Adam. *An Inquiry into the Nature and Causes of the Wealth of Nations.* University of Chicago Press, 1976. Originally published in 1776.

Smith, Edmond. "The Global Interests of London's Commercial Community, 1599–1625: Investment in the East India Company." *Economic History Review* 71, no. 4 (2018): 1118–46.

Smith, S. A. *Russia in Revolution: An Empire in Crisis, 1890 to 1928.* Oxford University Press, 2017.

Sonenscher, Michael. *Before the Deluge: Public Debt, Inequality, and the Intellectual Origins of the French Revolution.* Princeton University Press, 2007.

Sonenscher, Michael. *Capitalism: The Story Behind the Word.* Princeton University Press, 2022.

Spang, Rebecca. "The Ghost of Law: Speculating on Money, Memory and Mississippi in the French Constituent Assembly." *Historical Reflections* 32, no. 1 (2005): 3–25.

Stanley, Amy Dru. "Histories of Capitalism and Sex Difference." *Journal of the Early Republic* 36, no. 2 (2016): 343–50.

Stedman Jones, Gareth. *Languages of Class: Studies in English Working Class History, 1832–1982*. Cambridge University Press, 1983.

Stein, Stanley, and Barbara Stein. *Silver, Trade, and War: Spain and America in the Making of Early Modern Europe*. Johns Hopkins University Press, 2000.

Steinfeld, Robert. *The Invention of Free Labor: The Employment Relation in English and American Law and Culture, 1350–1870*. University of North Carolina Press, 1991.

Stephenson, Judy Z. "'Real' Wages? Contractors, Workers, and Pay in London Building Trades, 1650–1800." *Economic History Review* 71, no. 1 (2018): 106–32.

Stern, Philip. *The Company-State: Corporate Sovereignty and the Early Modern Foundations of the British Empire in India*. Oxford University Press, 2011.

Stigler, Stephen. *Casanova's Lottery: The History of a Revolutionary Game of Chance*. University of Chicago Press, 2022.

Stokes, Eric. *The English Utilitarians and India*. Oxford University Press, 1959.

Sweeney, Stuart. "Indian Railways and Famine, 1875–1914: Magic Wheels and Empty Stomachs." *Essays in Economic and Business History* 26 (2008): 147–57.

Sylvester, Louise M., Mark C. Chambers, and Gale R. Owen-Cocker, eds. *Medieval Dress and Textiles in Britain: A Multilingual Sourcebook*. Boydell, 2014.

t'Hart, Marjolein. *The Making of a Bourgeois State: War, Politics and Finance During the Dutch Revolt*. Manchester University Press, 1993.

Tawney, R. H. *Religion and the Rise of Capitalism: A Historical Study*. Harcourt, Brace, 1926.

Taylor, Eric. *If We Must Die: Shipboard Insurrections in the Era of the Atlantic Slave Trade*. Louisiana State University Press, 2006.

Temin, Peter, and Hans-Joachim Voth. *Prometheus Shackled: Goldsmith Banks and England's Financial Revolution After 1700*. Oxford University Press, 2013.

Thompson, E. P. *The Making of the English Working Class*. Vintage, 1963.

Thompson, E. P. "Time, Work-Discipline, and Industrial Capitalism." *Past & Present* no. 38 (December 1967): 56–97.

Thompson, E. P. *Whigs and Hunters: The Origin of the Black Act*. Allen Lane, 1975.

Thorsheim, Peter. *Inventing Pollution: Coal, Smoke, and Culture in Britain Since 1800*. Ohio University Press, 2006.

Timmins, Geoffrey. *The Last Shift: The Decline of Handloom Weaving in Nineteenth-Century Lancashire*. Manchester University Press, 1993.

Tomlins, Christopher. "Early British America, 1585–1830: Freedom Bound." In *Masters, Servants, and Magistrates in Britain and the Empire, 1562–1955*, edited by Douglas Hay and Paul Craven. University of North Carolina Press, 2004.

Tomlins, Christopher. *Freedom Bound: Law, Labor, and Civic Identity in Colonizing English America, 1580–1865*. Cambridge University Press, 2010.

Tracy, James. *A Financial Revolution in the Habsburg Netherlands: Renten and Renteniers in the County of Holland, 1515–1565*. University of California Press, 1985.

Trebilcock, Clive. *The Industrialization of the Continental Powers, 1780–1914*. Longman, 1981.

Trivellato, Francesca. *The Promise and Peril of Credit: What a Forgotten Legend About

Jews and Finance Tells Us About the Making of European Commercial Society. Princeton University Press, 2019.

Uchida, Jun. *Brokers of Empire: Japanese Settler Colonialism in Korea, 1876–1945.* Harvard University Press, 2014.

Uekoetter, Frank. *The Age of Smoke: Environmental Policy in Germany and the United States, 1880–1970.* University of Pittsburgh Press, 2009.

United Nations. *World Urbanization Prospects: 2007 Revision.* United Nations, 2008.

Valentinov, Nikolay. *Encounters with Lenin.* Oxford University Press, 1968.

van Bavel, Bas, and Oscar Gelderblom. "The Economic Origins of Cleanliness in the Dutch Golden Age." *Past & Present* 205, no. 1 (2009): 41–69.

van Bavel, Bas, and Jan Luiten van Zanden. "The Jump-Start of the Holland Economy During the Late-Medieval Crisis, c. 1350–c. 1500." *Economic History Review* 57, no. 3 (2004): 503–32.

Vanthemsche, Guy. *Belgium and the Congo, 1885–1980.* Cambridge University Press, 2012.

Velde, François. "Lottery Loans in the Eighteenth Century." Federal Reserve Bank of Chicago Working Paper WP 2018–17 (2018).

Vilar, Pierre. *A History of Gold and Money, 1450–1920.* New Left Books, 1976.

Volckart, Oliver. *The Silver Empire: How Germany Created Its First Common Currency.* Oxford University Press, 2024.

von Glahn, Richard. *Fountain of Fortune: Money and Monetary Policy in China, 1000–1700.* University of California Press, 1996.

von Glahn, Richard. "Myth and Reality of China's Seventeenth-Century Monetary Crisis." *Journal of Economic History* 56, no. 2 (1996): 429–54.

Voth, Hans-Joachim. *Time and Work in England, 1750–1830.* Clarendon Press, 2000.

Wang, Luman. *Chinese Hinterland Capitalism and Shanxi Piaohao: Banking, State, and Family, 1720–1910.* Routledge, 2021.

Weber, Max. *The Protestant Ethic and the Spirit of Capitalism.* Routledge, 2001. Originally published in 1930.

Wennerlind, Carl. *Casualties of Credit: The English Financial Revolution, 1620–1720.* Harvard University Press, 2011.

Westfall, Richard. *Never at Rest: A Biography of Isaac Newton.* Cambridge University Press, 1980.

Whitney, Gordon G. *From Coastal Wilderness to Fruited Plain: A History of Environmental Change in Temperate North America, 1500 to the Present.* Cambridge University Press, 1994.

Williams, Eric. *Capitalism and Slavery.* University of North Carolina Press, 1944.

Wright, Gavin. *Old South, New South: Revolutions in the Southern Economy Since the Civil War.* Louisiana State University Press, 1986.

Wright, Gavin. "Slavery and Anglo-American Capitalism Revisited." *Economic History Review* 72, no. 2 (2020): 1–31.

Wright, Gavin. "Slavery and the Rise of the Nineteenth-Century American Economy." *Journal of Economic Perspectives* 36, no. 2 (2022): 123–48.

Wrightson, Keith. *Earthly Necessities: Economic Lives in Early Modern Britain*. Yale University Press, 2000.

Wrigley, E. A. *Energy and the English Industrial Revolution*. Cambridge University Press, 2010.

Zahedieh, Nuala. "Regulation, Rent-Seeking, and the Glorious Revolution in the English Atlantic Economy." *Economic History Review* 62, no. 4 (2010): 865–90.

Zelin, Madeline. *The Merchants of Zigong: Industrial Entrepreneurship in Early Modern China*. Columbia University Press, 2006.

INDEX

Page numbers in italics refer to figures and tables.
Page numbers after 248 refer to endnotes.